THE EVERYTHING®

Grammar and Style Book
2nd Edition

Dear Reader,

I've been an English teacher for more than thirty years, so I've encountered thousands of students. When I run into former students, many say something along the lines of "You know, Mrs. Thurman, I really wish I'd paid more attention in your class, but then I didn't realize how important correct grammar and good writing skills would be in my adult years."

My hope in writing this book is to make grammar and writing easier to learn and more engaging for all students—whether they're still in school or have already graduated.

In the years since the first edition of *The Everything® Grammar and Style Book* was published, a number of people have been gracious enough to contact me to tell me they have enjoyed and benefited from the book. Readers have said the book has helped in writing for their jobs, in creating screenplays and novels, even in understanding the rules of Chinese grammar (now that's a use for my book that I never dreamed of!).

Whatever your reason for reading this book, I hope it helps you become a grammar guru and writing wizard.

Sincerely,

Susan Thurman

Welcome to the EVERYTHING Series!

These handy, accessible books give you all you need to tackle a difficult project, gain a new hobby, comprehend a fascinating topic, prepare for an exam, or even brush up on something you learned back in school but have since forgotten.

You can read an *Everything*® book from cover to cover or just pick out the information you want from our five useful boxes: e-questions, e-facts, e-link, e-ssentials, and e-alerts. We give you everything you need to know on the subject, but throw in a lot of fun stuff along the way, too.

We now have more than 400 *Everything*® books in print, spanning such wide-ranging categories as weddings, pregnancy, cooking, music instruction, foreign language, crafts, pets, New Age, and so much more. When you're done reading them all, you can finally say you know *Everything*®!

QUESTIONS?

Answers to
common questions

FACTS

Important snippets
of information

E-LINK

Informative URLs for
further learning

ESSENTIALS

Quick
handy tips

ALERTS!

Urgent
warnings

Editorial

Director of Innovation: Paula Munier

Editorial Director: Laura M. Daly

Executive Editor, Series Books: Brielle K. Matson

Associate Copy Chief: Sheila Zwiebel

Acquisitions Editor: Lisa Laing

Development Editor: Elizabeth Kassab

Production Editor: Casey Ebert

Production

Director of Manufacturing: Susan Beale

Production Project Manager: Michelle Roy Kelly

Prepress: Erick DaCosta, Matt LeBlanc

Design Manager: Heather Blank

Interior Layout: Heather Barrett, Brewster Brownville, Colleen Cunningham

Visit the entire Everything® *series at* www.everything.com

THE EVERYTHING®

GRAMMAR AND STYLE BOOK

2ND EDITION

All you need to master
the rules of great writing

Susan Thurman

Adams media
Avon, Massachusetts

As always, for my husband Mike

An Everything® Series Book.
Everything® and everything.com® are registered trademarks of F+W Publications, Inc.

Published by Adams Media, an F+W Publications Company
57 Littlefield Street, Avon, MA 02322 U.S.A.
www.adamsmedia.com

ISBN 10: 1-59869-452-9
ISBN 13: 978-1-59869-452-9

Printed in the United States of America.

J   I   H   G   F   E   D   C   B   A

Library of Congress Cataloging-in-Publication Data
available from the publisher.

This publication is designed to provide accurate and authoritative information with regard to the subject matter covered. It is sold with the understanding that the publisher is not engaged in rendering legal, accounting, or other professional advice. If legal advice or other expert assistance is required, the services of a competent professional person should be sought.

—From a *Declaration of Principles* jointly adopted by a Committee of the American Bar Association and a Committee of Publishers and Associations

Many of the designations used by manufacturers and sellers to distinguish their products are claimed as trademarks. Where those designations appear in this book and Adams Media was aware of a trademark claim, the designations have been printed with initial capital letters.

This book is available at quantity discounts for bulk purchases.
For information, please call 1-800-289-0963.

Contents

Acknowledgments

The author gratefully acknowledges the inspiration of:

Paula Fowler, who never failed to know just the right word or phrase to use, and whose interest and encouragement spurred me on countless times

The generous folks on Copyediting-L, busy people who nevertheless tirelessly share their ideas, suggestions, and wit

Peter Niblo, whose compliments and kindness began a friendship that sprang from his reading of the first edition of this book

Lisa Laing, the Adams Media editor whose "So, what's new in the world of grammar?" question was the springboard for this second edition

Top Ten Reasons for Using this Book

1. You understand the necessity of overcoming your grammar phobia.

2. You want people at your class reunion to think you weren't really sleeping in English class.

3. You yearn for a badge in the grammar police.

4. You wonder about the difference between "What's going on, Bob?" and "What's going on Bob?"

5. You recognize the importance of knowing for whom the bell tolls.

6. You know the embarrassment of misplacing your modifier.

7. You speculate about how to suitably split an infinitive.

8. You don't except what you meant to accept.

9. You realize that a misplaced comma might cost your company millions (see *tinyurl.com/ympf2v*).

10. You are itching to bring out your inner grammar guru.

Introduction

▶ ARE YOU SOMEONE who gripes that English was always your worst subject in school? Do you say that even today, you can't tell a clause from a conjunction from a colon; you always write *their* when you should have written *there*; you're never sure if that thing that goes in words like *don't* and *we're* is an apostrophe or a comma; and you get shivers just thinking about when to use *who* and when to use *whom*?

And your writing—well, forget about it! Your papers were covered in so much red ink that your instructors should have had stock in companies that manufactured it. What did *not parallel* or *dangling modifier* mean, for heaven's sake? And what exactly were those transitional words you were supposed to add, not to mention the clichés you were to delete and the fragments you were to fix? Grrr!

If any of this rings true, *The Everything® Grammar and Style Book, 2nd Edition* is just what the (grammar and writing) doctor ordered.

First, let's have a little history. In Western culture, the study of grammar goes back many years—to the days of the ancient Greeks. As time passed, Greek influenced Latin, and Latin in turn influenced the Romance languages that sprang from it. English developed separately from Latin but was influenced in some ways by it. Even after it ceased to be an everyday language, Latin was considered the language of the learned because it was still used in churches and scientific circles.

In the early days of modern English, writers hoped the language would be more standardized and refined, so they began publishing books of grammar. English, of course, traveled across the Atlantic with settlers who came to the colonies, and as schools here were established and grew, so did grammar studies. The works of one-time colonist Lindley Murray, the "Father of English Grammar," became major forces in grammar for many years. (Incidentally, Murray had a little trouble with the American Revolution—he was a Loyalist, and he fled to England after the United States won the war—but the books he published there were even more popular in the land he had abandoned.) Books on grammar and writing have been published ever since.

All of this brings us to your study of grammar and writing, using *The Everything® Grammar and Style Book, 2nd Edition*. Save yourself a little time by noting that this book has three main parts: grammar, types of writing, and vocabulary. In the first part of the book, you'll find grammar rules spelled out in an easy-to-understand format. Impossible, you say, for someone with brain freeze about grammar? Just take a little time to look and you'll see how easy correct grammar—and punctuation and usage—really can be.

The middle of the book details many types of writing that may interest you or may be a requirement for your academic life or your employment. In this section, you'll also find a number of ways to devise and develop ideas for your writing, as well as suggestions for revising and proofing your material to make it shine.

New to this edition of *The Everything® Grammar and Style Book* are its last chapters; these deal with vocabulary, both English and foreign words that are commonly used in material written in English. You can use all of this information to add flavor to your own writing.

Interspersed in all the chapters are addresses of Internet sites that provide interactive quizzes (but don't worry—no grades!) on different segments in the chapters. A special feature of this book is the shortened URLs that I devised in order to save you the frustration of possibly mistyping those URLs that seem to go on forever. All of the shorter forms begin with *tinyurl.com/*, followed by a combination of just six additional letters and/or numbers, so you'll have far fewer characters to type than with the conventional URL.

At the end of each chapter is a section called Checkpoint, which you can use to test yourself on various points highlighted in the chapter. (Again—no grades!)

So, are you ready to overcome those leftover fears or uncertainties? Come on and jump right in—the grammar's fine (or it will be soon)!

Chapter 1

What's in a Word?

Let's begin our explorations into the wonderful world of grammar and style with the most elemental unit through which you communicate meaning: the word. A single word includes a world of significance.

Spelling It All Out

You probably remember a few rules about spelling from your elementary school days. The poem that most students deem unforgettable is this one:

I before e,
Except after c,
Or when sounded as <u>a</u>,
As in <u>neighbor</u> or <u>weigh</u>.

That's certainly a helpful mnemonic—most of the time. It works for words such as *beige, ceiling, conceive, feign, field, inveigh, obeisance, priest, receive, shield, sleigh,* and *weight.*

But take a look at these words that don't follow the rule from the poem: *ancient, caffeine, codeine, conscience, deify, deity, efficient, either, feisty, foreign, forfeit, height, heist, kaleidoscope, leisure, nucleic, protein, reimburse, reincarnation, science, seize, sleight, society, sovereign, species, sufficient, surfeit,* and *weird.*

You see enough exceptions to wonder about the rule, don't you?

You do know, of course, not to rely on the spell check feature of your word processor to catch all your spelling mistakes. Off coarse ewe due. Ewe no the programme that ewe ewes two cheque mite look threw and thru an knot find awl your miss takes. An it wont tell ewe what ewe kneed too change the word two.

Here are some rules that generally apply to English nouns. (Note the word *generally.*) English has adopted words from many languages, and those languages have differing ways of changing word forms. That means, unfortunately, that every rule will have an exception (and probably more than one, as you've seen). Although the whole enchilada can be pretty confusing, these rules provide you with some useful guidelines for making your spelling decisions.

Making More: Forming Plurals of Nouns

Let's say you're making a list of items from your home to take to a local charity. Are you donating two chairs or two chaires? three clocks or three clockes? five knives or five knifes? a picture of six deers or a picture of six deer? You get the picture; plurals in English are formed in any number of ways.

1. To form the plural of most English words that don't end in -s, -z, -x, -sh, -ch, or -ss, add -s at the end:

   desk = desks, book = books, cup = cups

2. To form the plural of most English words that end in -s, -z, -x, -sh, -ch, and -ss, add -es at the end:

   bus = buses, buzz = buzzes, box = boxes, dish = dishes, church = churches, kiss = kisses

   Exceptions to this rule include *quizzes*, *frizzes*, and *whizzes*. (Note the doubled –z.)

3. To form the plural of some English words that end in -o, add -es at the end:

   potato = potatoes, echo = echoes, hero = heroes

To make things interesting, other words that end in -o add only -s at the end:

auto = autos, alto = altos, two = twos, zoo = zoos

And—just to keep you on your toes—some words ending in -o can form the plural in multiple ways:

buffalo = buffalo/buffaloes/buffalos, cargo = cargoes/cargos, ghetto = ghettos/ghettoes

When in doubt about which form to use, consult your dictionary (check to see if your instructor or company prefers a particular dictionary) and use the plural form listed first.

4. To form the plural of most English words that end in a consonant plus *-y*, change the *y* to *i* and add *-es:*

   lady = ladies, candy = candies, penny = pennies

5. To form the plural of most English words that end in a vowel plus *-y*, add *-s:*

   joy = joys, day = days, key = keys

6. To form the plural of most English words that end in *-f* or *-fe*, change the *f* to *v* and add *-es:*

   knife = knives, leaf = leaves, wife = wives

   Some exceptions to this rule (didn't you know there would be exceptions?) include *chef, cliff, belief, tariff, bailiff, roof,* and *chief.* All simply add *-s* to form their plural.

7. Some words form their plurals in ways that defy categories:

   child = children, mouse = mice, foot = feet, person = people, tooth = teeth, ox = oxen

8. And—to confuse matters further—some words are the same in both singular and plural:

   deer, offspring, crossroads

QUESTION?

What's odd about these nouns: *ides, means, mathematics, outskirts, goods, economics, cattle, clothes, alms*?
They're among the nouns that don't have a singular form.

At the end of this chapter, you'll find spelling rules about prefixes and suffixes.

Many words that have come into English from other languages retain their original method of constructing plurals. Here are some of them:

Latin

one alumnus   *two alumni*
one radius   *two radii*

Greek

one analysis   *two analyses*
one diagnosis   *two diagnoses*

So Many Rules!

These are just some of the rules of spelling, but you'll find lots of others. Many Internet sites are devoted to spelling rules. Just type in "English spelling rules" on a major search engine, and you'll get scores of hits.

Make sure that any site you visit pertains to spelling rules for American English rather than British English; as you'll discover, there's quite a difference. Also, depending on your background, you may find it helpful to look at Internet sites that deal with English as a foreign language.

The English Way

You probably know the meanings of some words are different in Britain than in the United States, such as the British usage of *chips* for what Americans call *French fries* and *lorry* for what Americans call a *truck*. But are you aware that the two languages have many variations in spelling as well? A few of the differences between American English and British English are these:

American English	British English
airplane	aeroplane
center	centre
check	cheque
color	colour
draft	draught
jail	gaol

plow	plough
spelled	spelt
theater	theatre
tire	tyre

Mind-Blowing Mnemonics

Let's face it—sometimes spelling rules just don't sink in. The English language has too many rules, and almost all of them have so many exceptions that learning them may not seem worth your time or trouble.

So how can you learn to spell properly? Many people create mnemonics (memory aids) to help them spell correctly. Listed here are some commonly misspelled words and suggested mnemonic forms to help you remember the right spelling.

After looking at these mnemonics, try developing some of your own for words that you often misspell (of course, look up the words in the dictionary first to get the right spelling). For mnemonics for some commonly confused words, see Chapter 12.

- **abundance:** Is it *–ance* or *–ence*? Remember: "An abun<u>dance</u> of people can <u>dance</u>."
- **ache:** Remember the first letter of each word of this sentence: "<u>A</u>ches <u>C</u>an <u>H</u>urt <u>E</u>verywhere."
- **acquire:** Most misspellings omit the *c*. Remember: "I want to <u>AC</u>quire <u>A</u>ir <u>C</u>onditioning."
- **across:** One *c* or two? Remember: "Walk across <u>a cross</u> walk."
- **address:** One *d* or two? Remember: "I'll <u>add</u> you to my <u>add</u>ress book."
- **aisle:** Remember the first letter of each word of this sentence: "<u>A</u>thletics <u>I</u>n <u>S</u>tadiums <u>L</u>ooks <u>E</u>asy."
- **Arctic:** Remember the first letter of each word of this sentence: "<u>A</u> <u>R</u>eally <u>C</u>old <u>T</u>ime <u>I</u>s <u>C</u>oming."
- **believe:** Remember: "Don't bel<u>ie</u>ve a <u>lie</u>."
- **business:** Remember: "I often take the <u>bus in</u> my <u>business</u>."
- **calendar:** Remember: "J<u>A</u>nu<u>A</u>ry is the first month of the c<u>A</u>lend<u>A</u>r."
- **cemetery:** Remember: "<u>E</u>pitaphs are in a c<u>E</u>m<u>E</u>t<u>E</u>ry."

- **defendant:** Remember: "At a picnic, it's hard to <u>defend</u> an <u>ant</u>."
- **dilemma:** Remember: "<u>Emma</u> faced a dil<u>emma</u>."
- **doctor:** Remember: "Get me to the doct<u>OR OR</u> else!"
- **environment:** Remember: "Lots of <u>IRON</u> is in the env<u>IRON</u>ment."
- **equivalent:** Remember: "Is <u>ALE</u> the equiv<u>ALE</u>nt of beer?"
- **escape:** Remember: "It's <u>e</u>ssential to <u>e</u>scape."
- **especially:** Remember: "I <u>ESP</u>ecially enjoy <u>ESP</u>."

FACT

Are you as exasperated with spelling as the famous playwright George Bernard Shaw was? Calling attention to various irregularities in spelling and pronunciation, Shaw once pointed out that *ghoti* was the correct way to spell *fish*. How could that be? In the word *enough*, he said, the letters *gh* make an *f* sound. In *women*, the *o* makes an *i* sound. In *fiction*, the *ti* makes an *sh* sound. Therefore *ghoti* is how *fish* really should be spelled.

- **exceed:** Remember: "Don's exc<u>EED</u> the sp<u>EED</u> limit."
- **expensive:** Remember: "Those <u>pens</u> were ex<u>pens</u>ive."
- **familiar:** Remember: "That <u>liar</u> looks fami<u>liar</u>."
- **February:** "Remember: "<u>BR</u>r, it's cold in Fe<u>br</u>uary.
- **generally:** Remember: "The gener<u>al</u> is your <u>ally</u>."
- **grammar:** Remember: "Bad gram<u>MAR</u> will <u>MAR</u> your chances for a good job."
- **handkerchief:** Remember: "<u>Hand</u> the <u>chief</u> a <u>hand</u>ker<u>chief</u>."
- **hindrance:** Remember the first letter of each word of this sentence: "<u>H</u>al <u>I</u>s <u>N</u>ot <u>D</u>riving <u>R</u>ight <u>A</u>nd <u>N</u>obody <u>C</u>an <u>E</u>xplain."
- **hoarse:** Remember: "When you're h<u>oarse</u>, you feel as if you have <u>oars</u> in your throat."
- **indispensable:** Remember: "That <u>sable</u> coat is indispen<u>sable</u>."
- **knowledge:** Remember: "I <u>know</u> that <u>ledge</u> is dangerous."
- **loneliness:** Remember: "<u>ELI</u> is known for his lon<u>ELI</u>ness."
- **maintenance:** Remember: "The <u>main ten</u> student workers got an <u>A</u> in <u>mainten</u>ance."

- **maneuver:** Remember the word is spelled with the first letter of each word of this sentence: "<u>M</u>ary <u>A</u>nd <u>N</u>ancy <u>E</u>at <u>U</u>gly <u>V</u>egetables—<u>E</u>ven <u>R</u>adishes."
- **marriage:** Remember: "You have to be a certain <u>age</u> for marri<u>age</u>."
- **mortgage:** Remember: "<u>Mort</u> thought his <u>mortgag</u>e rate was a <u>gag</u>."

FACT

Haplography is the accidental omission of a letter or letter group that should be repeated in writing, as in *mispell* for *misspell*. Haplology is the spoken contraction of a word by omitting one or more letters or syllables (as in *libary* for *library*).

- **niece:** Remember the first letter in each word of this sentence: "<u>N</u>iece <u>I</u>rma <u>E</u>xpects <u>C</u>ute <u>E</u>arrings."
- **parallel:** Remember: "Two para<u>ll</u>el lines are in the middle of <u>parall</u>el."
- **peculiar:** Remember: "That pecu<u>liar</u> fellow is a <u>liar</u>."
- **rhythm:** Remember: "Two syllables, two *h*s."
- **roommate:** Remember: "Two roommates, two *m*s."
- **separate:** Remember: "There's <u>A RAT</u> in sep<u>arat</u>e."
- **sincerely:** Remember: "Can I since<u>rely</u> RELY on you?"
- **skiing:** "Sk<u>ii</u>ng has two ski poles in the middle."
- **subtle:** Remember the first letter of each word of this sentence: "<u>S</u>ome <u>U</u>gly <u>B</u>oys <u>T</u>hrew <u>L</u>ogs <u>E</u>verywhere."
- **surprise:** Remember: "<u>U R</u> surprised when you receive a s<u>UR</u>prise." (Sound it out!)
- **villain:** Remember: "A <u>VILLA</u>in is in this <u>VILLA</u>."
- **Wednesday:** Remember: "Try to <u>wed</u> on <u>Wed</u>nesday."
- **weird:** Remember the first letter in each word of this sentence: "<u>W</u>eird <u>E</u>ddie <u>I</u>s <u>R</u>eally <u>D</u>aring."
- **wholly:** Remember: "<u>HOLLY</u> is in w<u>HOLLY</u>."

Unlocking the Secrets of Root Words, Prefixes, and Suffixes

A number of the words we use today are shaped from prefixes, root words, and suffixes that originally came from many other languages, especially Latin, Greek, Old English, and French. By learning some of these, you can analyze unfamiliar words, break them down into their component parts, and then apply their meanings to help unlock their definitions.

Root words (base words) can add either prefixes or suffixes to create other words. Take, for instance, the root word *bene*, meaning *good*. If you add various prefixes (letters that come at the beginning of a word) and suffixes (letters that come at the end of a word) to *bene*, you can create other words such as *benefit*, *benevolent*, *benediction*, and *unbeneficial*. Each prefix and suffix has a meaning of its own; so by adding one or the other—or both—to root words, you form new words. You can see the root word *bene* in each of the new words, and each of the new words still retains a meaning having to do with *good*, but the prefix or suffix changes or expands on the meaning. (The prefix *un-*, for instance, means "not." That gives a whole new meaning—an opposite meaning—to the word *unbeneficial*.)

In another example, look at the root word *chron*, which comes from Greek and means *time*. Adding the prefix *syn-* (meaning *together with*) and the suffix *-ize* (meaning *to cause to be*) creates the modern word *synchronize*, which means *to set various timepieces at the same time*. Use a different suffix, *-ology*, meaning *the study of*, and you have *chronology*, which means *the study that deals with time divisions and assigns events to their proper dates*.

Interesting, too, is the way ancient word forms have been used to create words in modern times. Two thousand years ago, for instance, no one knew there would be a need for a word that meant *sending your voice far away*—but that's what the modern word *telephone* means. It's a combination of *tele*, meaning *distant or far away*, and *phon*, meaning *voice or sound*.

In Appendix B, you'll find other common root words and some examples of modern English words that incorporate them.

The Last Word on Spelling

Here are some rules for spelling words to which prefixes or suffixes have been added.

1. Words that end in *-x* don't change when a suffix is added to them:

   fax = faxing, hoax = hoaxed, mix = mixer

2. Words that end in *-c* don't change when a suffix is added to them if the letter before the *c* is *a, o, u,* or a consonant:

   talc = talcum, maniac = maniacal

3. Words that end in *-c* usually add *k* when a suffix is added to them if the letter before the *c* is *e* or *i* and the pronunciation of the *c* is hard:

   picnic = picnickers, colic = colicky, frolic = frolicking

4. Words that end in *-c* usually don't change when a suffix is added to them if the letter before the *c* is *e* or *i* and the pronunciation of the *c* is soft:

   critic = criticism, clinic = clinician, lyric = lyricist

5. Words that end in a single consonant immediately preceded by one or more unstressed vowels usually remain unchanged before any suffix:

   debit = debited, credit = creditor, felon = felony

   Of course, you'll find exceptions, such as:
   program = programmed, format = formatting, crystal = crystallize

6. When a prefix is added to form a new word, the root word usually remains unchanged:

   spell = misspell, cast = recast, approve = disapprove

   In some cases, however, the new word is hyphenated. These exceptions include instances when the last letter of the prefix and the first letter of the word it's joining are the same vowel; when the prefix is being added to a proper noun; and when the new word formed by the prefix and the root must be distinguished from another word spelled in the same way but with a different meaning: anti-institutional, mid-March, re-creation (versus recreation).

7. When adding a suffix to a word ending in *-y*, change the *y* to *i* when the *y* is preceded by a consonant:

   carry = carrier, irony = ironic, empty = emptied

   This rule doesn't apply to words with an *-ing* ending:

   carry = carrying, empty = emptying

   This rule also doesn't apply to words in which the *-y* is preceded by a vowel:

   delay = delayed, enjoy = enjoyable

8. Two or more words that join to form a compound word usually keep the original spelling of each word:

   cufflink, billfold, bookcase, football

9. If a word ends in *-ie*, change the *-ie* to *-y* before adding *-ing*:

   die = dying, lie = lying, tie = tying

10. When adding *-full* to the end of a word, change the ending to *-ful*:

    armful, grateful, careful

Take a look at these Web sites for spelling rules, which range from very elementary to quite detailed.

   tinyurl.com/y93yvj   tinyurl.com/y8hr56
   tinyurl.com/yyvbmu

To test yourself with homonyms (words that sound alike but are spelled differently and have different meanings), try the online test at: *tinyurl. com/toupk.*

Checkpoint

Circle the correct plural for the following words. Check your answers in Appendix D.

1. wizard   wizards   wizzards
2. penny   pennys   pennies
3. wife   wifes   wives
4. ox   oxes   oxen
5. deer   deer   deers

Circle the correct spelling of the following words:

6. abundance   abundence
7. believe   beleive
8. defendant   defendent
9. envirnment   environment
10. February   Febuary
11. grammer   grammar
12. knowledge   knowlege
13. rhythm   rythm
14. seperate   separate
15. villian   villain

Chapter 2

Cracking the Code of Punctuation

Surely it's been awhile since you were introduced to punctuation rules. In elementary school, you learned that each punctuation mark sends a certain message. By applying the "code" of punctuation and capitalization properly, your readers are able to understand your words in the way you intended.

Avoiding the Problem of Miscommunication

When readers and writers don't use the same format—the same code—for applying capital letters and punctuation marks, confusion often results. Using the rules of the code enables you and your reader to understand the same things. Take a look at the following:

> *when the envelope arrived i opened it and screamed this is it i yelled in a voice that was loud enough to wake up the whole neighborhood running up from the basement my husband asked whats wrong nothings wrong i hastened to reply weve just become the latest winners in the state sweepstakes now well have enough money to go on that vacation weve dreamed about*

At this point you've probably given up trying to decipher what's being said. Obviously, the words are jumbled together without any capitalization or punctuation, so reading them requires both time and trouble on your part.

FACT

You shouldn't put a space between the last letter of the sentence and the end mark, but this mistake is commonly made. Other languages do insert a space, but in English the end mark comes immediately after the final word.

However, if the story is rewritten and uses appropriate capital letters and punctuation marks, then it's a snap to read.

> *When the envelope arrived, I opened it and screamed. "This is it!" I yelled in a voice that was loud enough to wake up the whole neighborhood.*
> *Running up from the basement, my husband asked, "What's wrong?"*
> *"Nothing's wrong," I hastened to reply. "We've just become the latest winners in the state sweepstakes. Now we'll have enough money to go on that vacation we've dreamed about."*

Much better, wouldn't you say? The same words are used, but now you can easily read and understand the story because capital letters and punctuation marks have been correctly inserted.

The End of the Road

Let's begin at the end—of sentences, that is. Three marks signal that a sentence is over: a period, a question mark, and an exclamation point.

Points about Periods

A period is most often used to signal the end of sentence that states a fact or one that gives a command or makes a request. For example:

The majority of the viewers stopped watching the program after the format was changed.

Hand me the pen that rolled near you.

If a sentence reports a fact that contains a question, a period should be used at the end. Look at this sentence:

I wondered if you could join me tonight for a night on the town.

The end punctuation should be a period because the sentence as a whole states a fact (that I'm wondering something) rather than asks a question. Periods are also used in abbreviations, such as *Dr.*, *Ms.*, *Rev.*, *i.e.*, and *et al.*

If your declarative or imperative sentence ends with an abbreviation that takes a period, don't put an additional period at the end. Write:

I'll be at your apartment to pick you up at 8 P.M.

not

I'll be at your apartment to pick you up at 8 P.M..

Answering Your Questions about Question Marks

News flash: Question marks go at the end of direct questions and sentences that end in questions. But you knew that, didn't you? Couldn't that information have been left out? You get the picture, don't you? Surely the point has sunk in by now, hasn't it?

A question mark is also used to show that there's doubt or uncertainty about something written in a sentence, such as a name, a date, or a word. In birth and death dates, such as (?–1565), the question mark means the birth date hasn't been verified. Look at this example:

The police are searching for Richard-O (?) in connection with the crime.

Here, the question mark means that the author is uncertain about the person's name. But look at this example:

Paul said he would donate five thousand dollars (?) to the charity.

The question mark means that the author is unsure about the exact amount of the donation.

Watch to see if a question mark is part of a title. If it is, be sure to include it in any punctuation that goes with the title:

I won't watch that new television program Can You Believe It?

Remember question marks go inside quotation marks if the quoted material forms a question. Otherwise, question marks go outside quotation marks. Notice the difference in these examples:

Brendan asked, "Where in the world are those reports?"

Did Brendan say, "I thought I gave you the reports"?

If you have a series of questions that aren't complete sentences, a question mark should be included after each fragment:

Can you believe that it's ten below zero? or that it's snowing? or that my electricity has gone off? or that the telephone has gone out?

They're Here! Exclamation Points

Another news flash: Exclamation points (exclamation marks) are used to express strong feelings! There's quite a difference between these two sentences:

Out of the blue, Marsha called Morris last night.
Out of the blue, Marsha called Morris last night!

The second sentence tells readers that there was something extraordinary about the fact that Marsha called Morris.

Only in informal writing should you use more than one question mark or exclamation mark:

Is this picture of our former roommate for real????

or

I can't believe that our former roommate is featured in Playboy*!!!*

In formal writing, don't use exclamation points (unless, of course, you're quoting a source or citing a title—or working for a tabloid magazine). In informal writing, you might include exclamation points after information that you find to be remarkable or information that you're excited about:

Paul said that he would donate five thousand dollars (!) to the charity.

or

Paul said that he would donate five thousand dollars to the charity!

Check to see if an exclamation point is part of a title. If it is, be sure to include it:

I won't watch that new television program I Can't Believe It!

May I Quote You on That?

Use quotation marks (" ") at the beginning and ending of words, phrases, or sentences to show which words belong to you (the writer) and which belong to someone else.

The term *double quotes* is synonymous with *quotation marks*. You'll learn about single quotes (' ') later.

The most common use of quotation marks is to show readers the exact words a person said, in the exact order the person spoke them. This is called a direct quotation. Note the difference in the following sentences:

Direct Quotation

Amber Posey said, "Give me the book."

Indirect Quotation

Amber Posey said to give her the book.

Direct Quotation

Carla Fenwick replied, "I don't have the book."

Indirect Quotation

Carla Fenwick replied she didn't have the book.

The same meaning is conveyed either way, but the quotation marks tell readers the words are stated exactly as they were spoken.

One of the most common mistakes that's made with quotation marks is to use them immediately after a word such as *said* or *asked*. Quotation marks are used *correctly* in sentences like these:

> *Harry asked, "Anna, will you pass me the butter?"*
> *Anna said, "We don't have any butter."*

The mistake comes in sentences that are indirect quotations (that is, the words after *said*, *asked*, and so on aren't the exact words, in the exact order, that the speaker used).

Consider this sentence, which gives the same information about Harry and Anna:

Harry asked if Anna would pass him the butter.

The mistake often made is to punctuate that sentence this way:

Harry asked, "If Anna would pass him the butter."

But the words inside the quotation marks aren't the exact words, in the exact order, that Harry used. Since these aren't the exact words, quotation marks can't be used.

To Help You Along: *Some Guidelines*

Guideline #1. Every time you change speakers, indent and start a new paragraph, even if the person quoted is just saying one word. This is the signal for readers to keep straight who's saying what. Take a look at this sequence:

When the telephone rang, Nick picked up the receiver and said, "Hello." Nora screamed into her end of the phone, "Who is this?" "Nick." "Nick who?" "Well, who is this?" "You know darned well who this is. You've sure called me often enough to know the sound of my voice!" "Huh?" "That's right. I'm hopping mad, and you know why."

Are you confused yet? Written that way, readers can't follow who's saying what. The dialogue should start a new paragraph each time the speaker changes. Then readers can identify the speaker. This is the way the passage should be written:

When the telephone rang, Nick picked up the receiver and said, "Hello." Nora screamed into her end of the phone, "Who is this?"
"Nick."
"Nick who?"
"Well, who is this?"
"You know darned well who this is. You've sure called me often enough to know the sound of my voice!"
"Huh?"
"That's right. I'm hopping mad, and you know why."

Guideline #2. If you're quoting more than one sentence from the same source (a person or a manuscript), put the closing quotation marks at the end of the speaker's last sentence of that paragraph *only*, not at the end of each sentence. This helps readers know that the same person is speaking. For example:

> *At the diner, Leslie said, "I'll start with a cup of coffee and a large orange juice. Then I want scrambled eggs, bacon, and toast for breakfast. May I get home fries with that?"*

No quotation marks come after *juice* or *breakfast*. That tells readers that Leslie hasn't finished speaking.

Guideline #3. If you're quoting more than one paragraph from the same source (a person or a manuscript), put beginning quotation marks at the start of each paragraph of your quote and closing quotation marks *only* at the end of the last paragraph. This lets readers know that the words come from the same source, without any interruption. Take a look at this example:

> *The ransom letter read:*
> *"We'll expect to receive the ransom money by this afternoon. You can get it from your Grandfather Moss. We know he's loaded.*
> *"Tell him not to try any funny stuff. We want the money in unmarked bills, and we don't want any police involved."*

At the end of the first paragraph the word *loaded* isn't followed by quotation marks, and quotation marks are placed at the beginning and end of the second paragraph. This tells readers that the same person is speaking or the same source is being quoted. The closing quotation marks designate when the quotation ends.

Guideline #4. Use quotation marks to enclose the titles of short works (short poems, short stories, titles of articles from magazines or newspapers, essays, chapters of books, songs, and episodes of television or radio programs):

> *To get the information for my book, I'm consulting a chapter called "The Art of Detection" from the book* How Mysteries Are Written.
> *Mary Lynn and Pat decided their favorite song is "Love Letters," from the CD* ABC and XYZ of Love.

Guideline #5. If you're using slang, technical terms, or other expressions outside their normal usage, enclose the words or phrases in quotation marks (alternately, you may put the words or phrases in italics):

My grandmother didn't know if it was a compliment or an insult when I described my best friend as being "phat."
In computer discussion groups, what does "start a new thread" mean?

Using the quotation marks lets readers know which particular words or phrases you're emphasizing.

Guideline #6. Remember that periods and commas go *inside* closing quotation marks; colons and semicolons go *outside* closing quotation marks. If you examine a work closely, you'll see that following this rule doesn't really look right (and it isn't adhered to in British English), but it's the correct punctuation in the United States. Look at this sentence:

I was reading the short story "Scared Out of My Wits," but I fell asleep in spite of myself.

See the comma after *Wits* and before the closing quotation marks? The actual title of the story is "Scared Out of My Wits" (there's no comma in the title). However, the sentence continues and demands a comma, so U.S. English requires a comma to be placed *inside* the closing quotation marks. Now look at this sentence:

I was reading the short story "Scared Out of My Wits"; I didn't find it to be scary at all.

The semicolon is *outside* the closing quotation marks after *Wits*.

Guideline #7. Deciding on placement of the two other end marks of punctuation—the question mark and the exclamation mark—is tricky: These go either *inside* or *outside* the closing marks, depending on what's being quoted. Take, for instance, a question mark. It goes *inside* the closing quotation if what is being quoted is a question:

Jica said, "Did you fall asleep reading the story?"

The words that Jica said form the question, so the question mark goes *inside* the closing quotation mark to show readers what she said. Look at this example:

Pat shouted, "I hope you know what you're doing!"

Again, the words that Pat said form the exclamation, so the exclamation mark goes inside the closing quotation marks. Now take a look at this example:

Did Martha say, "You must have fallen asleep"?

Now that the words that Martha said ("You must have fallen asleep") don't form a question; the sentence as a whole does. The question mark goes outside the closing quotation marks to show readers that.

Martha actually said, "You must be right"!

Again, the words that Martha said don't form an exclamation; the sentence as a whole does (probably expressing surprise). The exclamation mark goes *outside* the closing quotation marks to show readers that.

What do you do when both the sentence as a whole *and* the words being quoted form a question or an exclamation? Use only *one* end mark (question mark or exclamation mark) and put it *inside* the closing quotation marks. Look at this example:

Did I hear Martha say, "Who called this afternoon?"

Quotes Within Quotes: Single Quotation Marks

In the United States, single quotation marks are used for a quotation within a quotation:

"Mark Lester said, 'I'll be fine,' but then he collapsed," cried Marrin Wright.
"I'm reading the story 'Plaid Blazers and Other Mysteries,'" said Tara Hoggard.

Do you see that what Mark said ("I'll be fine") and the name of the short story ("Plaid Blazers and Other Mysteries") would normally be enclosed with double quotation marks? But since these phrases come inside material that's already in double marks, you show readers where the quotation (or title) begins by using a single quotation mark.

Try the interactive quizzes on quotation marks at this Web site:

tinyurl.com/ydyll7

Have some fun viewing misused quotation marks at links at *tinyurl .com/yjkehp.*

When not to use quotation marks with quotes: If you're using the writing guidelines from the Modern Language Association (MLA) or the American Psychological Association (APA), keep in mind that these groups have specific rules for block quotations (passages of a certain length). In spite of the fact that you're quoting, you don't use quotation marks. You do, however, have a definite format for letting readers know that the material you're citing is verbatim from the original text. Consult the specific guidelines for each group to see how to format this material.

Checkpoint

Decide which of the following sentences is punctuated correctly. Check your answers in Appendix D.

1. A. I asked myself if I'd done the right thing?
   B. I asked myself if I'd done the right thing.
2. A. Pat, Erin, and Ryan enjoy the revival of the television program *What's My Line?*
   B. Pat, Erin, and Ryan enjoy the revival of the television program *What's My Line.*

3. A. When did the boss say, "Have that information this afternoon?"
   B. When did the boss say, "Have that information this afternoon"?
4. A. The neighbor shouted that the house was on fire.
   B. The neighbor shouted, "That the house was on fire."
5. A. The bank robber said to, "Hand over the money."
   B. The bank robber said, "Hand over the money."
6. A. Jessica Page stated, "I have to get a gift card, a new coat, and some wrapping paper." "Do you want me to pick up anything for you?"
   B. Jessica Page stated, "I have to get a gift card, a new coat, and some wrapping paper. Do you want me to pick up anything for you?"
7. A. So far, the hardest chapter in the book *Why I Love Grammar* is titled "Quirky Quotation Marks."
   B. So far, the hardest chapter in the book "Why I Love Grammar" is titled "Quirky Quotation Marks."

Chapter 3

More Fun with Punctuation

Since you've mastered periods, question marks, exclamation points, and quotation marks, are you ready to take on a few more punctuation marks? The following shouldn't be too difficult, and this chapter makes the task as painless as possible.

The Dreaded Apostrophe

People often become confused about the purpose of apostrophes and end up using them in all sorts of creative ways. Perhaps you've done so yourself. If so, take heart, because you're certainly not alone. You can walk into almost any store and see signs like the following that feature the incorrect use of the apostrophe:

> *Special price's this week!*
> *Rent two movie's today!*
> *Five can's for $4.00!*

In these examples, none of the words that has an apostrophe needs one. Each is a simple plural, and you almost never need to use an apostrophe to denote a plural. Using an apostrophe correctly doesn't have to be difficult.

There are three basic situations in which an apostrophe would be the correct choice:

- contractions
- possession
- forming a plural (rare)

Let's start with the easiest use of the apostrophe, the contraction.

Cutting It Short: Contractions

An apostrophe often indicates that at least one letter has been omitted from a word, and the word that's formed is called a contraction. For example, the contraction *don't* stands for *do not*; the *o* in *not* has been omitted. *I'll* is a short form of *I will*; in this case the *wi* of *will* has been omitted.

Do you know the contractions formed from these words?

she will	she'll
you have	you've
he is	he's

Sometimes authors will use apostrophes in contractions to help readers understand dialect. For instance, an author might write, "Alice is goin' swimmin' today." Readers understand that the final *-g*s are omitted from *going* and *swimming*, and that the author is trying to duplicate the type of speech (the dialect) a character uses.

What's Mine Is Yours: Possession

Before using an apostrophe to show possession, first make sure the phrase you're questioning actually denotes possession and isn't simply a plural. For instance, in the phrase *the babies' rattles*, the babies possess rattles (so an apostrophe indicates this to readers); however, in the phrase *the babies in their cribs*, the babies aren't possessing anything and an apostrophe isn't needed.

Here are some guidelines to help you make sense of it all.

Guideline #1. If a singular noun doesn't end in *-s*, its possessive ends in *-'s*. Say what? Take a look at this sentence:

The cars engine was still running.

The word *cars* needs an apostrophe to indicate possession, but where does the apostrophe go?

Use this mental trick: Take the word that needs the apostrophe (*cars*) and the word that it's talking about (*engine*) and mentally turn the two words around so that the word you're wondering about is the object of a preposition. (This rule may be easier for you to understand this way: Turn the words around so that they form a phrase. Usually the phrase will use *of*, *from*, or *belonging to*.)

When you change *cars engine* around, you come up with *engine of the car*. Now look at the word *car*. *Car* is singular and doesn't end in *-s*, so the original should be punctuated *-'s*. You should have:

The car's engine was still running.

Try the trick again with this sentence:

Donna Moores wallet was lying on the seat.

Mentally turn *Donna Moores wallet* around so that you have *the wallet of (belonging to) Donna Moore.*

After you've turned it around, you have the words *Donna Moore,* which is singular (in spite of being two words) and doesn't end in -*s.* That lets you know that you need to use -'*s.* The sentence should be punctuated this way:

Donna Moore's wallet was lying on the seat.

One of the most common mistakes with apostrophes comes with possessive pronouns (*its, yours, his, hers, theirs, ours, whose*). Remember that the only one of these words that ever takes an apostrophe is *its,* and that happens only when the word means *it is.*

Guideline #2. When you have plural nouns that end in -*s* (and most do), add an apostrophe after the final -*s.* This tells readers that you're talking about several people, places, or things. The same mental trick of turning the two words into a phrase applies.

This sentence talks about two girls who had been reported missing:

The girls coats were found at the bus station.

Now just apply the trick. Take the phrase *girls coats,* and turn it around so that you have *coats of (belonging to) the girls.*

When you've turned the phrase around this time, the word *girls* ends in -*s.* This lets you know that you should add an apostrophe after the -*s* in *girls,* so the sentence is punctuated this way:

The girls' coats were found at the bus station.

Although most English plurals end in -*s* or -*es,* our language has a number of exceptions (and didn't you know there would be?), such as *children, women,* and *deer.* If a plural doesn't end in -*s,* the possessive is formed with an -'*s* (that is, treat it as if it were singular).

Again, the turnaround trick applies. Take the sentence:

The childrens coats were covered with mud.

Mentally turn *childrens coats* into the phrase *coats of the children.* Since *children* doesn't end in -*s,* its possessive would be -*'s;* so the correct punctuation would be:

The children's coats were covered with mud.

So far, so good? You have just one tricky part left to consider. It concerns singular words that end in -*s.* Two ways of punctuating these words are common. Guideline #3 is used more often than Guideline #4, but many people find that Guideline #4 is easier to grasp. You'll have to ask instructors or employers if they have a preference as to which you should follow.

Guideline #3. If a singular word ends in -*s,* form its possessive by adding -*'s* (except in situations in which pronunciation would be difficult, such as *Moses* or *Achilles*). Look at this sentence:

Julie Jones information was invaluable in locating the missing girls.

Applying the turnaround trick would make the phrase that needs the apostrophe read this way: *information from Julie Jones.*

Guideline #3 would tell you that, since *Jones* is singular and ends in -*s,* you'd form the possessive by adding -*'s.* Therefore, the sentence would be punctuated this way:

Julie Jones's information was invaluable in locating the missing girls.

However, you may be told to use another rule:

Guideline #4. If a singular word ends in -*s,* form its possessive by adding an apostrophe after the -*s.* In this case, the sentence would be written this way:

Julie Jones' information was invaluable in locating the missing girls.

If using Guideline #4 is okay with your teacher or employer, then you have to remember only two rules about placing the apostrophe in possessives:

1. After you mentally turn the phrase around, if the word in question doesn't end in *-s*, add *-'s*.
2. After you mentally turn the phrase around, if the word in question ends in *-s*, add an apostrophe after the *-s*.

Joint Versus Individual Possession

One use of apostrophes shows readers whether the people you're talking about possess (own) something jointly or individually. Take a look at this sentence:

> *Jim and Allisons cars were stolen.*

The question is, did Jim and Allison own the cars together or separately? If, say, Jim and Allison were a married couple and they had the misfortune of having two of their cars stolen, then the sentence would be punctuated this way:

> *Jim and Allison's cars were stolen.*

The possessive comes after the last person's name *only*. This usage tells readers that Jim and Allison had joint ownership of the cars.

But maybe Jim and Allison were neighbors, and a rash of car thefts had taken place on their block. The sentence would then be punctuated this way:

> *Jim's and Allison's cars were stolen.*

The possessive comes after *both* names. This tells readers that Jim and Allison had separate ownership of the cars.

A Rare Occasion: Using an Apostrophe to Form a Plural

Take another look at the store signs mentioned at the beginning of this section that incorrectly used an apostrophe:

> *Special price's this week!*

Rent two movie's today!
Five can's for $4.00!

The words that have apostrophes are just plain ol' plurals; they don't show ownership in any way and so don't need apostrophes. (If you're unsure about whether you should use an apostrophe, ask yourself if the word in question owns or possesses anything.)

Also, if you have proverbial expressions that involve individual letters or combinations of letters, use apostrophes to show their plurals.

Dot your i's and cross your t's.

In these examples, some style academic or company guides dictate that you shouldn't italicize the letter you're making plural; other guides take the opposite view. Be sure to consult the guide suggested by your instructor or company.

Another time that you should use an apostrophe to form a plural is if your reader would be confused by reading an –s alone (for instance, when an –s is added to an individual letter or letter combination or to numbers used as nouns).

s = **s**'s *(instead of* **s***s)*
Write 7's (instead of 7s) in the graph.

For interactive quizzes on apostrophes, see these Internet sites:

tinyurl.com/yffxje   *tinyurl.com/ydogxa*
tinyurl.com/rnted   *tinyurl.com/yx7rhc*

Commendable Comma Comments

Commas are used more frequently than any other punctuation mark. Like all other punctuation marks, use a comma to keep your readers from being confused. When readers see a comma, they know a slight pause comes at that place in the sentence, and they can tell how particular words or phrases relate to other parts of the sentence. Take a look at this sentence:

Will you call Mary Alice Lee and Jason or should I?

What's being said here? This sentence has entirely different meanings, depending on how commas are placed in it.

Will you call Mary, Alice, Lee, and Jason, or should I?
Will you call Mary Alice, Lee, and Jason, or should I?
Will you call Mary, Alice Lee, and Jason, or should I?

Using Commas with a Series

If you have a series of items, use a comma to separate the items. Take a look at this sentence:

The convertible 2008 Ford and Chevy pickup were involved in a wreck.

How many vehicles were involved? With the following punctuation, you'd see that three vehicles were involved.

The convertible, 2008 Ford, and Chevy pickup . . .

However, this punctuation shows that only two vehicles were involved.

The convertible 2008 Ford and Chevy pickup . . .

Use a comma between two or more adjectives (words that explain or describe or give more information about a noun or pronoun) that modify a noun (the name of a person, place, thing, or idea):

The man in the torn, tattered jacket moved quickly through the crowded, unlit street.

If the first adjective modifies the idea expressed by the combination of subsequent adjectives and the noun, then you don't need commas. Look at this sentence:

Many countries don't have stable central governments.

Since *central governments* would be considered a single unit, you don't need to separate it from the adjective modifying it *(stable)* with a comma.

If you're using *and*, *or*, or *nor* to connect all the items in the series, don't use commas:

The flag is red and white and blue.
The flag might be red or white or blue.
The flag is neither red nor white nor blue.

Some style guides mandate that the final two items in a series (also referred to as the "serial comma," "Harvard comma," or "Oxford comma") always be separated by commas; other guides dictate that it be eliminated, except in cases where the meaning would be misconstrued without it. You should find out which style your instructor or company prefers.

Using Commas with Compound Sentences

If you have two independent clauses (that is, two thoughts that could stand alone as sentences) and they're joined by *but*, *or*, *yet*, *so*, *for*, *and*, or *nor* (use the mnemonic *boysfan* to help you remember), join them with a comma:

It was more than three hours past lunchtime, and everybody was grumbling about being hungry.

The exception: You may eliminate the comma if the two independent clauses are short and if the sentence would still be clear without the comma. For example:

We filled up with gas and we went on our way.

If you have a simple sentence with a compound verb, don't put a comma between the verbs:

I wanted to get some rest [no comma] but needed to get more work done.

Using Commas with Quoted Material

If a quoted sentence is interrupted by words such as *he said* or *she replied*, use commas in this way:

"For this contest," he said, "you need three pencils and two pieces of paper."

The first comma goes before the closing quotation mark and the second comma goes before the beginning quotation mark.

If the words being quoted make up a question or an exclamation, don't include a comma:

"Put that down right now!" Barry cried.

Avoid using a comma with words that are generally thought of as pairs—even if they're in a series. For instance, you'd write:

I ate an apple, an orange, and peanut butter and jelly every day while I was in grade school.

Since peanut butter and jelly are often though of as one food, don't put a comma after *butter.*

Using Commas with Clauses, Phrases, Appositives, and Introductory Words

Use commas to set apart clauses (groups of words that have a subject and a predicate), participle phrases (see Chapter 8), and appositives (words or phrases that give information about a noun or pronoun) that aren't necessary to the meaning of the sentence.

Take a look at this sentence:

The handsome man over there, the only one who works in the deli at Sam's Supermarket, has black hair and brown eyes.

If you took out the clause *the only one who works in the deli at Sam's Supermarket*, you'd still have the same essential parts of the sentence. You don't need to know where the man works in order to learn his hair and eye color. (The nonessential part of this sentence is called a nonrestrictive clause. See Chapter 8 for more information.) Here's another way of looking at it: If you can take out the part in question (the part you're questioning for commas) and the sentence still makes sense, then you should use the commas. Now look:

The only man who works in the deli at Sam's Supermarket was arrested for stealing four grapes and five apples.

In this case, if you removed *who works in the deli at Sam's Supermarket*, you'd have *The only man was arrested for stealing four grapes and five apples*. That isn't the meaning of the original sentence. Remember: If you need the extra words for the meaning, you don't need the commas.

Commas are also used after introductory words such as exclamations, common expressions, and names used in direct address that aren't necessary for the meaning of a sentence. If you have words that begin a sentence and you could understand the sentence without them, use a comma to separate them from the rest of the sentence. For example:

Why, don't you look nice tonight!
Now, what was I supposed to remember?
If you must know, I have been dyeing my hair for the past ten years.

A comma is also used before these same types of words and phrases when they appear at the end of a sentence, as long as they're not necessary for the meaning:

Don't you think that new CD really rocks, Madison?
You're not going to the party, are you?
Call me back at your convenience, if you please.

Use commas around words that interrupt a sentence (these words are called parenthetical expressions), as long as the words aren't necessary for the meaning:

The answer to the next question, Paula, can be found on page thirty-six.
This textbook, unlike the one I had before, is written in a style I can understand.

Use a comma after an introductory verbal (a verbal is a participle, gerund, or infinitive) or verbal phrase:

Weeping at the sight of the destruction, the news reporter broke down on camera.
To try to regain her composure, Allison took several deep breaths.

Use a comma after an introductory adverb clause. (An adverb clause is a group of words that has a subject and a verb, and describes a verb, adjective, or other adverb.) For example:

Because Reagan didn't stop at the red light, she got a ticket.
If Grant comes in town tonight, the whole family is going to get together for a picnic.

Using Commas in Addresses

When writing out a mailing address as text (not on separate lines), put a comma between the person's last name and the start of the street address, then after the street address, then between the city and the state. Don't put a comma between the state and the zip code. For example:

Please remit the payment to Cooper Bartlett, 4238 Old Highway 41 North, Nicholasville, KY 42309.

If you're putting address information on separate lines, use a comma only between the city and state:

Cooper Bartlett
4238 Old Highway 41 North
Nicholasville, KY 42309.

If you mention a city and state in text, put commas around the state:

I have to visit Clinton, Iowa, on my next sales trip.

The same is true if you mention a city and country; put commas around the country:

Using Commas in Dates

Put a comma after the day of the week (if you've stated it), the day of the month, and the year (if the sentence continues):

John Abbott will meet you on Friday, February 22, 2008, at half past seven.

If you're writing only the day and month or the month and year, no comma is necessary:

John Abbott will meet you on February 22.
John Abbott will meet you in February 2008.

Using Commas in Letters

Put a comma after the greeting (salutation) of all friendly letters and the closing of all letters:

Dear Aunt Helen,
Sincerely,

Using Commas with Titles or Degrees

If a person's title or degree follows his or her name, put commas after or around it:

Please call Robert Householder, Ph.D., at your convenience.
The deposition was given by Edward Shuttleworth, M.D.

FACT

A mistake that seems to be cropping up more and more is using a comma to separate a verb from its subject (As in "The flour, had been infested with bugs"). The comma after *flour* should be eliminated.

Using Commas with Long Numbers

Using commas helps readers understand long numbers more easily. If, for instance, you read the number 1376993, you'd have to stop, count the numbers, and then group them in threes before you could understand the number. Using commas to divide the numbers makes for quicker interpretation:

Is it my imagination, or does this book list 1,376,993 rules for commas?

E-LINK

For interactive quizzes on commas, see these Web sites:

tinyurl.com/yjy5br   *tinyurl.com/ybs2vn*
tinyurl.com/yg8wbs   *tinyurl.com/ygyml3*

Checkpoint

Rearrange and write the following phrases to use a possessive. You may use either Guideline #3 or Guideline #4, depending on your instructor's or employer's preference: Check your answers in Appendix D.

1. the computer belonging to Chris

   _____

2. the chair belonging to Lois

   _____

3. the hairstyle of Mrs. Williams

   _____

4. the house of Mr. Harris

   _____

5. the cards belonging to Katherine Mears

   _____

Chapter 4

Punctuation Pairs

A few punctuation marks—in particular, colons and semicolons, hyphens and dashes, and parentheses and brackets—are closely linked in appearance, if not in function. This can cause confusion for the writer—and has even been known to strike fear into the heart of some. But fear no more! This chapter will clear up any ambiguity surrounding these punctuation pairs and will give you the tools you need to be able to use them with confidence.

Cleansing Your Colon

Use a colon to introduce particular information. One of the most common uses of a colon is to signal to readers that a list will follow:

On the camping trip, please bring the following: a flashlight, a sleeping bag, two boxes of matches, and food for six meals.

ALERT!

If you have a list that is the object of a verb or of a preposition, you don't need a colon:

On the camping trip, please bring a flashlight, a sleeping bag, two boxes of matches, and food for six meals.

(The list is the object of the verb *bring*.)

On the camping trip, please bring your supplies to Tom, Sally, Mykela, or Fernando.

(The list is the object of the preposition *to*.)

To be on the safe side, use an expression such as *the following* or *as follows* before a colon.

Use a colon to explain or give more information about what has come before it in a sentence:

I have a number of complaints against the tenant: damaged plaster, dog-stained carpet in every room, and three months of unpaid rent.

In formal papers, a colon usually precedes a lengthy quotation:

In his Gettysburg Address, Abraham Lincoln stated:
Four score and seven years ago, our forefathers brought forth on this continent a new nation, conceived in liberty and dedicated to the proposition that all men are created equal.

To determine what is meant by "lengthy," consult the style guide designated by your instructor or employer.

Here are other times to use a colon:

- in the greeting of a business letter
  To Whom It May Concern:

- between the hour and minutes in time
  a meeting at 4:15 P.M.

- in dividing a title from its subtitle
  My Favorite Punctuation Marks: Why I Love Colons

- in naming a chapter and verse of the Bible
  Genesis 2:10

- in naming the volume and number of a magazine
  Time 41:14

- in citing the volume and page number of a magazine
  U.S. News and World Report 166: 31

- between the city and the publisher in a bibliographical entry
  London: Covent Garden Press

Try this Web site to test yourself on using colons correctly: *tinyurl .com/yypo58.*

The Serviceable Semicolon

I have grown fond of semicolons in recent years. . . . It's almost always a greater pleasure to come across a semicolon than a period. —Lewis Thomas, M.D., from *The Medusa and the Snail* (1979)

Although most people probably don't get as excited over semicolons as award-winning author and scientist Mr. Thomas did, these punctuation marks can be very useful in their own way.

Semicolons signal a pause greater than one indicated by a comma but less than one indicated by a period. The most common use for a semicolon is joining two complete thoughts (independent clauses) into one sentence.

Look at the following sentences:

The bank teller determined the bill was counterfeit. No serial number was on it.

Each of these sentences stands alone, but they could be joined by using a semicolon:

The bank teller determined the bill was counterfeit; no serial number was on it.

Often semicolons are used with conjunctive adverbs and other transitional words or phrases, such as *on the other hand* or *therefore*. In this case, be sure that you put the semicolon at the point where the two thoughts are separated. For example:

Right: *There is more to this case than meets the eye; however, you'll have to wait to read about it in the newspapers.*

Wrong: *There is more to this case than meets the eye, you'll; however, have to read about it in the newspapers.*

FACT

In English, many transitional words and phrases are commonly used. Here are a few of them:

first	second	third
next	finally	then
moreover	likewise	similarly

Semicolons are sometimes used at the end of bulleted or numbered lists, depending on the style and the sentence construction. (Sometimes commas or periods are used, and sometimes there's no punctuation at all.) A list may appear like this:

In order to receive your award, you must do the following:
1. verify that you have been a member for at least three years;
2. submit copies of civic or charitable work done in the name of the club;
3. have at least three letters of recommendation.

Now it's time to break a rule about semicolons. Sometimes you use a semicolon when a comma might seem to be the correct punctuation mark. Look at this sentence:

The manhunt took place in Los Angeles, Nashville, Indiana, Stratford, Connecticut, Enid, Oklahoma, Dallas, and Olympia.

Commas came after the name of each city and each state, as the rule on commas says they should. However, readers will probably be confused about the true meaning of the sentence. Consider that a semicolon is a "notch above" a comma. By substituting a semicolon in places where you'd ordinarily use a comma, you make the material clearer for readers by showing which cities go with which states. Look at how the sentence should be punctuated:

The manhunt took place in Los Angeles; Nashville, Indiana; Stratford, Connecticut; Enid, Oklahoma; Dallas; and Olympia.

Reading the sentence with semicolons used in this way, readers can tell that the manhunt took place in Nashville, Indiana, as opposed to Nashville, Tennessee. Also, readers can identify that Enid is located in Oklahoma.

When Semicolons Won't Work

Semicolons won't work if the two thoughts aren't on the same playing field (that is, if they're not logically connected). Look at these two sentences:

The teller wore a blue suit. The police were called immediately.

Although both are sentences, they have no logical link. If a semicolon were used between these two sentences, readers would be scratching their heads, thinking they were missing something.

Semicolons also won't work if one of the thoughts isn't a complete sentence. Look at this example:

The police were called immediately; screeching through the streets.

The first part of the sentence is a complete thought (*the police were called immediately*), but the second part isn't (*screeching through the streets*).

The Power to Divide and Unite: The Hyphen

Hyphens and dashes are another tricky punctuation pair. A hyphen is a short horizontal line (next to a zero on a keyboard); a dash is longer. But the differences between them go much deeper than just a few fractions of an inch.

The most common use of the hyphen is to divide words at the ends of lines. The important rule to remember is that you may divide words only between syllables. Why is this important, you ask? Read the following lines:

Sarah was unhappy with her oldest child, her nineteen-year-old da-ughter Lindsay. Lindsay was still relying on her mother to get her up wh-en the alarm clock rang in the mornings, to see that her various deadli-nes for typing papers for school were met, to take her side in the cons-tant squabbles with her boyfriend, Harry.

See how difficult this is to read? That's because you've learned to read in syllables. When words aren't divided correctly, readers have to go back to the previous line and put the syllables together, and that's confusing and time-consuming.

The text should read:

Sarah was unhappy with her oldest child, her nineteen-year-old daugh-ter Lindsay. Lindsay was still relying on her mother to get her up when the alarm clock rang in the mornings, to see that her various dead-lines for typing papers for school were met, to take her side in the con-stant squabbles with her boyfriend, Harry.

If you're not sure where syllables occur, consult a dictionary. In addition, most word processing software contains automatic hyphenation tools you may use. Since you may divide a word only between its syllables, one-syllable words may not be divided.

No matter where the words are divided, be careful to leave more than one letter at the end of a line (or more than two at the beginning of a line) so that readers' eyes can adjust quickly.

You wouldn't write:

Beth wondered if the employment agency would call her back a-gain for another interview.

Nor would you write:

Beth killed her chances for another interview when she contact-ed the company president by telephone.

You should also avoid hyphenating acronyms (such as UNESCO or NAACP), numerals (such as 1,200 or 692), and contractions (such as haven't, didn't, couldn't). Also, some style guides say that proper nouns (those that are capitalized) shouldn't be hyphenated.

Also try to avoid dividing an Internet or e-mail address. Since these addresses often contain hyphens as part of the address, inserting an extra hyphen would certainly confuse readers. If angle brackets aren't used (see Chapter 5), extending the address to the second line without any extra punctuation would make the address clear for your reader. You should do that this way:

When I tried to order, I was directed to this site: www.anglosaxon.com/rebates/year/1066/.

Hyphens with Numbers

Use a hyphen (not a dash) between two dates and between two page numbers:

Prohibition (1919–1933) came about as a result of the Eighteenth Amendment.
See the section on the Roaring Twenties (pp. 31–35) for more information.

Technically, both of these instances use what's called an "en dash," which is longer than a hyphen and shorter than a normal dash, which is usually called an "em dash." Are you confused? Don't be. Most word processing programs have an **INSERT** icon or a character map that you can use to access en and em dashes, as well as other symbols.

Another common use of the hyphen comes when numbers are written as words instead of numerals. You probably do this already, but the rule says to hyphenate numbers from twenty-one to ninety-nine. If you look at words printed without a hyphen (e.g., *sixtyfour*, *eightyseven*), you see that they're difficult to read. Using hyphens makes reading easier.

Hyphens with Compound Adjectives

When a compound adjective (two or more adjectives that go together to form one thought or image) precedes the noun it modifies, it should be hyphenated. Look at these sentences:

> *Charles Dickens was a nineteenth-century writer.*

In this case, *nineteenth-century* is an adjective (it modifies the noun *writer*), and so it's hyphenated. Notice the difference:

> *Charles Dickens was a writer who lived in the nineteenth century.*

Here, *nineteenth century* is a noun, so it's not hyphenated.

Use a hyphen to join adjectives only if together they form the image. If they're separate words describing a noun (as *big, bulky package*), then don't use a hyphen. Take a look at this example:

> *loyal, long-time friend*

Long and *time* go together to form the image that describes the friend, so they're hyphenated. If the hyphen weren't there, then readers would see *long time friend* and would wonder what a *long friend* was or what a *time friend* was.

ALERT!

If a modifier before a noun is the word *very* or is an adverb that ends in *-ly*, you don't need a hyphen. You should write:

> *a very condescending attitude*   *a strictly guarded secret*
> *a very little amount of money*   *the highly publicized meeting*

Hyphens for Clarification

Sometimes you should use a hyphen to clarify the meaning of your sentence. For instance, look at this example:

My favorite sports star resigned!

Should you be elated or upset? The way the sentence is punctuated now, the star will no longer play; his or her fans will be upset. If, however, the writer intended to get across that the star had signed another contract, the sentence should contain a hyphen and be written this way:

My favorite sports star re-signed!

Now you understand the writer's intent. Not many words have this idiosyncrasy (*recreation* and *recollect* are two others), but be careful of those that do.

May I Interrupt? The Dash

The dash is a handy device, informal and essentially playful, telling you that you're about to take off on a different tack but still in some way connected with the present course—only you have to remember that the dash is there, and either put a second dash at the end of the notion to let readers know that he's back on course, or else end the sentence, as here, with a period.—Lewis Thomas, M.D., from *The Medusa and the Snail* (1979)

Ah, the "playful" dash. As Mr. Thomas writes, a dash provides a window for some informality in writing, allowing the writer to introduce an abrupt change in thought or tone. Look at this sentence:

The odometer just reached thirty thousand miles, so it's time to call the garage for—oops! I just passed the street where we were supposed to turn.

The dash tells readers that a sudden idea interrupted the speaker's original thought.

Use a dash to give emphasis to something that's come before. Look at this sentence:

Elizabeth spent many hours planning what she would pack in the van—the van that she had rented for two weeks.

Another time a dash may be used is in defining or giving more information about something in a sentence. Read this sentence:

Margaret knew that when she finally arrived at her sorority house, she would be warmly greeted by her sisters—Bea, Kwila, and Arlene.

The last example could also be punctuated by using parentheses or a colon in place of the dash. You might have written the same sentence this way:

Margaret knew that when she finally arrived at her sorority house, she would be warmly greeted by her sisters (Bea, Kwila, and Arlene).

or this way:

Margaret knew that when she finally arrived at her sorority house, she would be warmly greeted by her sisters: Bea, Kwila, and Arlene.

You can see that punctuating the sentence with colons is much stuffier than using a dash or parentheses. Generally speaking, save the colon for formal writing.

The Inside Scoop: Parentheses

You know what parentheses are (and—in case this comes up when you're on *Who Wants to Be a Millionaire?*—the singular of the word is *parenthesis* and the plural is *parentheses*), but you may not be completely sure of when and how to use them. You may know very little about square brackets, which, after all, are only used infrequently.

Using parentheses tells readers that you're giving some extra information, something that isn't necessary to the meaning of the sentence but is helpful in understanding what's being read. For example:

For a complete study of Hitchcock's movies, see Chapter 8 (pages 85–96).

When readers see parentheses, they know that the material enclosed is extraneous to the meaning of the sentence. If the information is necessary for the sentence to be read correctly, you shouldn't use parentheses. For instance, if you're comparing statistics about two floods that occurred in different years, you might have a sentence like this:

The high-water mark of the 2008 flood came in early April, as compared to the high-water mark of the 1956 flood, which occurred in late May.

You can't put *of the 2008 flood* or *of the 1956 flood* in parentheses because you need that information for the sentence. However, if you have a sentence written like this:

I haven't recovered from my latest (and, I hope, my last) adventure with blind dates.

You could omit the material inside the parentheses and you'd still have the essence of the sentence. Granted, the sentence wouldn't be as cleverly worded, but the gist would be the same.

Another time parentheses are commonly used is in citing dates, especially birth and death dates.

Dame Agatha Christie (1890–1976) wrote twelve novels featuring Miss Marple.

In addition, use parentheses to enclose numbers or letters that name items in a series. Sometimes both the parentheses marks are used, and sometimes just the mark on the right-hand side is used:

Before checking the patient, you should (a) wash your hands; (b) make sure the patient's chart is nearby; (c) call for the attending nurse to supervise.
Before checking the patient, you should a) wash your hands; b) make sure the patient's chart is nearby; c) call for the attending nurse to supervise.

Whether you use both parentheses or just one, be consistent. Also, be aware that if you use one parenthesis only, your reader may easily get the letter mixed up with the preceding word.

In material that covers politics, you'll often see parentheses used to give a legislator's party affiliation and home state (in the case of national politics) or city or county (in the case of state politics).

Senator Willa Liberi (D-R.I.) met in her Washington office with a number of constituents, including Representative Mark Digery (R-Providence).

Another—though less common—use for parentheses is to show readers that an alternate ending for a word may be read. Take a look at this sentence:

Please bring your child(ren) to the company picnic.

Keep in mind that parentheses would not be used this way in more formal writing; the sentence would be reworded to include both *child* and *children*.

Making a Rare Appearance: Square Brackets

Ordinarily, square brackets aren't used very often, except in dictionaries. A detailed dictionary will often use brackets to show the etymology, or the history, of the word being defined. (Now be honest—you've never noticed brackets in dictionaries, have you?)

One use of square brackets is to make certain that quoted material is clear or understandable for readers. Suppose you're quoting a sentence that contains a pronoun without its antecedent, as in this example:

"He burst onto the party scene and began to take society by storm."

Just who is *he?* Unless the previous sentences had identified him, readers wouldn't know. In that case, you'd use square brackets this way:

"He [Justin Lake] burst onto the scene and began to take society by storm."

Here's another example:

"It came as a big surprise to everyone at the party."

Readers would have no idea what *it* was. An announcement of retirement? an unexpected large check? a stripper popping out of a cake?

To explain the pronoun so that readers understand the material more clearly, you might use brackets in this way:

"It [the fact that a thief was in their midst] came as a big surprise to everyone at the party."

Along the same lines, you use brackets to alter the capitalization of something you're quoting so that it fits in your sentence or paragraph. For example:

"[T]he river's bank has eroded sufficiently to warrant major repair."

Use brackets for quoted material only if their use doesn't change the meaning of what's being quoted.

ALERT!

Remember! Just as with love and marriage and that horse and carriage, you can't have one side of parentheses or brackets without the other (except in display lists).

Another time that brackets are used occurs even less frequently. If you need to give information that you'd normally put in parentheses—but that information is already in parentheses—use brackets instead. This may sound confusing, but take a look at this and you'll see how the rule applies:

The man responsible for the arrest (James Bradson [1885–1940]) was never given credit.

Normally, you put a person's birth and death dates in parentheses, but since those dates are placed in material that's already in parentheses, you use brackets instead.

Depending on the type of writing you do, you might add the Latin word *sic* to the information that you're quoting. You don't know what *sic* means? *Sic* shows that what you're quoting has a mistake that you're copying. By seeing the *sic* designation, readers know that the mistake was made by the original author and not you. Look at this sentence:

"This painting was donated to the museum on September 31 [sic]."

Now, you know and I know that "thirty days hath September"—not thirty-one, as stated in the example. By using [sic] readers can tell that you copied the mistake as it was written in the original form. Note that *sic* is enclosed in brackets (many handbooks or style guides dictate that it be italicized as well).

Most style guides allow you to use either brackets or parentheses to let readers know that you've added italics to quoted material. The only rule is that you keep using the same choice of punctuation throughout the manuscript. Take your pick:

"The time of the accident is as equally important as is the date [italics added]."

"The time of the accident is as equally important as is the date (italics added)."

Generally speaking, you'll use brackets rarely—unless you're writing in a particular style. As with any writing, if you're told to use a particular style guide (say, for instance, *The Chicago Manual of Style*), consult it for the other infrequent times that brackets are used.

Checkpoint

Read and complete the following story starter and insert parentheses and brackets where they're needed. You may have to change some of the punctuation marks already in place. Check your answers in Appendix D.

It all started because I was so tired. I had my chapter notes in front of me, and what I had written said, "Test Monday on chapters 3–6 pages 48–194." I opened my history book to page 48, where I saw a picture of Robert Fulton 1765–1815.

I certainly learned quite a number of interesting facts. Among them this was on page 57 was this:

"It the Clermont, Fulton's first boat sped along at the amazing rate of five miles an our. sic"

Chapter 5

Wrapping It All Up

Congratulations! You've almost finished the refresher course on punctuation. That wasn't so bad, was it? We'll wrap it up with some punctuation symbols that aren't used every day but that certainly come in handy on occasion: italics (underlining), angle brackets, ellipses, and slashes.

Getting Fancy: Italics and Underlining

What's the difference between underlining and italics? None. As a reader, you understand the same code when you see italics or underlining. With the use of computers, clicking a button and italicizing a word is just as easy as underlining it. But sometimes (if you're writing longhand or using a type-writer), the option to italicize isn't available. Just remember to consistently use either underlining or italicizing throughout your document. A good idea is to ask if your instructor or company has a policy regarding a preference for italicizing or underlining. (Just so you know, the standard is normally to italicize, rather than to underline.)

So when is italicizing or underlining used? The most common use is in titles, but only titles of long works, such as books. For titles of short works—such as short stories, short poems, and essays—use quotation marks. In the following example, the left-hand column shows the format for the name of a book; the right-hand column shows the name of a short story within that book:

The Complete Sherlock Holmes   *"The Speckled Band"*

or

<u>*The Complete Sherlock Holmes*</u>

Titles of sacred books don't require any punctuation, nor do books of the Bible.

I read the Bible for a half an hour today.
A copy of the Koran was on his bedside table.

Here's a more complete list of works that should be italicized (underlined):

- book-length poems and collections of poems: *Leaves of Grass*
- plays: *A Raisin in the Sun*
- operas: *Carmen*
- movies: *Casablanca*
- pamphlets: *What To Do Before You See the Doctor*

- television programs (the title of an episode from a program uses quotation marks): *The X-Files*
- works of art: *Mona Lisa*
- long musical works (a CD would be italicized or underlined; a song from the CD uses quotation marks): *Greatest Love Songs of the New Century*
- magazines and newspapers (an article title from the magazine or newspaper would have quotation marks around it): *Time*
- ships, aircraft, spacecraft, trains: *Titanic*, U.S.S. *Cole* (don't italicize the U.S.S.); *Spirit of St. Louis*; *Endeavor*; *Orient Express*

FACT

In the Internet world, another common use for italics and underlining is in citing a URL, or Internet address; some style guides, however, require that angle brackets be used instead:

I purchased film study guides from the site at tinyurl.com/23bzk8.

Keep in mind that articles (*a*, *an*, and *the*) are italicized (underlined) only when they're part of the actual title. For instance:

I read Sharyn McCrumb's book *The Rosewood Casket*.

The is part of the title of the book. On the other hand, you would write:

I spent time aboard the *Mir* spacecraft.

Mir is the name of the spacecraft; *the* isn't part of its name.

Take Two: Emphasis—Another Use of Italics (Underlining)

Look at the following sentences and see if you can tell the difference:

I'm certain *I'm going to have to arrest you,"* Chief Amanuel Tekle said slyly.
"I'm certain I'm *going to have to arrest you,"* Chief Amanuel Tekle said slyly.
"I'm certain I'm going to *have* to arrest you," Chief Amanuel Tekle said slyly.

"I'm certain I'm going to have to arrest you," Chief Amanuel Tekle said slyly.

"I'm certain I'm going to have to arrest you," Chief Amanuel Tekle said slyly.

Can you see that the only difference in the five sentences is the words that are italicized? This illustrates another use of italics. In this case, the use of italics tells readers where emphasis should be placed. This helps the writer let readers know the speech patterns being used, and it also helps readers understand those patterns.

Be careful not to overuse italics for emphasis. If you use italics or underlining too frequently, you lose the emphasis you want to communicate, and—even worse—your reader soon loses interest. Look at this sentence and you'll see that the device is overdone:

"Chief, the *culprit's Mark*, not *me*. I wasn't *there* when the *wreck* happened," Bill cried *sullenly*.

With so many words italicized, the emphasis has lost its effectiveness.

Remember that you never use two end marks of punctuation at the end of the sentence.

Take Three: Unusual Usage

Read the following sentence and see if it makes sense to you:

The angry editor said to the reporter, "You imbecile! You used robbery when you should have used burglary."

Say what? Is the editor telling the reporter that he or she committed the wrong crime? No, and if the writer had used the correct punctuation marks, then the sentence would make sense.

The rule is that when words, numbers, or letters are used outside of their normal context, they should be italicized (underlined). So the sentence really should be written this way:

The angry editor said to the reporter, "You imbecile! You used *robbery* when you should have used *burglary*."

Written this way, readers understand that the reporter used the words *robbery* and *burglary* incorrectly in a story.

Some style guides also mandate that you apply this rule if you're reproducing a sound through a word (if you're using a form of onomatopoeia), as in

Brrr! *I didn't know it was this cold outside*

or

When Jerri dropped her new calculator, she cringed as it went kerplunk *when it landed.*

The Final Take: Foreign Terms

The last use of italics is related to the previous one. This rule says you should italicize or underline a foreign word or phrase.

I was wavering about whether to go to the festival with my friends, but I decided *carpe diem*.

If a foreign word or phrase has become so widely used in English that readers wouldn't question its meaning (like per diem or summa cum laude), don't italicize it.

Try the interactive quiz on italics or underlining at this Web site: *tinyurl .com/y8xp2c*

Be careful to apply italics only to punctuation (commas, periods, question marks, exclamation marks, and the like) if that punctuation is part of the title.

May screamed, "There's never been a better mystery than *The Murder of Roger Ackroyd!*"

The title of the book *The Murder of Roger Ackroyd* has no exclamation point, so the exclamation point shouldn't be italicized.

May screamed, "There's never been a better mystery than *The Murder of Roger Ackroyd*!"

The exclamation point and the ending quotation mark aren't italicized, since they aren't part of the title of the book.

Angling for Some Attention: Angle Brackets

Before Internet usage became so commonplace, you'd see angle brackets used only in a mathematical context, with > being the symbol for *greater than* and < being the symbol for *less than*.

Today, however, angle brackets are often used before and after URLs (Internet addresses). Using angle brackets helps eliminate a problem that occurs with URLs. Many URLs contain miscellaneous marks of punctuation, including hyphens and periods, so readers have trouble determining whether a particular punctuation mark is part of the URL. Look at this sentence:

Be sure to check out the information about this book and lots of our other fine publications at *<www.-i-love-angle-brackets.net/~angle.brackets>*.

By putting the URL inside brackets this way, readers can tell that the closing period is the end of the sentence and isn't part of the URL. If you've ever typed a URL incorrectly, you'll know how frustrating it can be to try to find one little mistake. Using angle brackets can help eliminate that.

Some style guides will dictate that you put e-mail addresses in angle brackets, too.

E-mail me at <anglebracketsRfun@newyork.net>

What You're Not Saying . . . Ellipsis Points

Ellipsis points or marks (three spaced periods) let readers know that some material from a quotation has been omitted. Look at this sentence:

Marilyn asked Frank to pick up a hat she had ordered and to stop for milk at the grocery store.

If you needed to quote that sentence but the part about Frank picking up the hat had no relevance to what you were saying, you could use ellipsis points in this way:

Marilyn asked Frank . . . to stop for milk at the grocery store.

You should use ellipsis points only if the meaning of the sentence isn't changed by what you omit.

Suppose you have this sentence:

The policeman reported, "The car involved in the accident had been stolen and then driven by a woman whom friends called 'Honest Harriet.'"

You shouldn't use ellipsis marks to shorten it this way:

The policeman reported, "The car involved in the accident had been . . . driven by a woman whom friends called 'Honest Harriet.'"

In doing so you would've left out some rather vital information.

If the material you're omitting occurs at the end of a sentence, or if you omit the last part of a quoted sentence but what is left remains grammatically complete, use four ellipsis points, with the first one functioning as a period. Take this original passage:

"A number of new people have joined the secret club. In fact, its membership has never been higher. Because the club is devoted to reading classical literature, however, its secret enrollment numbers haven't been questioned by the public at large."

You could use ellipsis marks in these ways:

> *"A number of new people have joined the secret club. . . . Because the club is devoted to reading classical literature, however, its secret enrollment numbers haven't been questioned by the public at large."*

Another use for ellipsis marks comes if you're quoting someone and trying to show that there's a deliberate pause in what the person said. Read the following paragraph:

> *Jimmy thought to himself, "If I can just hold on to the ball long enough to get it over to Mike, I know he can get the shot off. . . . I have to pace myself. . . . Twenty-five seconds . . . Fifteen seconds . . . Eight seconds . . . Time for a pass."*

The ellipsis marks tell your readers that they're reading all of Jimmy's thoughts and that Jimmy wasn't interrupted by anything, he just didn't have any conscious thoughts in the intervening time indicated by the ellipsis marks.

Slash It All! The Slash/Virgule/Solidus

What? You say you didn't know that a slash is also called a *virgule* and a *solidus*? Now, aren't you glad that you bought this book?

A virgule/slash/solidus is commonly used to mean *or.* Thus:

> *a slash/virgule/solidus = a slash or virgule or solidus*
> *You may bring your spouse/significant other to the picnic. = You may bring your spouse or significant other to the picnic.*

In mathematics, the slash means *per,* as in this sentence:

> *There are 5,280 feet/mile.*

It's also used in fractions:

> *365/296 (meaning 365 divided by 296)*

In literature, the slash separates lines of poetry that are written in a block style, as in this passage from Edgar Allan Poe's "The Raven":

Once upon a midnight dreary, while I pondered, weak and weary, / Over many a quaint and curious volume of forgotten lore—/"

Because of the popularity of the Internet, today the most common use of a slash is in URLs. If you've ever inadvertently omitted a slash when you're typing an address, you know that getting the site to open is impossible.

E-LINK

Now that you've learned all the punctuation marks, try the interactive quizzes at these Web sites:

tinyurl.com/y2s88y   *tinyurl.com/yx6njv*
tinyurl.com/y2kvh9   *tinyurl.com/wwdt6*
tinyurl.com/yyopl8

Checkpoint

Use angle brackets, ellipsis marks, and slashes where appropriate in the following story starter. Check your answers in Appendix D.

Janet kept trying to get to the right Internet site. The URL that she had written down was http://www.help-me-out.edu/hrcc/macleroy/, but she was unsuccessful every time she tried that site. She just knew that if she went to that site, she'd find the words to "The Star-Spangled Banner," and she needed those words in order to get extra credit in her music class.

She began humming to herself, "Oh, say, can you see, by the dawn's early light, O'er the land of the free and the home of the brave."

(You finish the story.)

_____

_____

_____

_____

_____

Chapter 6

Parts of Speech— the Big Eight

You remember the parts of speech— your English teachers talked about them all the time. But maybe you're wondering why on earth anyone other than an English teacher would be interested in the parts of speech—a valid question. The answer is that the parts of speech are basically the building blocks for good grammar and usage, and any writer who isn't familiar with them will, sooner or later, run into problems.

Step Right Up and Name Your Noun

A noun simply names a person *(Sammy, man)*, place *(Philadelphia, city)*, or thing *(Toyota, car)*. Some definitions of *noun* also include another category: idea (e.g., *philosophy, warmth*). For purposes of capitalization and points of grammar, nouns are divided into various categories. Knowing the terms will come in handy when we get to the discussion of subject-verb agreement.

Notice that some of the nouns mentioned in the previous paragraph were capitalized and some weren't. Proper nouns (particular persons, places, things, or ideas) are capitalized, but common nouns (everyday names of places, things, or ideas) aren't.

Proper Noun	Common Noun
February	month
Egypt	country

Nouns are also classified as concrete or abstract. Concrete nouns, which most nouns are, name things that can be seen, felt, heard, touched, or smelled *(star, water, album, television)*. Abstract nouns name concepts, beliefs, or qualities *(freedom, capitalism, courage)*.

Some nouns are called compound nouns; these nouns consist of more than one word but count as only one noun. Look at this name:

Henderson County Community and Technical College

It's a compound noun made up of six words, but it's only one noun (it's only one place).

Nouns are also classified as either count or noncount nouns. Count nouns are persons, places, or things that can be (surprise!) counted (thirteen *colonies*, seventy-six *trombones*). Noncount nouns are persons, places, or things that can't be counted *(unease, happiness)* and are always singular.

Collective nouns are names of persons, places, or things that are sometimes counted as one unit (they're considered to be singular) and sometimes counted separately (they're considered to be plural). *Army, herd*, and *family* are all collective nouns.

In a sentence, a noun will act either as a subject or some type of complement (predicate nominative, direct or indirect object of a verb, or object of a preposition).

The sunset was beautiful.

(The subject of this sentence is *sunset.*)

Cathy is a police officer.

(Here *police officer* is a predicate nominative, completing the verb *is.*)

Michael recently bought a new car.

(*Car* is the direct object of *bought.*)

George gave Lucy his keys.

(*Lucy* is the indirect object of the verb *gave*; *keys* is its direct object.)

Jon and Allison went into the restaurant.

(*Restaurant* is the object of the preposition *into.*)

Try the interactive quizzes on nouns at these Web sites:

> *tinyurl.com/wt344*   *tinyurl.com/y8nsue*
> *tinyurl.com/y899fu*   *tinyurl.com/smgeo*

Pithy Pronouncements on Pronouns

The textbook definition of a pronoun is "a word that takes the place of a noun." Okay, just what does that mean? Read this paragraph:

When Mrs. Anne Shreiner came into the room, Mrs. Anne Shreiner thought to Mrs. Anne Shreiner's self, "Is the situation just Mrs. Anne Shreiner, or is the temperature really hot in here?" Mrs. Anne Shreiner went to the window and opened the lower part of the window, only to have a number of mosquitoes quickly fly right at Mrs. Anne Shreiner. Mrs. Anne Shreiner said a few choice words, and then Mrs. Anne Shreiner began swatting the pesky mosquitoes, managing to hit a few of the mosquitoes when the mosquitoes came to rest on Mrs. Anne Shreiner's arm.

Isn't that the most boring paragraph you've ever read? That's because no pronouns were used. Now read the same paragraph, but with pronouns inserted in the right places:

When Mrs. Anne Shreiner came into the room, she thought to herself, "Is it just me, or is it really hot in here?" She went to the window and opened the lower part of it, only to have a number of mosquitoes quickly fly right at her. She said a few choice words, and then she began swatting the pesky mosquitoes, managing to hit a few of them when they came to rest on her arm.

What a difference a few pronouns make!

Like nouns, pronouns are divided into various classifications. To determine a pronoun's classification, follow a simple rule that will help you with all of the parts of speech: Look at the way the word is used in a sentence. Personal pronouns, one of the classifications, represent people or things: *I, me, you, he, him, she, her, it, we, us, they, them.*

I came to see you and him today.

Possessive pronouns show ownership (possession): *mine, yours, hers, his, theirs, ours.*

"These parking spaces are yours; ours are next to the door," the teachers explained to the students.

Demonstrative pronouns point out (demonstrate) someone or something: *this, that, these, those.*

This is his umbrella; that is yours.

Relative pronouns relate one part of the sentence to another: *who, whom, which, that, whose.*

The man whom I almost hit last night was taken to the police station.

(*Whom* relates to *man.*)

One country that I'd like to visit someday is France.

(*That* relates to *country.*)

Reflexive pronouns (or intensive pronouns) reflect to someone or something else in the sentence: *myself, yourself, himself, herself, itself, ourselves, yourselves, themselves.*

I said I'd do it myself!

(*Myself* relates back to *I.*)

You must ask yourself what you would do in such a situation.

(*Yourself* relates back to *you.*)

One of the most pretentious mistakes writers and speakers make is using a reflexive pronoun when a simple personal pronoun (*I, me, you, he, him, she, her, it, we, us, they, them*) will do. A simple rule to follow is to refrain from using a reflexive pronoun in a sentence if you haven't already specified whom or what you're talking about. Say what? For instance:

Please call Allan Contlesworth and myself at your earliest convenience.

You haven't said who "myself" is. The word *myself* should be replaced with *me* so that the sentence should be written:

Please call Allan Contlesworth and me at your earliest convenience.

Interrogative pronouns ask a question.

Whom can I turn to in times of trouble?
What in the world was that politician talking about?

E-LINK

Try the interactive quizzes on pronouns at these Web sites:

tinyurl.com/tfvys   *tinyurl.com/v4lfy*
tinyurl.com/y8q54s

Indefinite pronouns, contrary to their label, sometimes refer to a definite (specific) person, place, or thing that has already been mentioned in the sentence. Indefinite pronouns include *all, another, any, anyone, anything, everybody, everything, few, many, more, most, much, neither, no one, nobody, none, nothing, one, other, others, several, some, someone,* and *something.*

Keep in mind that *all, any, more, most, none,* and *some* sometimes are singular and sometimes are plural.

Three Little Questions for Adjectives

The textbook definition of an adjective is "a word that modifies a noun or pronoun." Said a different way, an adjective describes, elaborates on, or gives more information about a person, place, or thing.

One way to determine if a word is an adjective is to ask yourself if the word in question gives you more information about a noun or pronoun.

During the earthquake, the framed picture came crashing down.

You think the word *framed* is an adjective, and you ask yourself if it gives you more information about a noun. Since *framed* gives you information about *picture*, and *picture* is a thing (a noun), *framed* must be an adjective.

If that method of checking for an adjective doesn't work for you, try this one: Ask yourself if the word answers which one, what kind of, or how many? In the example, you can see that *framed* answers both *which one?* (which picture? the framed one) and *what kind?* (what kind of picture? the framed one), so it must be an adjective.

E-LINK

Try the interactive quiz on adjectives at these Web sites:

tinyurl.com/yl97x2   *tinyurl.com/hvsjm*
tinyurl.com/yy2m77

A special category of adjectives—articles—consists of just three words: *a, an,* and *the. A* and *an* are called indefinite articles because they don't indicate anything specific *(a house, an honor); the* is called a definite article because it names something specific *(the owl, the transit system).*

Another subcategory of adjectives is called determiners. These are adjectives that make specific the sense of a noun; they help determine to which particular units the nouns are referring (e.g., *the country*, *those apples*, *seven pencils*).

When you're trying to decide if a word is an adjective, examine the way it's used in your sentence. Take a look at these sentences:

I'll go to either game.
I'll go to either the basketball or the football game.

In the first sentence, *either* gives more information about (modifies) the noun *game*; so it's used as an adjective. In the second sentence, *either* is an indefinite pronoun (referring to the word *game*). Look at these sentences:

The tense situation became much more relaxed when the little boy arrived.
What is the tense of that verb?

In the first sentence, *tense* describes *situation* (a thing), so it's an adjective. Looking at it another way, *tense* answers the question *what kind?* about *situation* (a thing), so it's an adjective. In the second sentence, *tense* is simply a thing, so it's a noun.

Show Me the Action (and the Being): Verbs

Verbs are divided into two main categories: action verbs and verbs of being (or linking verbs). Let's start with the easier of the two, action verbs.

The Movers and the Shakers: Action Verbs

Verbs that express action are action verbs (not too difficult to understand, is it?). Action verbs are the more common verbs, and they're easy to spot. Look at these sentences:

Lynn petted the puppy when Mike brought it home to her.

(*Petted* and *brought* both show action.)

The frog sits on top of the lily pad in the lake.

(*Sits* shows action—well, not much action, but you get the picture.)

Action verbs are divided into two categories: transitive and intransitive. The textbook definition of a transitive verb is "a verb that takes an object." What does that mean? If you can answer *whom?* or *what?* to the verb in a sentence, then the verb is transitive.

I carried the injured boy to the waiting ambulance.

Carried whom or what? Since *boy* answers that question, the verb *carried* is transitive in that sentence.

Exhausted, I sank into the sofa.

Sank whom or what? Nothing in the sentence answers that, so the verb *sank* is intransitive in that sentence.

Knowing about transitive and intransitive verbs can help you with some easily confused verbs, such as *lie* and *lay*, and *sit* and *set.* You'll be able to see that *lie* is intransitive (I lie down), *lay* is transitive (I lay the book down), *sit* is intransitive (I'll sit here), and *set* is transitive (Beth set the vase here).

Just "Being" Verbs: Getting Linked

Granted, the action verb is easy to spot. But what in the world is meant by a definition that says a verb "expresses being"? That usually means the word is a form of the verb *be.* But that's another problem because, except for *been* and *being*, most forms of *be* don't look remotely like *be.*

It would be nonstandard to say, for instance:

I be sitting on the dock of the bay.

You should say:

I am sitting on the dock of the bay.

In that case, *am* is a form of *be.* Looking at the past tense, it would be nonstandard to say:

Yesterday she be sitting on the dock of the bay.

Instead, you should write:

Yesterday she was sitting on the dock of the bay.

So *was* is a form of *be*.

Here are the forms of *be*: *am, is, are, was, were, be, being, been*. These forms also include *has been, have been, had been, should have been, may be, might have been, will have been, should be, will be, may have been*, and *might be*.

Unusual Linking Verbs and Helping Verbs

Notice that the definition for "be verbs" says they "usually" are forms of "be." Just to complicate the situation, the words in the following list can sometimes be used as linking verbs.

The following verbs can be either linking verbs or action verbs:		
appear	become	feel
grow	look	prove
remain	seem	smell
sound	stay	taste

So when are these twelve verbs action verbs, and when are they linking verbs? Use this test: If you can substitute a form of *be* (*am, is, was*, and so on) and the sentence still makes sense, by golly, you've got yourself a linking verb. Look at these examples:

The soup tasted too spicy for me.

Substitute *was* or *is* for *tasted* and you have this sentence:

The soup was (is) too spicy for me.

It makes perfect sense. You have a linking verb. Now look at this one:

I tasted the spicy soup.

Substitute *was* or *is* for *tasted* and you have this sentence:

I was (is) the spicy soup.

That doesn't make much sense, does it? Since the substitution of a *be* verb doesn't make sense, you don't have a linking verb. You can try the same trick by substituting a form of *seem*:

The soup tasted too spicy for me.

Substitute *seemed* and you have the following:

The soup seemed too spicy for me.

The sentence makes sense, so *tasted* is a linking verb.
If you try the same trick with this sentence:

I tasted the spicy soup.

You get:

I seemed the spicy soup.

That doesn't make sense, so *tasted* isn't a linking verb in this sentence.

Another type of verb that may appear in a sentence is a helping (auxiliary) verb. This can join the main verb (becoming the helper of the main verb) to express the tense, mood, and voice of the verb. Common helping verbs are *be*, *do*, *have*, *can*, *may*, and so on. (The first two sentences of this paragraph have helping verbs: *may* and *can*.)

Breaking It Down: The Principal Parts of Verbs

You may be familiar with the phrase "the principal parts of verbs," a reference to basic forms that verbs can take. English has four principal parts: the present infinitive (the one that's the main entry in a dictionary), the past tense, the past participle, and the present participle. Take a look at the principal parts of these verbs:

Present Infinitive	Past Tense	Past Participle	Present Participle
hammer	hammered	hammered	hammering
bring	brought	brought	bringing
rise	rose	risen	rising

The first three examples all form their past and past participle by adding -*d* or -*ed* to the present infinitive. Most English verbs do this; they're called regular verbs. The last three examples, however, aren't formed in the regular way; these are called (surprise!) irregular verbs. All verbs form the present participle by adding -*ing* to the present infinitive.

Admirable Advice about Adverbs

An adverb is a word that modifies (describes, elaborates on) a verb, adjective, or other adverb.

> *Yesterday the quite relieved soldier very quickly ran out of the woods when he saw his comrade frantically waving at him.*

The adverbs in that sentence are *yesterday* (modifies the verb *ran*), *quite* (modifies the adjective *relieved*), *very* (modifies the adverb *quickly*), *quickly* (modifies the verb *ran*), and *frantically* (modifies the verb *waving*).

If you still need help finding adverbs, try this method: Ask yourself if the word you're wondering about answers one of these questions: *how, when, where, why, under what circumstances, how much, how often,* or *to what extent?*

In the example, *yesterday* answers the question *when?*; *quite* answers the question *to what extent?*; *very* answers the question *to what extent?* (or *how much?*); *quickly* answers the question *how?* (or *to what extent?*); and *frantically* answers the question *how?*

The Joiners: Conjunctive Adverbs

Conjunctive adverbs are in a category of their own. These words join independent clauses into one sentence.

Common conjunctive adverbs		
accordingly	however	nevertheless
also	incidentally	next
besides	indeed	otherwise
consequently	instead	still

Common conjunctive adverbs (cont'd)		
finally	likewise	therefore
furthermore	meanwhile	thus
hence	moreover	

Use conjunctive adverbs to join short sentences into complex thoughts; however, (did you notice the conjunctive adverb there?) be sure that:

1. you have a complete thought on either side of the conjunctive adverb
2. you put a semicolon before it and a comma after it
3. you're joining two closely related thoughts
4. you've used the right conjunctive adverb

English has a small group of adverbs known as intensifiers or qualifiers. These words increase the intensity of the adjectives and other adverbs they modify. Common intensifiers are *awfully, extremely, kind of, more, most, pretty, quite, rather, really, somewhat, sort of, very,* and *too.*

Try the interactive quizzes on adverbs at these Web sites:

tinyurl.com/ybjkf6   tinyurl.com/yj969s
tinyurl.com/yaswv2   tinyurl.com/yzv877

What's Your Position on Prepositions?

A preposition is a word that links a noun or pronoun to some other word in a sentence. Take, for example, these short sentences:

Jack and Jill went up the hill.

(*Up* is a preposition connecting *went* and *hill.*)

Little Jack Horner sat in a corner.

(*In* is a preposition connecting *sat* and *corner.*)

Sing a song of sixpence.

(*Of* is a preposition connecting *song* and *sixpence.*)

The most common prepositions				
about	behind	down	off	to
above	below	during	on	toward
across	beneath	except	onto	under
after	beside	for	out	underneath
against	between	from	outside	until
along	beyond	in	over	up
among	but	inside	past	upon
around	by	into	since	with
at	concerning	like	through	within
before	despite	of	throughout	without

Some prepositions (called compound prepositions) consist of more than one word, like *in spite of, next to, on top of,* and *together with.*

If you're trying to determine if a particular word is a preposition, here's a little trick that works for many prepositions: See if the word will fit in this sentence:

It went _____ the thing(s).

If the word in question makes sense in that sentence, it's a preposition. (Note that *of* is the most notable exception.)

Here's another way of remembering what a preposition is. Look at the last eight letters of the word *preposition*; they spell *position.* A preposition sometimes tells the position of something: *under, over, above,* and so forth.

Here's a rule you've probably heard: Never end a sentence with a preposition. Well, sometimes that rule is correct and sometimes it isn't. Generally, your writing sounds better if you can structure a sentence so that it doesn't end with a preposition. However, sometimes you want a more colloquial or conversational tone, and—let's face it—in speaking, we often end sentences with prepositions.

> *With whom are you going to the party?*

That's the "no-preposition-at-the-end" construction.

> *Whom are you going to the party with?*

That's the way the sentence normally is said.

Try the interactive quizzes on prepositions at these Web sites:

tinyurl.com/yx3crt   *tinyurl.com/k3wka*
tinyurl.com/y42mqh

Who Put the Junction in Conjunction?

A conjunction joins words in a sentence; that is, it provides a junction between words. Conjunctions are divided into three categories: coordinating, correlative, and subordinating.

Coordinating conjunctions include *and, but, or, nor, for, so,* and *yet.* Correlative conjunctions can't stand alone; they must have a "relative" nearby, usually in the same sentence. The pairs include *both/and, either/or, neither/nor, not only/also,* and *not only/but also.* Use subordinating conjunctions at the beginning of dependent (subordinate) clauses.

Common subordinating conjunctions		
after	how	than
although	if	that
as in	order that	though
as if	in that	unless
as long as	inasmuch as	until
as much as	now that	when

Common subordinating conjunctions (cont'd)		
as soon as	once	where
assuming that	providing that	whenever
because	since	wherever
before	so long as	whether
even though	so that	while

Heavens to Betsy! and Other Interjections

Egads! You don't remember what an interjection is? It's a word or phrase that expresses surprise or some other emotion or is used as filler. An interjection often stands alone (*gosh*, *darn*). If an interjection is part of a sentence, it doesn't have a relation to other words in the sentence; if it's taken out of the sentence, the meaning is unchanged. Take a look at these sentences:

> *Hey, dude.*
> *Like, what's going on?*
> *Ouch! Did you step on my toe?*

Hey, *like*, and *ouch* are interjections.

When you're expressing a strong emotion or surprise (as in *Stop!* or *Darn it all!*), use an exclamation point. If you're using milder emotion or merely using a filler (as in *like* or *well*), use a comma.

A note of caution about interjections: use them in moderation, if at all. In dialogue, interjections are used far more often than in more formal writing, where they're hardly ever used.

FACT

Interjections that are considered too off-color for readers are often denoted by using various symbols, in no particular order.

"I've been stood up by that $@# guy for the last time!" Lolita cried.*

Checkpoint

Try this fun activity to test your knowledge of the parts of speech. Check your answers in Appendix D.

Tom Swifties

Who says adverbs can't be fun? Tom Swifties are puns that use adverbs. The adverbs create a "punny" description between how Tom asked or said something (the adverb) and the words he's quoted as saying. For example, here's a Tom Swifty: "Which way is the cemetery?" Tom asked gravely. (Get it? The word *gravely* is a play on the word *cemetery*.) See if you can fill in the adverbs that will make these Tom Swifties complete:

1. "Would you turn the light on?" Tom asked _____.
2. "That's nothing; I've had a transplant," Tom's father countered _____.
3. "I can't tell if that is sleet or hail," Tom said _____.
4. "You're driving too fast!" Tom cried _____.
5. "The florist has run out of flowers," Tom lamented _____.
6. "This is the end of our relationship," Tom declared _____.
7. "It's too warm in here!" Tom bellowed _____.
8. "Because of my new job, I'll have to relocate," Tom remarked _____.
9. "Play ball!" Tom shouted _____.
10. "Let's go see a baseball game in Atlanta," Tom suggested _____.

Chapter 7

More Pieces of the Puzzle

In addition to the eight main parts of speech, English has three other parts (participles, gerunds, and infinitives), which are called verbals. Also important are the three main parts of a sentence: a subject, a predicate (verb), and complements (words that complete the meaning of the subject and predicate). Jump right in and see if you can tackle these not-so-tricky trios.

Here Come the Hybrids: Verbals

Verbals are called hybrids because they're part verb. However, they don't act as verbs; instead, they act as other parts of speech. This isn't as complicated as it sounds; you probably use verbals all the time without realizing it.

Part This and Part That: Participles

A participle is part verb and part something else, but it's used as an adjective. In the last chapter, you learned that adjectives answer one of three questions: *which one? what kind of?* or *how many?* That will come in handy here, too. Some participles consist of a verb plus *-ing*, as in these sentences:

Let sleeping dogs lie.

Sleeping consists of the verb *sleep* plus the ending *-ing*, and it acts as an adjective in the sentence. It describes *dogs*, and it answers the question *which ones?*

Shivering when they came in, Peter and Sylvia Niblo made a mad dash for the coffeepot.

Shivering consists of the verb *shiver* plus the ending *-ing*, and it acts as an adjective in the sentence. It describes *Peter and Sylvia Niblo*, and it answers the question *what kind of?* or *which one?* The previous examples illustrate present participles.

Other participles consist of a verb plus *-d* or *-ed*, as in these sentences:

Exhilarated from the victory, the entire team embraced the cheering fans.

Exhilarated consists of the verb *exhilarate* plus the ending *-d*, and it acts as an adjective in the sentence. It describes *team*, and it answers the question *which ones?*

Stained with both mustard and ketchup, my new shirt went right into the washing machine.

Stained consists of the verb *stain* plus the ending *-ed*, and it acts as an adjective in the sentence. It describes *shirt*, and it answers the question *which one?* The previous examples illustrate past participles.

So what's the big deal about a participle? Sometimes it's used in the wrong way, and that creates a dangling participle (hanging participle or unattached participle). Take a look at this sentence:

Babbling incoherently, the nurse quickly wrapped his arms around the child.

The way the sentence is written, the nurse was babbling (a participle) incoherently. What the writer means (at least, what we hope he or she means) is that the *child* was babbling incoherently. The sentence should be rewritten, perhaps this way:

The nurse quickly wrapped his arms around the babbling child.

Here's another dangling participle:

Tired from shopping at the mall, the recliner looked like the perfect spot for Kathy Wethington.

How in the world could a recliner have a tiring day shopping? That participle (*tired*) and the rest of the words that go with it (its phrase: *tired from shopping*) should be moved. A better way to word that sentence would be:

The recliner looked like the perfect spot for Kathy Wethington, who was tired from the long day shopping.

The Jolly Gerund

A gerund is a word that begins with a verb and ends in *-ing*. Wait a minute! Isn't that what a present participle is? Glad you were paying attention. Now for the rest of the story. A gerund begins with a verb, ends in *-ing*, and acts like a noun (that is, it names a person, place, or thing).

Running up hills for the last six months has improved Cathe's stamina.

Running is a gerund. It's composed of a verb (*run*), ends in *-ing*, and is used as a noun.

This rule is often ignored: Use a possessive noun or possessive pronoun (*my, your, his, her, its, our,* and *their*) before a gerund. Look at this sentence:

David continues to be amazed by (Susan, Susan's) singing.

Use the possessive *Susan's* before the gerund *singing*.
The same is true for this sentence:

Steve and Diana weren't happy about (us, our) leaving so early.

Use the possessive pronoun *our* before the gerund *leaving*.

Look at the different uses of *addressing* in these sentences:

Addressing the problem made Pat Davis realize what she must do.

Addressing the audience, Donna and Jim White felt a connection.

Anthony and Ruth Hazelwood mailed the invitations as soon as they finished addressing the envelopes.

In the first sentence, *addressing* is a gerund (a verb plus *-ing*, functioning as a noun). In the second sentence, *addressing* is a participle (a verb plus *-ing*, functioning as an adjective). In the last sentence, *addressing* is a verb (showing action).

To Be or Not to Be: Infinitives

The good news is that infinitives are easy to spot—usually. Infinitives are composed of *to* plus a verb (e.g., *to go, to carry*). Most often infinitives are used as nouns, but sometimes they crop up as adjectives or adverbs.

"I want to go home!" cried the youngster.

To go is an infinitive acting as a noun.

We come to bury Caesar.

To bury is an infinitive that acts as an adverb; it tells why we came.

Harry was the first guy in our crowd to marry.

To marry is an infinitive that acts as an adjective; it describes *guy*.
Now for the bad news. Sometimes the *to* part of an infinitive is omitted.

"Please help me mow the lawn," Arthur said to his wife.

That sentence means the same as

"Please help me to mow the lawn . . . "

Once you get used to looking at sentences in this way, you'll find that recognizing infinitives without the *to* will become automatic.

Many years ago grammarians decided that splitting an infinitive (that is, inserting a word—an adverb, to be exact—between *to* and the verb, as in *to plainly see* and *to hastily wed*) was wrong. Thankfully, that rule has gone by the wayside for all but the stuffiest editors.

Why was the "no split infinitive" rule created in the first place? In the days when the study of Latin was a mandatory part of the curriculum in many schools, rules of Latin grammar often affected rules of English grammar. Since a Latin infinitive is written as one word, it can't be split; therefore, grammarians said, the English infinitive should never be split either.

Look at the following sentence (with a split infinitive):

Georgia needed to better understand the rules of English grammar.

Now look at this sentence:

To really understand split infinitives, look at their construction.

That sentence constructed without using a split infinitive would be worded like this:

To understand really split infinitives, look at their construction.

or

Really to understand split infinitives, look at their construction.

Those don't do justice to the meaning of the sentence, do they?
But now take a look at a sentence like this:

You're usually safe to make the split.

In that instance, if you split the infinitive, you'd end up with a sentence like this:

You're safe to usually make the split.

or

You're safe to make usually the split.

Neither of those sounds right either. Better to leave the infinitive whole in that case. The moral of the story here is that you have to let your ear tell you if a split infinitive works. If it does, then by all means use it; if not, leave the infinitive alone.

E-LINK

Try the interactive quizzes on verbals at these Web sites:

tinyurl.com/3c6tp5   *tinyurl.com/2rdmqm*
tinyurl.com/82579

The Starring Roles: Subject and Predicate

Now on to the parts of a sentence. As you probably know, a sentence can be very short or very long. By definition, a sentence must have the following: (1) a predicate (usually called a verb), (2) the subject of that verb, and (3) words that form a complete thought.

The complete subject is the person, place, or thing that the sentence is about, along with all the words that modify it. The complete predicate is what the person, place, or thing is doing, or what condition it is in.

Complete Subject	Complete Predicate (Verb)
The elderly, white-haired gentleman	walked quickly down the hallway.

The simple subject of a sentence is the fundamental part of the complete subject—the main noun(s) and pronoun(s) in the complete subject. In this example, the simple subject is *gentleman*.

The simple predicate (verb) of a sentence is the fundamental part of the complete predicate—the verb(s) in the complete predicate. In the example, the simple predicate is *walked*.

A sentence may also have compound subjects and predicates.

The elderly, white-haired gentleman and his wife walked quickly down the hallway.

This sentence has a compound subject: *gentleman* and *wife*.

The elderly, white-haired gentleman walked quickly down the hallway and then paused to speak to me.

This sentence has a compound verb: *walked* and *paused*.

The elderly, white-haired gentleman and his wife walked quickly down the hallway and then paused to speak to me.

This sentence has a compound subject—*gentleman* and *wife*—and a compound verb—*walked* and *paused*.

If you have trouble locating the subject of a sentence, find the verb and then ask *who* or *what* did the verb. Read this sentence:

After a tiring morning at the gym, Justin fell onto the floor in exhaustion.

The verb is *fell*. If you ask, "Who or what fell?" you answer *Justin*, which is the subject.

Some imperative sentences written in the second person are called "you understood" sentences. You know the subject of the sentence is *you*, even though *you* isn't spoken or written. Look at this sentence:

"Go get me some lemonade."

You understand that the meaning is "You go get me some lemonade."

Remember that the subject of a sentence is never in a prepositional phrase. If the sentence is a question, the subject sometimes appears after the verb. To find the subject, turn the question around so that it resembles a declarative sentence. Then proceed in the normal way. Look at this sentence:

What is Willa going to do with that leftover sandwich?

Now, turn the wording around so that you have:

Willa is going to do what with that leftover sandwich?

Willa answers the *who?* or *what?* question about the verb *is going.*
Finding the subject of a sentence helps you use verbs and pronouns correctly.

E-LINK

Try the interactive quiz on sentence subjects at this Web site:

tinyurl.com/3bwzks

Making It Complete: Complements

Although some sentences are complete with only a subject and a predicate, many others need something else to complete their meaning. These additional parts of a sentence are called complements, and English has five types: direct object, object complement, indirect object, predicate adjective, and predicate nominative. Predicate adjectives and predicate nominatives are considered subject complements.

Direct Objects

One type of complement used with a transitive verb is a direct object: the word or words that receive the action of the verb. Direct objects are nouns (usually), pronouns (sometimes), or noun clauses (rarely). You can find a direct object by applying this formula:

1. First, find the subject of the sentence.
2. Second, find the verb, and make sure it's transitive.
3. Third, say the subject and predicate, and then ask *whom?* or *what?* If a word answers either of those questions, it's a direct object.

All of this sounds more complicated than it is. Look at this sentence:

The little boy constantly dribbled the basketball in the outdoor playground.

You can find the subject *(boy)* and the verb *(dribbled)*, so all you do is say *boy dribbled whom or what?* The word that answers that question *(basketball)* is the direct object. Easy enough, huh?

Object Complements

Another kind of complement used with a transitive verb is an object (objective) complement; it elaborates on or gives a fuller meaning to a direct object. Object complements can be nouns, pronouns, or adjectives. Take a look at this sentence:

Helen and Ruth asked their sister Marie for a ride home.

In this sentence the direct object is *Marie* (Helen and Ruth asked whom or what? *Marie.*), and the noun *sister* is the object complement. Object complements that act in this way—that is, they elaborate on the direct object—are nouns or pronouns.

Object complements can also be adjectives. Look at this sentence:

On a whim, both George and Lucy painted their fingernails blue.

In this sentence the direct object is *fingernails* (both painted whom or what? *fingernails*), and the adjective *blue* is the object complement. Object complements that act in this way—that is, they describe the direct object—are adjectives.

Indirect Objects

The third type of complement used with a transitive verb is an indirect object. It comes before a direct object and answers the question *to whom?* or *for whom?* after the subject and verb. An easy formula for finding an indirect object is this:

1. First, find the subject of the sentence.
2. Second, find the transitive verb.
3. Third, say the subject and the predicate, and then ask *to whom?* or *for whom?* If a word answers that question, it's an indirect object.

FACT

In order for a sentence to have an indirect object, *to* or *for* must be implied, not stated. If either of those words is stated, then you have a prepositional phrase, not an indirect object.

Bob and Sara Payne made us a spaghetti dinner.

When you ask *Bob and Sara Payne made for whom?* the answer is *us*. *Us* is an indirect object.

Bob and Sara Payne made a spaghetti dinner for us.

Since *for* is in the sentence, *for us* is a prepositional phrase, not an indirect object.

Look at this example:

Drew reluctantly gave Courtney the keys to his new car.

In this sentence, the subject is *Drew* and the verb is *gave*. Using the formula of asking *to whom?* or *for whom?* after the subject and verb, you would say *Drew gave to whom?* The answer is *Courtney*.

Subject Complements

Other kinds of complements, called subject complements, are used only with linking verbs. (Linking verbs, you'll remember, are all forms of *be* and, in certain situations, *appear, become, feel, grow, look, remain, smell, sound, stay,* and *taste.*) Subject complements do just what their name implies—they complete (give you more information about) the subject. Predicate adjectives and predicate nominatives are the two types of subject complements.

Predicate Adjectives

A predicate adjective is an adjective that comes after a linking verb and describes the subject of the sentence. To find a predicate adjective, apply this formula:

1. First, make sure the sentence has a linking verb.
2. Second, find the subject of the sentence.

3. Third, say the subject, say the linking verb, and then ask *what?* If a word answers the question *what?* and is an adjective, then you have a predicate adjective.

Here's an example of a predicate adjective:

Members of the Outlook Book Club are all intelligent.

Apply the formula for this sentence: (1) you know that *are* is a linking verb; (2) you find *members* as the subject of the sentence; (3) you say *members are what?* Since *intelligent* answers that question, and *intelligent* is an adjective, then you know that *intelligent* is a predicate adjective.

Predicate Nominatives

The other type of subject complement is the predicate nominative (predicate noun). It also comes after a linking verb and gives you more information about the subject. Here's a formula for finding a predicate nominative:

1. First, make sure the sentence has a linking verb.
2. Second, find the subject of the sentence.
3. Third, say the subject, say the linking verb, and then ask *who?* or *what?* If a word answers the question *who?* or *what?* and is a noun or pronoun, you have a predicate nominative.

FACT

Any kind of complement may be compound.

I played basketball and football in high school.
(compound direct objects)

Lynne and Dick bought their dogs Bow and Wow new engraved collars.
(compound object complements)

Lucy is my aunt and my friend.
(compound predicate nominatives)

Look at this sentence:

That man over there is DeShawn.

Apply the formula for this sentence: (1) you know that *is* is a linking verb; (2) you find *man* as the subject of the sentence; (3) you say *man is who?* Since *DeShawn* answers that question, and *DeShawn* is a noun (it names a person), then you know that *DeShawn* is a predicate nominative.

Checkpoint

Look at the following story starter and identify the subject, predicate, and type of complement (direct object, object complement, indirect object, predicate adjective, or predicate nominative) in each sentence. Check your answers in Appendix D.

Gail and Leo seemed very nervous about their upcoming job interviews. Both were good candidates, but they felt uneasy about their chances. Gail called Leo on the phone right before she left. "This is Gail. I will give you a ride to the interview."

"There is no need for you to come by here. I do, however, have some news for you."

1. Gail and Leo seemed very nervous about their upcoming job interviews.

   Subject: _____

   Predicate: _____

   Complement: _____

2. Both were good candidates, but they felt uneasy about their chances.

   Subject: _____

   Predicate: _____

   Complement: _____

3. Gail called Leo on the phone right before she left.

   Subject: _____

   Predicate: _____

   Complement: _____

4. This is Gail.

   Subject: _____

   Predicate: _____

   Complement: _____

5. I will give you a ride to the interview.

   Subject: _____

   Predicate: _____

   Complement: _____

6. There is no need for you to come by here.

   Subject: _____

   Predicate: _____

   Complement: _____

7. I do, however, have some news for you.

   Subject: _____

   Predicate: _____

   Complement: _____

You finish the story.

_____

_____

_____

_____

_____

Chapter 8

Let's Have a Few Words

You have to crawl before you walk. In the first few chapters, you were crawling through grammar—re-examining punctuation, parts of speech, and parts of a sentence. Now you can progress to walking—putting punctuation and words together in more complex forms.

Finding Fundamental Phrases

A phrase is a group of words that acts as a particular part of speech or part of a sentence but doesn't have a verb and its subject. The most common type of phrase is the prepositional phrase.

A prepositional phrase is a group of words that begins with a preposition and ends with a noun or pronoun (the object of the preposition). Here are a few examples:

during the terrible storm
after Tom and Norma's dinner
through the open doorway
for Rufie and Phyllis

In a sentence, prepositional phrases act as adjectives (they describe nouns or pronouns; they also answer the question *which one?* or *what kind of?*) or adverbs (they describe verbs, adjectives, or other adverbs; they also answer the question *when? where? how? why? to what extent?* or *under what condition?*).

Adjective Phrases

Adjective phrase: Several friends from my job are getting together tonight.

From my job is a prepositional phrase that acts as an adjective. It's an adjective phrase because it modifies or describes the noun *friends*. If you look at it in another way, *from my job* is an adjective phrase because it answers the question *which ones?* An adjective phrase is almost always placed right after the word or words it modifies.

Adverb Phrases

Adjective phrase: Tom and Debbie will meet at Wolf's Restaurant later tonight.

At Wolf's Restaurant is a prepositional phrase that acts as an adverb. It's an adverb phrase because it modifies or describes the verb *meet*. If you look at it in another way, *at Wolf's Restaurant* is an adverb phrase because it answers the question *where?*

Participial Phrases

Another type of phrase is the participial phrase, which is composed of a participle and any words that modify it or are related to it. A participle, you remember, is a word formed from a verb plus an ending. A participle acts as an adjective; that is, it describes a noun or pronoun in your sentence. Present participles always end in *-ing*; past participles usually end in *-d* or *–ed*, but English has many exceptions. For example:

Fleeing from the sudden storm, picnickers Leslie and Dino sought refuge in the shelter house at the park.

Fleeing is a present participle; it has a verb *flee* plus *-ing*, and it describes the noun *picnickers*. *Fleeing* and the words that go with it—*from the sudden storm*—make up the participial phrase.

A third type of phrase is the gerund phrase, which is a gerund and any words that modify it or are related to it in your sentence. Remember that a gerund is a word that is formed from a verb plus *-ing*. Since a gerund acts as a noun, it can be a subject or an object. Look at this sentence:

Singing the night away helped Charles and Catherine forget their troubles.

Singing is a gerund; it's composed of the verb *sing* plus *-ing*. In this sentence, it acts as the subject. *Singing* and the words that go with it—*the night away*—make up the gerund phrase.

Infinitive Phrases

A fourth type of phrase is the infinitive phrase, which is an infinitive and any words that modify it. An infinitive, you know, is *to* plus a verb. An infinitive can act as several parts of speech—a noun, an adjective, or an adverb. For example:

"To go home right now is my only wish," sighed the tired mother.

To go is an infinitive; it's composed of *to* plus the verb *go*. In this sentence, it acts as the subject of the sentence. The infinitive *To go* and the word that goes with it—*home*—make up the infinitive phrase.

Appositive Phrases

The final type of phrase is an appositive phrase, which is an appositive and any words that modify it or are related to it. An appositive is a noun (usually) or pronoun (rarely) that gives details or identifies another noun or pronoun. Here's an example:

> *My favorite book, a dog-eared copy of* To Kill a Mockingbird, *has accompanied me on many vacations.*

Copy is an appositive that refers to *book*. In this sentence, *copy* and the words that go with it—*a dog-eared*—make up the appositive phrase: *a dog-eared copy of To Kill a Mockingbird.*

Bringing It Up a Notch: Clauses

A clause is just a notch more complicated than a phrase. Like a phrase, a clause is used as a particular part of speech or part of a sentence; however, unlike a phrase, a clause has a verb and its subject. Independent and subordinate are the two main types of clauses.

The Declaration of Independent Clauses

An independent (main) clause is a group of words that has a verb and its subject. Also, this group of words could stand alone as a sentence; that is, the words could make sense if they were by themselves. Here's an example:

> *The index cards fell to the floor.*

This is one independent clause. It has a subject *(cards)* and a verb *(fell)*, and it stands alone as a sentence. Now, look at this sentence:

> *The index cards scattered on the floor, and Ora Lou and Gene had to pick them all up.*

This sentence has two independent clauses. The first—*the index cards scattered on the floor*—has a subject *cards* and a verb *scattered*; it could stand alone as a sentence. The second—*Ora Lou and Gene had to pick them all up*—has subjects *(Ora Lou* and *Gene)* and a verb *(had)*; it also could stand alone as a sentence.

Remember that independent clauses joined by *and, but, for, or, nor, so,* or *yet* are separated by a comma. Other independent clauses are separated by a semicolon.

Now look:

Ora Lou and Gene had just alphabetized the index cards when the cards fell on the floor and scattered everywhere.

The independent clause in this sentence is *Ora Lou and Gene had just alphabetized the index cards.* Although the rest of the sentence—*when the cards fell on the floor and scattered everywhere*—has a subject *(cards)* and verbs *(fell* and *scattered)*, it can't stand alone as a complete thought; because of this, it's not an independent clause.

In a State of Dependency: Subordinate Clauses

A subordinate (dependent) clause has a verb and its subject, but it can't stand alone as a sentence. When you read the words of a subordinate clause, you can see a subject and a verb but the words don't make sense by themselves. In order for a subordinate clause to make sense, it has to be attached to another part (to some independent clause) of the sentence. A subordinate clause usually begins with a subordinating conjunction or a relative pronoun. Look at the last example in the discussion about independent clauses:

Ora Lou and Gene had just alphabetized the index cards when the cards fell on the floor and scattered everywhere.

In this sentence, *when the cards fell on the floor and scattered everywhere* is a subordinate clause. It has a subject *cards* and verbs *fell* and *scattered.* But read the words alone:

when the cards fell on the floor and scattered everywhere

So, what about them? What happened next? If the terminology of clauses seems complicated, think of the relationship this way: since a subordinate clause can't stand alone, it's secondary (subordinate) to the main clause of the sentence. Or, a subordinate clause relies (is dependent) on another clause (an independent clause) that's in the same sentence.

English has three types of subordinate clauses, and each acts in a different way in a sentence.

Adjective Clauses

An adjective clause is a subordinate clause that acts as an adjective; it modifies or describes a noun or pronoun. Looked at a different way, an adjective clause answers *which one?* or *what kind of?* An adjective clause is sometimes called a relative clause because relative pronouns *(who, whose, whom, which,* and *that)* often begin adjective clauses and relate the clause to the person, place, or thing that they describe.

That man, whom I knew in high school, walked right by as if he'd never met me.

Whom I knew in high school is an adjective clause. It has a verb *(went)* and its subject *(I),* and it can't stand alone as a sentence—that's what makes it a subordinate clause. It's an adjective clause because it describes the noun *man;* in addition, it answers the question *which one?* about *man.*

Careful! Just to confuse you, sometimes an adjective clause has *that* deleted from it.

The new CD that Bill and Becky Brown want has not yet been released.
The new CD Bill and Becky Brown want has not yet been released.

Because an adjective clause modifies a noun, it can modify a subject, direct object, indirect object, predicate nominative, or object of a preposition.

Noun Clauses

A noun clause is a subordinate clause that acts as a noun; it can be the subject, predicate nominative, appositive, object of a verb, or object of a preposition. A noun clause answers *who? whom?* or *what?*

Kevin, Lynda, and Mike couldn't believe what they heard at the library.

What they heard at the library is a noun clause. It has a subject (*they*) and a verb (*heard*) and it can't stand alone as a sentence, so it's some type of subordinate clause. Because it's the direct object of *couldn't believe* (and therefore functions in the sentence as a noun), it's a noun clause.

FACT

A noun clause is often introduced by *if, how, that, what, whatever, when, where, whether, which, who, whoever, whom, whomever, whose,* or *why.*

Adverb Clauses

An adverb clause is a subordinate clause that acts as an adverb; it can modify or describe a verb, an adjective, or another adverb. Looked at in a different way, an adverb clause answers *when? where? how? why? to what extent? with what goal or result?* or *under what condition or circumstances?* An adverb clause is introduced by a subordinating conjunction, such as *after, although, as (if), because, once, until,* and *while.*

Mr. Kasenow visited Kim because he was attracted to her.

Because he was attracted to her is an adverb clause. It has a subject (*he*) and a verb (*was attracted*). It can't stand alone as a sentence, so it's some type of subordinate clause. Because it modifies the verb *visited*, it's an adverb clause.

Remember to use a comma after an introductory adverb clause, as in this example:

Whenever he came to visit, Mr. Kasenow brought Kim a box of candy.

Using Clauses

By eliminating the noun or pronoun and changing the verb, you can change clauses into phrases; in the same vein, you can add a subject and verb to a phrase and create a clause. Why would you want to change clauses into phrases (or vice versa)? After you've written a paragraph, you might notice that you've used the same style in several sentences, and because of that your writing seems monotonous or "sing-songy." Reconstructing your sentences by changing clauses and phrases might help eliminate that effect and make your paragraph livelier. Notice the difference here:

Adjective clause: The green van that is on the used car lot caught my eye.

Adjective phrase: The new green van on the used car lot caught my eye.

By the same token, you can convert a subordinate clause into an independent clause by adding a few words:

The green van on the used car lot caught my eye. The lot is on the corner of Elm and Second.

Try the interactive quizzes on phrases and clauses at these Web sites:

tinyurl.com/yp2wxk   tinyurl.com/24bqw5
tinyurl.com/2dsfuo   tinyurl.com/2yujyr

A Matter of Necessity: Restrictive and Nonrestrictive Clauses

Clauses are also divided in another way, depending on whether they're necessary in a sentence. A restrictive clause (essential clause or a defining clause) is necessary to the basic meaning of the sentence; a nonrestrictive clause (nonessential clause or nondefining clause) can be eliminated from the sentence without changing its basic meaning.

The car that Donald and Shirley Wathen had just purchased was stolen.
The car, which was stolen last Saturday, has been found.

In the first example, the clause *that Donald and Shirley Wathen had just purchased* is necessary to complete the meaning of the sentence. In the second example, including the clause *which was stolen last Saturday* isn't necessary in order to understand what the sentence says. In this instance, the clause is merely extra information.

QUESTION?

What's the difference between a phrase and a clause?
A clause has a verb and its subject; a phrase doesn't.

Notice in the preceding examples the word *that* introduces restrictive clauses, and *which* introduces nonrestrictive clauses. In general, note how particular words introduce different types of clauses. In determining parts of speech, look at the way the word is used in the sentence; in determining a type of clause, look at the way the clause is used in the sentence.

Putting It All Together: Constructing Sentences

Congratulations. Now that you've examined words, phrases, and clauses, you can put 'em all together and—*voilà!*—make sentences. Or can you? The truth is, you need a few additional facts.

Grammarians get technical with sentences, just as they do with the parts that make up the sentences. Sentences are classified in both the way they're arranged (this is called sentence type) and in the way they function.

Surveying Sentence Types

You can determine the type of sentence by looking at *what kind* of clauses the sentence has and *how many* clauses the sentence has. Sentence types come in one of four categories: simple, compound, complex, and compound-complex.

A simple sentence has one independent clause and no subordinate clause:

The man on the dapple gray horse confidently rode into town.

This sentence has one subject *(man)* and one verb *(rode)*.

A simple sentence may have compound subjects or verbs, but it has only one complete thought (one independent or main clause).

A compound sentence has at least two independent clauses (two main clauses) but no subordinate clause (no dependent clause):

The man on the dapple gray horse confidently rode into town, and the towns-people began to fear for their lives.

This sentence has two independent clauses joined by *and*.

ALERT!

Remember that independent clauses are joined by a comma plus one of the *boysfan* words *(but, or, yet, so, for, and,* or *nor)* or by a semicolon.

A complex sentence has one independent clause (main clause) and one or more subordinate clauses (dependent clauses):

Although he had been warned not to come, the man on the dapple gray horse confidently rode into town.

This sentence has one independent clause *(the man on the dapple gray horse confidently rode into town)* and one subordinate clause *(although he had been warned not to come).*

Using complex and compound-complex sentences helps to keep your writing from being monotonous. A compound-complex sentence has at least two independent clauses (main clauses) and one or more subordinate clauses (dependent clauses):

Although he had been warned not to come, the man on the dapple gray horse confidently rode into town, and the townspeople feared for their lives.

This sentence has one subordinate clause *(although he had been warned not to come)* and two independent clauses *(the man on the dapple gray horse confidently rode into town* and *the townspeople feared for their lives).*

Fathoming Sentence Function

Sentences function in four different ways; they can be declarative, interrogative, imperative, or exclamatory.

A declarative sentence makes a statement:

Tomorrow we can talk about our weekend plans.

An interrogative sentence asks a question:

Do you think we can talk about our weekend plans tomorrow?

FACT

Sometimes you have a combination of sentence types.

I'll see you tomorrow, won't I?

The first part is a declarative sentence, and the second part is called a tag question.

An imperative sentence issues a command, makes a request, or gives instructions:

Come here so we can talk about our weekend plans.

An exclamatory sentence expresses strong emotion:

How I hope we can be together this weekend!

Keeping the Harmony: Subject-Verb Agreement

Do you ever notice some kind of incompatibility in your sentences? When you read your sentences, do you hear a jarring ring that tells you that something's wrong? The problem may be that you have disagreement between your subjects and verbs. To smooth out the situation, all you need to do is be sure that you follow the rule about subject-verb agreement: You must make verbs agree with their subjects in number and in person.

Okay, that's the rule, but what does it mean? The first part *(make the verb agree with its subject in number)* is just this simple: If you use a singular subject, you have to use a singular verb; if you use a plural subject, you have to use a plural verb. Nothing hard about that, is there?

Well, as you probably suspect, a number of situations can arise to make the rule tricky.

The Problem of Prepositions

One problem comes with using the wrong word as your subject. To keep from making this mistake, remember this hint: Mentally disregard any prepositional phrases that come after the subject. Prepositional phrases will just distract you. Take a look at these sentences:

*The tray of ice cubes (*has, have*) fallen on the kitchen floor.*

Since you know to disregard the prepositional phrase *of ice cubes*, you then have:

*The tray ~~of ice cubes~~ (*has, have*) fallen on the kitchen floor.*

Now, you're left with the subject of the sentence *(tray)*. Of course, you would say,

"The tray has fallen on the kitchen floor."

Look at another example:

*Katie and Matt, along with their dog Pretzel, (*was, were*) walking down Hillcrest Boulevard.*

Again, mentally cross off the prepositional phrase—no matter how long it is—and you have:

Katie and Matt, ~~along with their dog Pretzel,~~ (was, were) walking down Hill-crest Boulevard.

You'd have no problem saying "Katie and Matt were walking down Hill-crest Boulevard," so that lets you know the correct verb to use.

Pinpointing the Pronouns

If an indefinite pronoun is the subject of your sentence, you have to look at the individual pronoun. Sometimes this is a snap, as with the plural pronouns that take a plural verb *(both, few, many, others, several).* Look at these sentences:

*"Several scouts are [not **is**] in the stands at tonight's game," whispered the coach.*
*A few of us want [not **wants**] to go camping this weekend.*

Just as some plural indefinite pronouns are easy to spot, so are some singular indefinite pronouns *(another, anybody, anyone, anything, each, either, everybody, everyone, everything, much, neither, no one, nobody, nothing, one, other, somebody, someone, something).* The problem with indefinite pronouns is that a few of them are considered to be singular, even though they indicate a plural number (e.g., *each, everybody, everyone, everything*). For example:

*Everybody is [not **are**] here, so we can start the trip.*
*No one is [not **are**] going to complain if you pick up the tab for tonight's meal.*

Now comes a tricky rule: Five pronouns *(all, any, most, none, and some)* sometimes take a singular verb and sometimes take a plural verb. How do you know which one to use? This is the time—the only time—you break the rule about disregarding the prepositional phrases. Take a look at these sentences:

*"Some of the money is [not **are**] missing!" cried the teller.*

*"Some of the people in the bank are [not **is**] the suspects," replied the policeman.*

*Most of my coworkers were [not **was**] cleared of any suspicion*

*Most of my jewelry is [not **are**] still missing.*

In each case, you have to look at the object of the preposition (*money, people, coworkers, jewelry*) to decide whether to use a singular or plural verb.

Seeking Solutions to Some Special Situations

Here are some more oddities of English grammar (as if you haven't seen enough of them already):

The phrase *the only one of those* uses a singular verb; however, the phrase *one of those* uses a plural verb. (Is your head spinning?) Maybe these examples will help:

*The only one of those people I feel comfortable with is [not **are**] Vicki Brand.*

*Vicki Brand is one of those people who always listen [not **listens**] when I have a problem.*

If you have a sentence with *every* or *many a* before a word or group of words, use a singular verb. For example:

*Many a good man is [not **are**] trying to please his wife.*

*Every wife tries [not **try**] to help her husband understand.*

When the phrase *the number* is part of the subject of a sentence, it takes a singular verb. When the phrase *a number* is part of the subject, it takes a plural verb. Look at these sentences:

*The number of people who came to the concert is [not **are**] disappointing.*

*A number of people are [not **is**] at home watching the finals of the basketball tournament.*

When the phrase *more than one* is part of the subject, it takes a singular verb:

*More than one person is [not **are**] upset about the outcome of the election.*

Another time that subjects may be singular or plural is with collective nouns. Collective nouns (*cast*, *fleet*, or *gang*) name groups. Use a singular verb if you mean that the individual members of the group act or think together (they act as one unit). Use a plural verb if you mean that the individual members of the group act or think separately (they have different opinions or actions). For example:

The couple is renewing its donation of $50,000 for scholarships.

(The two people were donating as a unit.)

The couple were cleared of the charges of embezzlement of $50,000.

(The two were cleared separately.)

Still another problem with singular and plural verbs comes with expressions of amount. When the particular measurement or quantity (e.g., of time, money, weight, volume, food, or fractions) is considered as one unit or group, then use a singular verb:

*Ten dollars to see this movie is [not **are**] highway robbery!*
*"Five hours is [not **are**] too long to wait for this plane to take off," complained the angry passenger.*
*I would estimate that two-thirds of the snow has [not **have**] melted.*

Some nouns look plural but actually name one person, place, or thing, and so they're singular:

*The United States is [not **are**] defending its title against the United Kingdom.*

(Although fifty states are in the United States, it's one country; therefore, you use a singular verb.)

*The Everything® Grammar and Style Book is [not **are**] the best grammar book I've ever read!*

(Even though six words are in the title, *The Everything® Grammar and Style Book* is one book; use a singular verb.)

*Because I find the subject fascinating, I think it's odd that economics is [not **are**] called "the dismal science."*

(*Economics* looks as if it's a plural word, but since it's one subject it needs a singular verb.)

Here's another special situation: When you use the words *pants, trousers, shears, spectacles, glasses, tongs,* and *scissors* alone, you use a plural verb:

*These pants are [not **is**] too tight since I returned from the cruise.*
*Do [not **Does**] these trousers come in another color?*

But put the words *a pair of* in front of *pants, trousers, shears, spectacles, glasses, tongs,* or *scissors,* and then you need a singular verb:

*This pair of pants is [not **are**] too tight since I returned home from the cruise.*
*Does [not **Do**] this pair of trousers come in another color?*

If you think about it, the logic behind the usage is strange since *pair* means *two,* and *two* denotes a plural. Oh, well . . .

Compounding the Problem: Using Compound Subjects

The first rule in this part is easy. Compound subjects (subjects joined by *and*) take a plural verb:

*Mike and Lynn are [not **is**] here.*
*Mr. and Mrs. Cox are [not **is**] joining us for an informal dinner tonight.*

Here's an exception: If you have two or more subjects joined by *and*—and the subjects are thought of as one unit—then use a singular verb.

Is spaghetti and meatballs the special at Rookie's Restaurant today?

The second rule is *almost* as easy. Singular subjects joined by *or* or *nor* take a singular verb:

The butcher, the baker, or the candlestick maker is [not are] coming to tomorrow's career fair.

Rule number three is along the same lines as rule number two (and it's also *almost* as easy as the first rule). Plural subjects joined by *or* or *nor* take a plural verb:

The Paynes or the Meaghers are [not is] visiting tonight.
The horses or the pigs are [not is] making too much noise tonight.

Did you notice the word *almost* in the second and third rules? The first rule was easy; all you had to do was look at subjects joined by *and*; then use a plural verb. The second and third rules require just a little more thought because you have to be sure that the subjects joined by *or* or *nor* are either *all* singular or *all* plural:

1. If all the subjects are singular, use a singular verb.
2. If all the subjects are plural, use a plural verb.

That covers all the examples in which the subjects are the same, but what if you have one singular subject and one plural subject joined by *or* or *nor*? Do you use a singular or plural verb? Simple: You go by the subject that's closer to the verb. So you would write:

*My cat or my three dogs are [not **is**, since* dogs *is plural and is closer to the verb] coming with me.*

Or, if you inverted the subjects, you'd write:

*My three dogs or my cat is [not **are**, since* cat *is singular and is closer to the verb] making me itch.*

Here, There, and Everywhere

Sometimes writers and speakers have a hard time with sentences that begin with *here* or *there*. Writing either

Here's the money Vincent owes Regina.

or

There's plenty of time left.

is fine because if you changed the contractions into the two words each represents, you'd have "Here is the money Vincent owes Regina" and "There is plenty of time left."

No problem, huh? Now look at these sentences:

Here's the books Marsha and Morris said they'd bring.
There's lots of sandwiches left, so help yourself.

In these examples if you change those contractions, you have "Here is the books Marsha and Morris said they'd bring " and "There is lots of sandwiches left, so help yourself." Obviously, you'd never say, "Here is the books" or "There is lots of sandwiches" (you wouldn't, would you?), so the verb form is wrong. Since each of those subjects is plural, you need the plural verb (*are*).

So the rule is this: If you begin a sentence with *here* or *there* and you have a plural subject, be sure to use a plural verb (usually the verb *are*).

Inside Out

In order to provide originality to their sentence structure or to keep their paragraphs from being too monotonous, good writers often change the word order of their sentences from the normal subject-verb pattern. Instead of writing the sentence as in the first example that follows, you might change the word order and present your sentence as it appears in the second example:

The soldiers came over the hill, determined to destroy the fortress
Over the hill came the soldiers, determined to destroy the fortress.

Both sentences have the subject (*soldiers*) and the verb (*came*), but the second sentence is written in what is called inverted order—the verb before the subject. The caution here is to be sure that the subject agrees with the verb, no matter in what order you write the sentence.

The same rule holds true for questions and for sentences that begin with here or there:

Here are all my friends in one room.
There go two of my oldest friends!

In both sentences, the normal pattern of subject-verb is reversed. In the first sentence, the subject is *friends* and the verb is *are*. In the second sentence, the subject is *friends* and the verb is *go*.

Mixed Numbers

If you have a sentence with a plural subject and a singular predicate nominative (or vice versa), use the verb that agrees with the subject, not the predicate nominative. For example:

Susie's favorite present is pink roses.
Pink roses are Susie's favorite present.

In the first sentence the subject (*present*) is singular, so use the singular verb (*is*). In the second sentence the subject (*roses*) is plural, so use the plural verb (*are*).

E-LINK

Try the interactive quizzes on subject-verb agreement at these Web sites:

tinyurl.com/ydtasn   tinyurl.com/yf7368
tinyurl.com/j2z75

Do It! No, Don't Do It!

For some reason, *do*, *does*, *doesn't*, and *don't* are particular problems for certain speakers and writers. Repeat three times: use *does* and *doesn't* only with singular subjects; use *do* and *don't* only with plural subjects:

*John doesn't [not **don't**] like the new supervisor anymore than Linda does.*
*It doesn't [not **don't**] matter if they like him or not; he's here to stay.*

Checkpoint

Take a look at the words in italics in the following paragraph, and decide if the words are A) an adjective prepositional phrase; B) an adverb prepositional phrase; C) a participial phrase; D) a gerund phrase; E) an infinitive phrase; F) an appositive phrase; G) an independent clause; H) an adjective clause; I) a noun clause; J) an adverb clause.

The long wait *on the bridge* was finally at an end, and the wreck *that had caused the delay* was cleared. *While I had been waiting*, I had finished a book on tape. *Listening to it* had sure helped to pass the time. *Whoever had been in the wreck* hadn't been injured seriously, *I knew*, because the ambulance had left *without any injured people*.

1. on the bridge _____
2. that had caused the delay _____
3. While I had been waiting _____
4. Listening to it _____
5. Whoever had been in the wreck _____
6. I knew _____
7. without any injured people _____

Chapter 9

Pertinent Points about Pesky Pronouns

Do you ever get confused about which pronoun to use? As handy as they are, pronouns sure can pose some problems for both speakers and writers. Yet using the proper pronoun is necessary to avoid both confusion and miscommunication.

Introducing the Pronoun

Consider the following:

> *Last night, the suspect was charged with hitting a fellow diner and knocking them to the floor. I spoke to E. J. and Pat earlier today, and I asked her if she had been there when it happened. She said that after the incident, the conversation between the other diners and she centered around thinking about whom would be questioned by the police. All the people who were discussing this they finally decided that if you were there, you probably were going to be questioned.*

Can you point out what's wrong in this paragraph? The story has examples of several common pronoun problems:

- a plural pronoun that refers to a singular antecedent
- a pronoun that isn't clear about which antecedent it refers to
- pronouns that shift points of view in the same sentence
- a pronoun that's not needed
- a pronoun that's in the wrong case
- confusion about when to use *who* and *whom*

Maybe it's time to take a look at these pesky pronoun problems.

Pronouns are words that take the place of nouns. They include:

I	herself	both
me	itself	each
you	ourselves	either
he	yourselves	everybody
him	themselves	everyone
she	this	everything
her	that	few
it	these	little
us	those	many

they	who	most
them	whom	much
mine	which	neither
yours	whose	no one
hers	what	nobody
his	all	none
theirs	another	nothing
ours	any	one
myself	anybody	other
yourself	anyone	others
himself	anything	several
some	somebody	someone

The Numbers Game: Problems with Agreement

Pronouns must agree in number with the words to which they refer (their antecedents). Read these sentences:

After I saw who wrote the letters, I tossed it in the wastebasket.
After I saw who wrote the letters, I tossed them in the wastebasket.

The first sentence doesn't make sense because *it* is the wrong pronoun. The noun that *it* refers to is *letters*, and *letters* is a plural noun. The pronoun used to replace *it* should also be plural. In the second sentence, *it* has been replaced by *them*, which is plural. That's why the second sentence makes sense.

Put another way, the rule is this: If a pronoun is plural, the word it refers to (also known as its antecedent) must be plural; if a pronoun is singular, the word it refers to must be singular.

So what's the problem? No one would write a sentence like the first example, right? But complications do arise where some of the indefinite pronouns are concerned.

Definite Problems with Indefinite Pronouns

Indefinite pronouns include the following:

all	everyone	none
another	everything	nothing
any	few	one
anybody	little	other
anyone	many	others
anything	most	several
both	much	some
each	neither	somebody
either	no one	someone
everybody	nobody	something

Anyone, anybody, anything, each, either, everybody, everyone, everything, neither, nobody, none, no one, one, somebody, something, and *someone* are all considered to be singular words, so they all require a singular pronoun. But, if you think about it, the word *each* implies more than one. If each person is doing something, that means more than one, right? The same can be said for *everybody, everything,* and *everyone.* This doesn't matter; all four words are considered singular. So you should write:

> *Everybody is seated, and each is waiting for the plane to take off.*
> *Each of the dogs needs its collar before it can be enrolled in obedience school.*
> *Everyone must bring a list of her prenatal vitamins. (Using only* her *in this sentence is perfectly fine since no men would be taking prenatal vitamins.)*

A common tendency in everyday speech is to use *they* or *their* in place of some singular pronouns. In the first example, you might hear the sentence spoken this way:

> *Everybody is seated, and they are waiting for the plane to take off.*

This usage is called the "singular they" because *they* refers to an antecedent that's singular.

Even though using the "singular they" is becoming more commonplace, its usage is still frowned on in many circles. However, this may be one of the rules of grammar that eventually changes. The advocates of the "singular they" point out that using it helps prevent an overuse of *his or her* or *he or she.*

Now it's time to break a rule. Remember the one that says to disregard any prepositional phrase when you're looking for the subject of a sentence? Well, this rule has a few exceptions. (This is also discussed in Chapter 8 about subject-verb agreement.) Take a look at these two sentences:

All of the money is missing from the safe.
All of the cookies are missing from the jar.

In both sentences, the subject is *all.* But the first sentence has a singular verb and the second sentence has a plural verb—and both are correct.

With five pronouns *(all, any, most, none,* and *some),* the "disregard the prepositional phrase" rule is canceled out. For those five pronouns, look at the object of the preposition to determine which verb to use.

When you have compound antecedents that are joined by *or* or *nor* (or *either . . . or, neither . . . nor*), make the pronoun agree with the one that's closer to the verb. Here's an example:

Either the lion or the monkeys have already gotten their food.

Since *monkeys* is plural and it comes nearer the pronoun, use the plural pronoun *their.*

Either the monkeys or the lion has already gotten its food.

Since *lion* is singular and it comes nearer the pronoun, use the singular pronoun *its.*

So, do you think you can pinpoint the mistake in the following paragraph? Pronouns and their antecedents should agree in number.

When I came down to breakfast, everybody in the family was eating, but nobody offered me even a piece of toast. At work, everyone was busy doing their different projects; they didn't even stop to look up when I came in.

By changing the incorrect pronouns, you should have:

When I came down to breakfast, everybody in the family was eating, but nobody offered me even a piece of toast. At work, everyone was busy doing his or her different projects; they didn't even stop to look up when I came in.

You can see, though, that there's a definite problem with that rewriting. While it may be grammatically correct, it sure doesn't read well. Contrary to rules of thirty or more years ago, using *his or her* rather than just *his* is now considered correct. But as you can see in the corrected paragraph, this can make for some rather awkward writing.

So what can you do to prevent this awkwardness? Rewriting the sentences to use plural nouns and pronouns instead of singular ones is far better. The paragraph could be rewritten this way:

When I came down to breakfast, all of my family were already eating, but nobody offered me even a piece of toast. At work, all of my associates were already busy doing their different projects; they didn't even stop to look up when I came in.

Much better, isn't it?

When in Doubt: Vague Pronoun References

One of the most common writing problems occurs in sentences that have unclear antecedents of the pronouns.

As you recall, pronouns are words that take the place of nouns; antecedents are the nouns that the pronouns refer to. For example:

Chelsea called to say she and Anthony would be glad to help decorate.

In this sentence, the pronoun *she* refers to *Chelsea*; therefore, *Chelsea* is the antecedent of *she*. Now, look at this example:

The movie's humor was rather sophomoric, and it didn't go over well with most of the audience.

The pronoun *it* refers to *humor*; *humor* is the antecedent of *it*.

In these examples, the antecedents are used correctly. They clearly refer to specific nouns (their antecedents). But take a look at this sentence:

Eddie invited Bud to the ranch because he enjoyed horseback riding.

Well, now. Just whom does the word *he* in the second part of the sentence refer to—Eddie or Bud? The antecedent of *he* isn't clear.

To make the sentence read clearly, it should be reworded:

Because Bud enjoyed horseback riding, Eddie invited him to the ranch.

or

Eddie, who enjoyed horseback riding, invited Bud to the ranch.

Now look at these sentences:

Pattye called Linda to report the unexpected news that she had gotten a raise. When Pattye told Claudia and Lorraine the news, she said that they should celebrate.

Are you confused? Who got the raise—Pattye or Linda? Who said that a celebration was in order—Pattye or Claudia or Lorraine? Who was to be included in the celebration—Pattye, Linda, Claudia, and Lorraine? Linda and Claudia and Lorraine? Pattye and Claudia and Lorraine? The way the two sentences are now worded, readers aren't sure.

You can correct the first sentence in several ways, depending on whom you're referring to by the words *she* and *they*. Suppose Pattye is the one who has received the raise. One way to recast the sentence to express that meaning is this way:

Pattye, who had received the unexpected news that she had gotten a raise, called her friend Linda.

Now there's no doubt about who received the raise. If Linda had received the raise, then the sentence could be reworded this way:

Pattye called Linda to report the unexpected news that Linda had gotten a raise.

In the second sentence, who's going to celebrate? To make the meaning clearer, that sentence could be reworded this way:

Pattye told Claudia and Lorraine the news, and she also said that they all should celebrate.

Now it's clear who announced the celebration and who was to be included in it.

Sometimes a pronoun has no reference at all. Read this sentence:

Cathy Blue was afraid he wouldn't remember to pick up the refreshments for the party.

Just who is *he*? Unless the man has been identified in an earlier sentence, readers are left out in the cold about his identity.

Remember that an antecedent has to refer to a specific person, place, or thing. Look at this sentence:

The young recording star was elated, but he kept it hidden.

What did the star keep hidden? Was *it* supposed to refer to the fact that he felt elated? In that case, the sentence would read:

The young recording star was elated, but he kept elated hidden.

Doesn't make sense, does it? The word *elated* can't be the antecedent of *it* because *elated* isn't a person, place, or thing. The sentence needs to be reworded something like this:

The young recording star was elated with his hit record, but he kept his elation hidden.

Along the same lines, sometimes a sentence has a noun that the pronoun refers to, but it's not the right noun; the correct reference is missing from the sentence. Read this sentence:

After a successful fishing trip with his brothers, Joe let them all go.

The way the sentence is worded, Joe let his brothers go. That's what *them* refers to in this sentence. But surely that's not what happened! What the writer means is that Joe let all the fish go. The sentence should be rewritten like this:

After a successful fishing trip with his brothers, Joe let all of their catch go.

When you're referring to people, use *who, whom,* or *whose,* not *which* or *that.* Here's an incorrect sentence:

I'm indebted to the people which helped me during the flood.

Here's the sentence in the correct way:

I'm indebted to the people who helped me during the flood.

Here's another example:

The new tax forms arrived today. They want me to fill out every line on the last three pages.

The tax forms want you to do the filling out? That's silly! What the writer meant was that the Internal Revenue Service, or an accounting firm—someone the writer failed to name—wants the tax forms filled out. The sentence needs to be reworded to make it clear who *they* are.

The new tax forms arrived today. Our accountant wants me to fill out every line on the last three pages.

Be careful not to use *they* when you refer to unnamed persons; *they* must refer to people you specify. The same holds true for any pronoun, but *they, he, she,* and *it* are the ones most commonly misused. If you think you may have an unclear reference, one way to test the sentence is to do this:

1. Find the pronoun.
2. Replace the pronoun with its antecedent—the noun it refers to.
3. If the sentence doesn't make sense, reword it.

One, Two, Three: What Person for Me?

Both pronouns and points of view are expressed in first person, second person, and third person. First-person pronouns include *I, me, my, mine, we, our,* and *us,* and the first-person point of view expresses the personal point of view of the speaker or author *(I will bring the book).* Second-person pronouns include *you, your,* and *yours,* and material expressed in the second-person point of view directly addresses the listener or reader *(You will bring the book).* Third-person pronouns include *he, she, him, her, his, hers, they, them, their,* and *theirs.* In the third-person point of view material is expressed from the point of view of a detached writer or other characters *(They will bring the book).* Check with your instructor or company to find out which person you should use. If you're in doubt, use third person.

Just Leave Me Out of It! Shifts in Person

One of the most common problems in writing comes with a shift in person. The writer begins in either first or third person and then—without reason—shifts to second person. Take, for example, this paragraph:

Even in a casual atmosphere, I can be embarrassed by someone else, and this causes you to become tense. For instance, somebody you know can embarrass you at a party or in a class. It's so simple for a stranger to embarrass you.

What's wrong with that paragraph? The writer begins in the first person (telling about himself or herself by using the pronoun *I)* and then shifts to second person. The constant use of *you* sounds as if the writer is preaching directly to readers. That writer doesn't know the readers and doesn't know if he or she can be easily embarrassed by others, and so on. Except for the beginning sentence, the entire paragraph should be rewritten and put into first person. Here is one way of doing that:

Even in a casual atmosphere, I can be embarrassed by someone else, and this causes me to become tense. For instance, somebody I know can embarrass me at a party or in a class. It's so simple for a stranger to embarrass me.

Repeat three times: Consistency is the key. Consistency is the key. Consistency is the key. If you begin in third person (which is the most common way of writing), stay in third person. If you begin in first person (the second most common way of writing), stay in first person. If you begin in second person, stay in second person. Consistency is the key.

(You did notice that the preceding paragraph is written in second person, didn't you? Actually, the first sentences are in second person. They're written in what's called a "you understood" form: even though the word *you* isn't included in the sentences, it's implied and readers understand that *you* is the subject of each sentence.)

May I Talk to You? Using the Second Person

For various reasons, most instructors usually disapprove of second person in formal writing. Is using second person ever acceptable? It is when you need an informal tone. Read something written in second person (remember, that means using *you* and *your*), and you'll find a more conversational tone than if it had been written in first or third person. Use second person when you want your words to come across in a casual way. Take a look at this paragraph:

> *You'll need to watch the mixture carefully, and you may have to stir it quite often. When you get to the last step, make sure you add the final three ingredients slowly. If you add them too quickly, you'll have a mess on your hands.*

You can easily read that paragraph. It's talking directly to you, telling you what to do in your cooking. But look at the same paragraph written in third person:

> *The mixture must be watched carefully, and it may have to be stirred quite often. At the last step, it's important that the final three ingredients be added slowly. If they're added too quickly, the combination may create a mess.*

Now, that's pretty boring and stilted, isn't it? The directions are far better if you write them in the second person.

Another time that second-person writing is used with frequency is in advertising. Consider this sign:

> *Come see the friendly folks at Abbotts' Used Car Lot!*

That's more inviting than if it were written in the third person:

Readers of this sign are invited to come see the friendly folks at Abbotts' Used Car Lot!

The friendly folks at Abbotts' probably wouldn't have much business with a sign like that, would they?

Making a Case for Pronouns

Pronouns are also one of three cases: subjective, objective, and possessive. The way you use a pronoun in a sentence determines which case you should use.

1. Subjective pronouns include *I, you, he, she, it, we,* and *they.*
2. Objective pronouns include *me, you, him, her, it, us,* and *them.* (Note that *you* and *it* are included on both lists; you'll see why later.)
3. Possessive pronouns include *my, your, his, her, its, our,* and *their.* (Possessive pronouns are regarded as adjectives by some grammarians. These pronouns won't be discussed in this section because people rarely have a problem with using them correctly.)

Writers often can't decide whether to use *we* or *us* when the pronoun comes right before a noun, as in these examples:

"(We, Us) seniors decided to play a prank on you," Matt told his instructors.

"You'd better rethink any decision to play a prank on (we, us) teachers," came the sharp reply.

To determine which pronoun is correct, just delete the noun that the pronoun refers to (*seniors* in the first sentence, *teachers* in the second sentence) and see how you would say the sentence.

No-Brainer, Part One: Subjective Pronouns

Here's the first part of a no-brainer: Subjective pronouns are used as the subjects of sentences (whom or what you're talking about). You would say, for instance:

I am going to leave for my appointment.
She is late already.

No problem seeing the right form in those sentences, is there? For some reason, though, a problem occasionally arises when subjects are compound. You might read, for instance:

His brothers and him are going to the ball game.
Margaret, Elizabeth, and me were at the mall for four hours yesterday.
Me and her see eye-to-eye on lots of things.

These pronouns are used incorrectly. Because the pronouns are used as subjects of the sentence, they should all be in the subjective case: *I, you, he, she, it, we,* or *they.* So, the sentences should read:

His brothers and he are going to the ball game.
Margaret, Elizabeth, and I were at the mall for four hours yesterday.
I and she see eye-to-eye on lots of things. (Actually, etiquette says to put the other person first, so it's better to word this sentence like this: She and I see eye-to-eye on lots of things.)

If you're not sure if you've used the right pronoun, try writing or saying the sentence with only one subject. You'd never say:

Him is going to the ball game.
Me was at the mall for four hours yesterday.
Me sees eye-to-eye on lots of things.
Her sees eye-to-eye on lots of things.

Since those pronouns sound wrong when they're by themselves, you know that they're the wrong case. Change the pronouns to the ones you'd normally use when there's just one subject.

No-Brainer, Part Two: Objective Pronouns

Here's part two of the no-brainer: Objective pronouns are used as the objects in sentences. You would say, for instance:

Hallie and Travis went to see her last night.
When Liz and Marvin celebrated their anniversary, Betty gave them a new CD.
"Give me the money right now!" the robber demanded.

As with compound subjects, problems arise with compound objects. People will write or say sentences like this:

The argument arose last night between Carla and she.
Please buy a raffle ticket from Fr. Hammerstein, Jane Ann, or I.
"The car sped by he and I, going 90 miles per hour," the witness testified.

Again, each pronoun is used incorrectly in these sentences. Because the pronouns are used as objects in these sentences, they should all be in the objective case: *me, you, him, her, it, us,* and *them.* So, the sentences should read:

The argument arose last night between Carla and her.
Please buy a raffle ticket from Fr. Hammerstein, Jane Ann, or me.
"The car sped by him and me, going 90 miles per hour," the witness testified.

Remember that pronouns that are predicate nominatives should be subject pronouns. Predicate nominatives, you recall, are nouns or pronouns used after linking verbs (usually forms of *be,* like *am, is, are, was,* and *were*).

The way to test yourself if you're not sure if you've used the right pronoun is to use the same trick that you used for the subjective pronoun problem, but substitute the objective form; that is, write or say the sentence with only one object. You'd never say:

The argument arose last night between she.
Please buy a raffle ticket from I.
"The car sped by he, going 90 miles per hour," the witness testified.
"The car sped by I, going 90 miles per hour," the witness testified.

Since those pronouns sound wrong when they're by themselves, you know that they're the wrong case. Change the pronouns to the ones you'd normally say when the sentence has only one object.

E-LINK

Try the interactive quizzes on pronoun forms at these Web sites:

tinyurl.com/w2lhx   *tinyurl.com/y7y8e9*
tinyurl.com/ysaujo

So why were *you* and *it* on the lists of both subjective and objective pronouns? Because, unlike other pronouns on the lists (*I* and *me*, for example), English uses the same form for those two words.

It was nice to get a surprise in the mail.

(*It* is a subject.)

I got it in the mail.

(*It* is an object.)

You called me at four o'clock?

(*You* is a subject.)

I called you back at five o'clock.

(*You* is an object.)

Some Sticky Situations with Than and As

Another problem with pronouns sometimes arises in a sentence with words that are omitted following *than* or *as*.

Look at the following examples:

Jim said to Donna, "I always thought Billy liked you more than me."
Jim said to Donna, "I always thought Billy liked you more than I."

When the words that have been omitted after *than* are restored, the real meaning of the sentences becomes clear:

Jim said to Donna, "I always thought Billy liked you more than (he liked) me."

Jim said to Donna, "I always thought Billy liked you more than I (liked you)."

(Either way, Jim's in quite a snit, isn't he?)

The same type of confusion can result when words following *as* have been omitted. For example, someone might say or write something along the lines of:

My husband finds physics as interesting as me.

This implies that, to the husband, physics and his wife are of equal interest. Now, look at the correction:

My husband finds physics as interesting as I (do).

This signifies that both spouses are equally interested in physics—which, one hopes, is the intended meaning here.

By mentally adding the missing verb at the end of a sentence using *than* or *as* in this way, you'll be able to tell which pronoun to use.

Who *and* Whom: *A Different Slant*

For many people, deciding whether to use *who* or *whom* may be the most difficult of all the problems with pronouns. Do you say, "The man who I called has already placed an order" or "The man whom I called has already placed an order"? How can you make your mind up between "The student who is early will get the best seat" and "The student whom is early will get the best seat"?

If you have trouble deciding whether to use *who* or *whom* (or *whoever* or *whomever*), try the following method. It substitutes *he* and *him* for *who* and *whom* and provides a mnemonic for remembering when you should use which pronoun.

FACT

The use of *whom* is gradually decreasing in casual speaking, although many people are still careful about its use. Generally, its use—its correct use—is still important in writing.

First, remember to look only at the clause (a set of words with a subject and its verb) associated with *who* or *whom*. Some sentences have only one clause, and that makes finding the right word easy. Often, though, a sentence has more than one clause (an independent clause and one or more dependent clauses).

Next, scramble the words of the clause (if you have to) so that the words form a statement, not a question.

Now, substitute either *he* or *him* for *who* or *whom*. This will tell you whether to use *who* or *whom*. Use the mnemonic *he = who, hiM = whoM* (the final *m* helps you remember the association). If your sentence is about females only, pretend they're males for the sake of your mnemonic.

Be on the lookout for predicate nominatives. After you scramble the words, if you have a linking verb rather than an action verb, use *he* (*who*) instead of *him* (*whom*).

Ready to put all this to a test? Try this sentence:

(Who, Whom) *telephoned late last night?*

Since the sentence has only one clause, all you need to do is see if it's necessary to scramble the words to make a statement. In this sentence, no scrambling is necessary. You can substitute *he* and have a perfectly good sentence: *He telephoned late last night.* Since you substituted *he* instead of *him* (remember that *he = who*), you know to use *who* in the original question.

Now, try this example:

(Who, Whom) *were you telephoning late at night?*

This sentence also has only one clause that you have to deal with. Scramble the words to make a statement; then substitute *he* or *him*, and you have the statement "You were telephoning him late at night." Since you used *him* in the new sentence, you know to use *whom* in the original question.

Now for a trickier example:

Eugene worried about (who, whom) *Ike would be teamed with in the competition.*

As you can tell, this sentence has two clauses (you could tell that, couldn't you?). Remember that you're *only* concerned with the clause that contains the *who/whom* question. In this case, take the words after *about*, scramble them to make a statement, substitute *he* or *him*, and you have "Ike would be teamed with him in the competition." Since you used *him*, you would know that the original sentence would use *whom* (remember the mnemonic *him = whom*). So the original sentence would read this way:

Eugene worried about whom Ike would be teamed with in the competition.

Try the interactive quizzes on *who* and *whom* at these Web sites:

tinyurl.com/yslsmc

tinyurl.com/23rpad

Here's another example that you have to stop and think about:

Was that (who, whom) *you thought it was?*

When you look *only* at the clause the *who/whom* is concerned with and you substitute *he/him*, you have "it was he/him." A light bulb goes off in your head because you recognize that *was* as being a linking verb. That tells you to use *he* (the predicate nominative).

An independent clause is a set of words with a subject and its verb that expresses a complete thought; it could stand alone as a sentence. A dependent clause—while having a subject and verb—makes no sense by itself; it can't stand alone as a sentence.

Checkpoint

Practice your proficiency with pronouns in the following exercises. Check your answer in Appendix D.

Problems with Pronouns

Read the following paragraph and try to make some sense of it (you'll be confused by the time you get to the second sentence). Then rewrite the paragraph by correcting the various problems with pronouns.

Kerri received two letters today, one from Theresa and one from Vera. Kerri was happy to read that she would be coming for a visit soon. It also mentioned that she would be bringing Andrea, somebody that Kerri had never met. Kerri thought that they could expect to have some fun-filled times because they were all people which were always up for some kind of adventure.

_____

_____

_____

_____

More Problems with Pronouns

Make the necessary changes in the story starter.

Looking out over the lake, Sarah was amazed to find that her and her sister seemed to be alone.

"It looks as if us two are the only ones still out. I saw Jody and Juan out in their boat just a few minutes ago. In fact, it was her who was rowing. Now I wonder what's happened to Jody and he," Sarah mused.

"Oh, I wouldn't worry about them. Him and her both said they were getting hungry and would probably head for shore. But if you want to try to beat them, I know you can row faster than her."

_____

_____

_____

_____

Who? Whom?

Use the _who, whom, he, him_ substitutions and see how many of these you get correct:

1. (Who, Whom) are you taking to the company party?
2. From (who, whom) did the large donation come?
3. (Who, Whom) was mentioned in that memo that came yesterday?
4. Isabelle Dixon said she was giving the prize to (who, whom?)
5. (Who, Whom) is going to the movies tonight?
6. (Who, Whom) drove up just as you did?
7. (Who, Whom) gave you the money for the down payment for the house?
8. (Who, Whom) were you trying to contact?
9. Paulette told Will that he would be called by (who, whom)?
10. (Who, Whom) let the dogs out?

Chapter 10

Figuring Out Some Finicky Forms

Without giving it a second thought, you probably use certain tenses to express particular time periods. Perhaps, however, you've never fully understood certain verb forms. This chapter will iron out all the complexities of the different verb forms for you so that choosing different tenses will never again make you, well, tense.

Let's Talk Tenses

English verbs are divided into three main tenses, all of which relate to time: present, past, and future. Each main tense is also subdivided into other categories: simple tense, progressive tense, perfect tense, and perfect progressive tense. These subcategories differentiate when a particular action has been done (or is being done or will be done).

Clear as mud? Take a look at this chart:

	Simple*	Progressive**	Perfect***	Perfect Progressive****
Present	hide	am/is/are hiding	have/has hidden	have/has been hiding
Past	hid	was/were hiding	had hidden	had been hiding
Future	will/shall hide	will be hiding	will have hidden	will have been hiding

*Indicates action that is usual or is repeated.
**Indicates action that is ongoing.
***Indicates action that is completed.
****Indicates ongoing action that will be completed at some definite time.

Each of these tenses signals the time something is done, will be done, or has been done relative to when it's being written or spoken about. You still don't quite get the whole thing? Don't worry; all will be cleared up in the next few pages, starting with explanations for each of the tenses. To lighten the mood, why don't we start with a little joke:

> *Professor Reynolds says to her student, "Conjugate the verb 'to walk' in the simple present tense."*
> *The student says, "I walk. You walk. He . . . "*
> *Interrupting, Professor Reynolds says, "More quickly, please."*
> *The student replies, "I run. You run. . . . "*

It's Elementary: The Simple Tense

The *simple present tense* tells an action that is usual or repeated:

> *I hide from the stalker.*

Looked at in a different way, the simple present tense relates actions that happen often or that state a fact or opinion.

To make sure they're using the correct verb form for the present tense, some writers find it helpful to begin the sentence with the word *today*:

> *Today I hide from the stalker.*

The *simple past tense* tells an action that began and ended in the past:

> *I hid from the stalker.*

To make sure they're using the correct verb form for the past tense, some writers find it helpful to mentally begin the sentence with the word *yesterday*:

> *Yesterday I hid from the stalker.*

The *simple future tense* tells an upcoming action that will occur:

> *I will hide from the stalker.*

To make sure they're using the correct verb form for the future tense, some writers find it helpful to mentally begin the sentence with the word *tomorrow*:

> *Tomorrow I will hide from the stalker.*

That's simple enough, isn't it? It's the simple present tense. After this, though, the explanations of the other tenses get a little tricky.

One Step Beyond: The Progressive Tense

Use the *present progressive tense* to show an action that's in progress at the time the statement is written:

> *I am hiding from the stalker today.*

Present progressive verbs are always formed by using *am*, *is*, or *are* and adding *-ing* to the verb. Use the *past progressive tense* to show an action that was going on at some particular time in the past:

> *I was hiding from the stalker yesterday.*

Past progressive verbs are always formed by using *was* or *were* and adding *-ing* to the verb. Use the *future progressive tense* to show an action that's continuous and that will occur in the future:

I will be hiding from the stalker tomorrow.

Future progressive verbs are always formed by using *will be* or *shall be* and adding *-ing* to the verb.

No Room for Improvement: The Perfect Tense

Use the *present perfect tense* to convey action that happened sometime in the past or that started in the past but is ongoing in the present:

I have hidden from the stalker for more than five years.

Present perfect verbs are always formed by using *has* or *have* and the past participle form of the verb. Use the *past perfect tense* to indicate past action that occurred prior to another past action:

I had hidden from the stalker for more than five years before I entered the Witness Protection Program.

Past perfect verbs are always formed by using *had* and the past participle form of the verb. Use the *future perfect tense* to illustrate future action that will occur before some other action:

I will have hidden from the stalker for more than five years before entering the Witness Protection Program.

Future perfect verbs are always formed by using *will have* and the past participle form of the verb.

Particulars of the Perfect Progressive Tense

Use the *present perfect progressive* to illustrate an action repeated over a period of time in the past, continuing in the present, and possibly carrying on in the future:

For the past five years, I have been hiding from the stalker.

Present perfect progressive verbs are always formed by using *has been* or *have been* and the past participle form of the verb.

Use the *past perfect progressive* to illustrate a past continuous action that was completed before some other past action:

> *Before I entered the Witness Protection Program, I had been hiding from the stalker for more than five years.*

Past perfect progressive verbs are always formed by using *had been* and adding *-ing* to the verb.

Use the *future perfect progressive* to illustrate a future continuous action that will be completed before some future time:

> *Next month I will have been hiding from the stalker for five years.*

Try the interactive quizzes on verb tenses at these Web sites:

> *tinyurl.com/2sz9up*   *tinyurl.com/2th72n*
> *tinyurl.com/3y5d6k*

Future perfect progressive verbs are always formed by using *will have been* and adding *-ing* to the verb.

Those Irritating Irregular Verbs

The good news is that most English verbs form their past and past participle by adding *-d* or *-ed* to the base form of the verb (the form you'd find listed first in the dictionary). These are called regular verbs.

The bad news is that English has a number of verb forms that aren't formed in that way; some people call them "those %*#@^ verbs," but usually they're called irregular verbs (clever, huh?). Here's a list of often-used irregular English verbs.

Verbs That Take an Irregular Form

Base (Infinitive)	Simple Past	Past Participle
abide	abode/abided	abode/abided
arise	arose	arisen
awake	awoke/awaked	awaked/awoken
be	was, were	been
beat	beat	beaten/beat
become	became	become
begin	began	begun
bend	bent	bent
bet	bet/betted	bet/betted
bid	bade/bid	bidden/bid
bind	bound	bound
bite	bit	bitten/bit
bleed	bled	bled
blow	blew	blown
break	broke	broken
breed	bred	bred
bring	brought	brought
build	built	built
burn	burned/burnt	burned/burnt
buy	bought	bought
catch	caught	caught
choose	chose	chosen
cling	clung	clung
come	came	come
creep	crept	crept
dig	dug	dug
dive	dived/dove	dived

Base (Infinitive)	Simple Past	Past Participle
do	did	done
draw	drew	drawn
dream	dreamed/dreamt	dreamed/dreamt
drink	drank	drunk
drive	drove	driven
eat	ate	eaten
fall	fell	fallen
feed	fed	fed
feel	felt	felt
fight	fought	fought
find	found	found
fit	fitted/fit	fit
flee	fled	fled
fling	flung	flung
fly	flew	flown
forsake	forsook	forsaken
freeze	froze	frozen
get	got	gotten/got
give	gave	given
go	went	gone
grind	ground	ground
grow	grew	grown
hang (to suspend)	hung	hung
has	had	had
have	had	had
hear	heard	heard
hide	hid	hidden/hid
hit	hit	hit

Base (Infinitive)	Simple Past	Past Participle
hold	held	held
hurt	hurt	hurt
input	input	input
inset	inset	inset
interbreed	interbred	interbred
keep	kept	kept
kneel	knelt/kneeled	knelt/kneeled
knit	knit/knitted	knit/knitted
know	knew	known
lay	laid	laid
lead	led	led
lean	leaned	leaned
leap	leaped/leapt	leaped/leapt
learn	learned/learnt	learned/learnt
leave	left	left
lend	lent	lent
lie (to rest or recline)	lay	lain
light	lighted/lit	lighted/lit
lose	lost	lost
make	made	made
mean	meant	meant
meet	met	met
mistake	mistook	mistaken
mow	mowed	mowed/mown
pay	paid	paid
plead	pleaded/pled	pleaded/pled
prove	proved/proven	proved/proven
quit	quit/quitted	quit/quitted

Base (Infinitive)	Simple Past	Past Participle
read	read	read
ring	rang	rung
rise	rose	risen
run	ran	run
say	said	said
see	saw	seen
sell	sold	sold
send	sent	sent
shoot	shot	shot
show	showed	shown/showed
sing	sang/sung	sung
sink	sank/sunk	sunk
sit	sat	sat
sleep	slept	slept
slide	slid	slid
smell	smelled/smelt	smelled/smelt
smite	smote	smitten/smote
sow	sowed	sown/sowed
speak	spoke	spoken
speed	sped/speeded	sped/speeded
spell	spelled/spelt	spelled/spelt
spend	spent	spent
spill	spilled/spilt	spilled/spilt
spin	spun	spun
spit	spat/spit	spat/spit
split	split	split
spoil	spoiled/spoilt	spoiled/spoilt
spring	sprang/sprung	sprung

Base (Infinitive)	Simple Past	Past Participle
stand	stood	stood
steal	stole	stolen
stick	stuck	stuck
sting	stung	stung
stink	stank/stunk	stunk
strew	strewed	strewn/strewed
stride	strode	stridden
strike	struck	struck/stricken
string	strung	strung
strive	strove	striven/strived
swear	swore	sworn
sweep	swept	swept
swell	swelled	swelled/swollen
swim	swam	swum
swing	swung	swung
take	took	taken
teach	taught	taught
tear	tore	torn
tell	told	told
think	thought	thought
throw	threw	thrown
tread	trod	trodden/trod
understand	understood	understood
wake	woke/waked	waked/woken
wear	wore	worn
weave	wove	woven
wed	wedded	wed/wedded
weep	wept	wept

Base (Infinitive)	Simple Past	Past Participle
wet	wet/wetted	wet/wetted
win	won	won
wind	wound	wound
wring	wrung	wrung

Just to keep you on your toes, two verbs—*hang and lie*—may be regular or irregular, depending on their meaning in the sentence. If *hang* means *to use a noose*, it's a regular verb. If it means *to affix to a wall*, it's irregular. For example:

> *Prison officials discovered a picture of the hanged man's mother had hung in his cell.*

If *lie* means *to tell a falsehood*, it's a regular verb. If it means *to rest or recline*, it's irregular. Here's an example:

> *Dave lay on the beach and lied when he phoned in sick.*

After you study the previous list of irregular verbs, try the interactive quizzes on them at these Web sites:

> *tinyurl.com/2sdofu*   *tinyurl.com/354n58*
> *tinyurl.com/33cbd6*   *tinyurl.com/o4hao*
> *tinyurl.com/3y9yzg*

What Kind of Mood Are You In?

In addition to tenses, English verbs are divided into moods, which show the writer's attitude toward what he or she is saying. The first two moods, indicative and imperative, aren't confusing at all, and, fortunately, they're used far more frequently than the third mood, subjunctive.

Almost all verbs are used in the indicative mood, which means that the verb's sentence states a fact or an actuality. All of these sentences are in the indicative mood:

I'll be seeing you later on tonight. Wear whatever you want. You look nice in anything. We're all casual dressers, so don't worry about your attire.

Verbs used in the imperative mood are in sentences that make requests or give a command. All of these sentences are in the imperative mood:

Please give me the phone.
Give it to me right now!
Give it to me—or else!

The subjunctive mood is the one that speakers and writers sometimes have problems with. Fortunately, it's used with only two verbs *(be* and *were)*, and in modern English, it's used in only two kinds of sentences:

1. statements that are contrary to fact (providing they begin with *if* or *unless)*, improbable, or doubtful

2. statements that express a wish, a request or recommendation, an urgent appeal, or a demand

The following are verb forms used in the subjunctive mood:

Present Subjunctive

Singular	Plural
(if) I be	(if) we be
(if) you be	(if) you be
(if) he/she/it be	(if)they be

Past Subjunctive

Singular	Plural
(if) I were	(if) we were
(if) you were	(if) you were
(if) he/she/it were	(if) they were

Here is an example:

It's important that everybody be [not is] at the meeting.

This is a wish or request—a strong request, at that.

After you've studied the forms of subjunctive mood, try the interactive quizzes at these Web sites:

tinyurl.com/oh3hd   tinyurl.com/39rnf3

Comparatively Speaking

Sometimes you need to show how something compares with or measures up to something else. Say, for example, you and your family enjoy watching horror movies. You may want to report about a new scary movie you've seen, deciding whether it's *scarier* than another one you've all recently watched together or perhaps even the *scariest* movie you've ever seen. A scary movie can become a *scarier* movie if it's compared to another one, or it can become the *scariest* movie if it's compared to several others.

In writing comparisons, you use one of three different forms (called degrees) of adjectives and adverbs:

- The positive degree simply makes a statement about a person, place, or thing.
- The comparative degree compares two (but only two) people, places, or things.
- The superlative degree compares more than two people, places, or things.

Positive	Comparative	Superlative
blue	bluer	bluest
happy	happier	happiest
tall	taller	tallest

Here are the rules to help you form the comparative and superlative:

- **Rule #1.** One-syllable adjectives and adverbs usually form their comparative form by adding -*er* and their superlative form by adding -*est* (see the examples *tall* and *blue* in the table).
- **Rule #2.** Adjectives of more than two syllables and adverbs ending in -*ly* usually form comparative forms by using *more* (or *less*) and superlative forms by using *most* (or *least*)

Positive	Comparative	Superlative
comfortable	more comfortable	most comfortable
qualified	less qualified	least qualified

- **Rule #3.** Confusion sometimes crops up in forming comparisons of words of two syllables only. Here's the rub: Sometimes two-syllable words use the -*er*, *est* forms, and sometimes they use the *more*, *most* (or *less*, *least*) forms. You knew there had to be some complications in there somewhere, didn't you?

Positive	Comparative	Superlative
sleepy	sleepier	sleepiest
tiring	more tiring	most tiring

So how do you know whether to use the -*er*, *est* form or the *more*, *most* form? You have to use a dictionary (a large dictionary, not a paperback one) if you're not sure. If no comparative or superlative forms are listed in the dictionary, use the *more*, *most* form.

Did you happen to notice the word *usually* in the first two rules? It's there because English has some exceptions to the rules. The good news is that the exceptions are few. Among them are:

Positive	Comparative	Superlative
bad	worse	worst
far	farther/further	farthest/furthest
little	littler/less/lesser	littlest/least
many	more	most
old (persons)	elder	eldest

One common mistake in both writing and speaking is to use the superlative form when the comparative should be used. If you're comparing two persons, places, or things, you use only the comparative form (not the superlative). Look at these sentences:

Of my two dogs, the cocker spaniel is the friendliest.
Tillie has two sons; Charlie is the eldest and Herb is the youngest.

In both of those sentences, the comparison is between only two *(two dogs, two sons)*, so the sentences should be written with the comparative form *(friendlier, younger)* instead of the superlative.

E-LINK

Try the interactive quizzes on comparative and superlative at these Web sites:

tinyurl.com/23fb98   tinyurl.com/ym9x4x
tinyurl.com/2ym2e7

Another frequent mistake in comparisons is in going overboard—using both the *-er* and *more* or *-est* and *most* forms with the same noun, as in *the most tallest statue* or *a more happier child*. Remember that one form is the limit (and, of course, it has to be the correct form). In the examples, *most* and *more* need to be eliminated.

Sometimes comparisons can be ambiguous. Because some comparisons can be interpreted more than one way, be sure you include all the words necessary to give the meaning you intend.

Read this sentence:

> *In the long jump, Adele could beat her rival Fern more often than her teammate Sherry.*

Constructed that way, readers don't know if the meaning is the following:

> *In the long jump, Adele could beat her rival Fern more often than her teammate Sherry could.*

or

> *In the long jump, Adele could beat her rival Fern more often than she could beat her teammate Sherry.*

Avoiding Double Negatives

Okay, now for the double negatives—two negative words used to stress denial or opposition, as in these examples:

> *After he had been laid off, Hal realized that he didn't need none of the luxuries he'd become accustomed to.*

(*Didn't* and *none* are negatives. The sentence should be "After he had been laid off, Hal realized that he didn't need any of the luxuries he'd become accustomed to.")

> *That man was not doing nothing but just standing there!*

(*Not* and *nothing* are negatives. The sentence should be "That man was not doing anything but just standing there!")

> *Allison wondered why Jason didn't call nobody when he became sick.*

(*Didn't* and *nobody* are negatives. The sentence should be "Allison wondered why Jason didn't call anybody when he became sick.")

> *Mr. Fowler said he ain't got none of those apples that you want.*

(*Ain't* and *none* are negatives—and you also know that *ain't* is considered nonstandard, don't you? The sentence should be "Mr. Fowler said he did not have any of those apples that you want.")

You'll often hear or read double negatives in colloquial speech:

> *You ain't heard nothin' yet!*
> *Ike said he hadn't seen Betty nowhere.*

Properly, these sentences should be "You haven't heard anything yet!" and "Ike said he hadn't seen Betty anywhere."

One exception to the rule of avoiding double negatives comes if you intend a positive or lukewarm meaning. Read this sentence:

> *I was not unhappy with my recent raise.*

The connotation in the double negatives *(not* and *unhappy)* tells readers that, while the writer wasn't unhappy, he or she wasn't exactly thrilled.

You may also use double negatives if you're using a phrase or clause for emphasis, as in this example:

> *"I will not take a bribe, not today, not tomorrow, not any time in my life," the politician cried.*

Since we began this chapter on a light note, let's end on one as well.

> *A linguistics professor was lecturing to his class one day. "In English," he said, "a double negative forms a positive. In some languages, such as Russian, a double negative is still a negative. However, there is no language wherein a double positive can form a negative."*
> *A voice from the back of the room piped up in reply, "Yeah, right."*

Checkpoint

Using the rules outlined previously, correct the mistakes in the story starter:

The reporter had just bursted on the scene, but already he could tell that the atmosphere was more edgier than he had anticipated. He stopped some of the neighbors who were standing around and sayed, "Is this the most excitingest thing that's ever happened here on Elm Street?"

Mrs. Atcheson turned to the reporter and said, "This ain't nothing! You should have been here last week when two burglars was holed up in my chimney. The fattest one kept screaming for help, and the skinniest one kept whispering to him that he should be quiet."

_____

_____

_____

_____

Chapter 11

Keeping It Coherent

Certain elements can make or break a sentence. For instance, if a sentence contains a misplaced modifier or is essentially illogical, it becomes confusing at best and silly at worst. This chapter gives you some pointers for looking critically at your sentence construction so that your writing (and your reputation!) remain solid.

Manglers of Meaning: Misplaced Modifiers

Misplaced modifiers aren't words or phrases that are lost; they're words or phrases that you've put in the wrong place. All of your words—whether they're single words, phrases, or clauses—should be as close as possible to whatever they modify (the words they describe or elaborate on). Take a look at this sentence, written with a single word in the wrong place:

After her wreck, Joanna could comprehend what the ambulance driver was barely saying.

The way the sentence is written, the ambulance driver is barely speaking—but surely that's not what the writer meant. *Barely* is out of its correct place because it modifies the wrong word. It should be moved so that it modifies the verb *could comprehend*. The sentence should be written this way:

After her wreck, Joanna could barely comprehend what the ambulance driver was saying.

In addition to being single words, misplaced modifiers can also be phrases, as in this example:

Witnesses reported that the woman was driving the getaway car with flowing black hair.

How interesting—a car with flowing black hair. *With flowing black hair* is in the wrong place in this sentence (it's misplaced) and should be placed after *woman*. That way, the sentence would read:

Witnesses reported that the woman with flowing black hair was driving the getaway car.

Clauses, too, can be put in the wrong place, as in the following sentence:

Paulette Dixon couldn't stop thinking about her sick baby running in the six-mile road race.

That's quite a baby who can run a six-mile road race (not to mention running while being sick). The clause *running in the six-mile road race* is out of place in this sentence; it should be closer to the noun it modifies *(Paulette Dixon)*. The sentence should be reworded this way:

Running in the six-mile road race, Paulette Dixon couldn't stop thinking about her sick baby.

ALERT!

A frequent problem often arises with the word *not*. In speaking, we frequently say something like this:

All the chairs in the office are not comfortable for the employees.

The problem with that blanket statement is that the word *not* may be in the wrong place. If the meaning was that some of the chairs were uncomfortable, then the sentence should be reworded this way:

Not all the chairs in the office are comfortable for the employees.

One of the most common problems with misplaced modifiers comes with what are called limiting modifiers—words like *almost*, *even*, *hardly*, *just*, *merely*, *nearly*, *only* (the one misplaced most often), *scarcely*, and *simply*. To convey the correct meaning, limiting modifiers must be placed in front of the words they modify.

Take a look at these sentences:

Already, Mr. Goulooze has almost eaten four slabs of ribs!

How does a person almost eat something? Did he have great willpower four different times? Or should the sentence be reworded to say that Mr. Goulooze has eaten almost four slabs of ribs?

Richard has nearly wrecked every car he's had.

Has Richard nearly wrecked the cars—in which case, he should be grateful for his luck—or has he wrecked nearly every car?

Dangling and Squinting Modifiers

Dangling modifiers are another problem in writing and speaking. Dangling modifiers have no word or phrase to describe; they just dangle, or hang, in a sentence without something to hold on to. Look at these sentences:

> *Long ears drooping on the floor, Julie wondered how the dog could walk.*

Is it time for Julie to consider plastic surgery?

> *While performing, the audience gasped as the singer forgot the words to the song.*

Why was the audience performing?

> *After getting a new paint job, reupholstering was now needed for the car.*

Why would reupholstering be painted?

Each of the sentences needs to be reworded so that the modifiers have something to attach to.

> *Julie wondered how the dog could walk with its long ears drooping on the floor.*
> *The audience gasped as the singer forgot the words to the song while he was performing.*
> *After getting a new paint job, the car needed to be reupholstered.*

Another problem comes with squinting modifiers (two-way modifiers). These are words that can logically modify or describe something on either side of them, but readers can't tell if the words modify what's on their left or right. Take a look at this sentence:

> *The instructor said after the semester ended that Keevie and Vonda were to retake the test.*

Try the interactive quizzes on modifiers at these Web sites:

> *tinyurl.com/2v2ud2   tinyurl.com/2tlgnl*

What does the phrase *after the semester ended* apply to? Did the instructor *tell* Keevie and Vonda this after the semester ended, or were Keevie and Vonda *eligible* to retake the test after the semester ended? The way this sentence is worded, the meaning isn't clear. To correct this sentence, change the placement of the modifier.

> *After the semester ended, the instructor said that Keevie and Vonda were eligible to retake the test.*
>
> *The instructor said that Keevie and Vonda were eligible to retake the test after the semester ended.*

Parallelism in Writing

For your work to be easily read—and, in some cases, for it to be coherent—using parallelism is important. This helps you give equality and balance to separate the points you make.

Puzzled? Not to worry. Understanding parallelism isn't as difficult as it may seem. You simply write all the similar parts of a sentence in the same way. If you've used two nouns, you don't suddenly switch to a gerund. If you've used verbs that have a certain tense, you don't suddenly change tenses. If you begin in one voice, you don't suddenly switch to another voice.

Take a look at some of the examples that follow, and you'll get a clearer understanding of what parallelism is and how important it is in your writing.

Parallelism Problem #1: Items in Pairs or in a Series

When naming items, you should present them all in the same way. Look at this problem sentence:

> *This afternoon Doris and Stefanie washed and waxed, and then they were vacuuming the car.*

Here is the problem viewed one way:

This afternoon Doris and Stefanie washed (past tense verb) and waxed (past tense verb), and then they were vacuuming (past progressive tense verb) the car.

Here is the problem viewed another way:

This afternoon Doris and Stefanie washed (-ed word) and waxed (-ed word), and then they were vacuuming (-ing word) the car.

Here's the repaired sentence that's now parallel:

This afternoon Doris and Stefanie washed, waxed, and vacuumed the car.

All the verbs are now in the same tense; all verbs are now *–ed* words.

This famous line uses parallelism effectively:

"With this faith we will be able to work together, to pray together, to struggle together, to go to jail together, to stand up for freedom together, knowing that we will be free one day."—Rev. Martin Luther King, Jr.

The following example shows the incorrect use of parallel items in a series when a colon is used:

A word processor has three helpful features that save time: you can quickly edit material you don't want, you can save drafts and revise them, and it can automatically correct words that you frequently misspell.

Here's the problem viewed one way:

A word processor has three helpful features that save time: you [second person] can quickly edit material you don't want, you [second person] can save drafts and revise them, and it [third person] can automatically correct words that you frequently misspell.

Here's the problem viewed another way:

A word processor has three helpful features that save time: you [you as subject] can quickly edit material you don't want, you [you as subject] can save drafts and revise them, and it [it as subject] can automatically correct words that you frequently misspell.

Here's the repaired sentence that's now parallel:

A word processor has three helpful features that save time: you can quickly edit material you don't want, you can save drafts and revise them, and you can automatically correct words that you frequently misspell.

Parallelism Problem #2: Clauses

When you're using more than one clause, keep the same voice and use the same type of introduction in each. Here's the problem sentence:

I was worried that Joan would drive too fast, that the road would be too slippery, and that the car would be stopped by the police.

Here's the problem viewed one way:

I was worried that Joan would drive too fast [active voice], that the road would be too slippery [active voice], and that the car would be stopped by the police [passive voice].

Here's the repaired sentence that's now parallel:

I was worried that Joan would drive too fast, that the road would be too slippery, and that the police would stop the car.

Now look at this problem sentence:

Mary Elizabeth and Ron promised that they would bring everything for the picnic, that they would be on time, and not to forget the bug repellent.

This is one way to look at the problem:

Mary Elizabeth and Ron promised that they would bring everything for the picnic [clause introduced with a subordinating conjunction], that they would be on time [clause introduced with a subordinating conjunction], and not to forget the bug repellent [clause introduced with an adverb and infinitive].

Or you can look at it this way:

Mary Elizabeth and Ron promised that they would bring everything for the picnic [clause introduced with that*], that they would be on time [clause introduced with* that*], and not to forget the bug repellent [clause introduced with* not to forget*].*

Here's the repaired sentence that's now parallel:

Mary Elizabeth and Ron promised that they would bring everything for the picnic, that they would be on time, and that they wouldn't forget the bug repellent.

Parallelism Problem #3: Placement

Items in a series should be placed in similar locations. Take a look at this problem sentence:

Mike is not only very kind but also is very good-looking.

Let's look at the problem:

Mike is not only [first part of a correlative conjunction not only *comes after the verb] very kind but also [second part of a correlative conjunction* but also *comes before the verb] is very good-looking.*

Here's the repaired sentence that's now parallel:

Mike is not only very kind but also very good-looking.

Parallelism Problem #4: Placement of Emphasis or Chronology

If the items in a list have different degrees of importance or if they occur at different times, you should order them according to their emphasis or chronology. Look at this problem sentence:

Misuse of the drug can result in fever, death, or dizziness.

Now, identify the problem:

Misuse of the drug can result in fever [something that's bad], death [something that's the worst of the three], or dizziness [something that's bad].

Here's the repaired sentence that's now parallel:

Misuse of the drug can result in fever, dizziness, or death.

In writing your sentence this way you've built up to the climax (the worst problem—death). You might also include a word or phrase before the last element to add to the buildup; for example, you could word the sentence like this:

Misuse of the drug can result in fever, dizziness, or even death.

Parallelism Problem #5: Missing Words

Be sure to include all the words you need for each item in your sentence. Look at this problem sentence:

Coach Tom Todd was honored for guiding his star player Cathy Rymer in her career, her schoolwork, and faith.

Identify the problem:

Coach Tom Todd was honored for guiding his star player Cathy Rymer in her career, her schoolwork, and faith [the word her *is not included in the last item of the list of how the coach guided Rymer].*

Here's the repaired sentence that's now parallel:

Coach Tom Todd was honored for guiding his star player Cathy Rymer in her career, her schoolwork, and her faith.

Parallelism Problem #6: Unclear Meaning

Include all the words necessary to indicate the items to which you're referring in the sentence. Look at this problem sentence:

In conducting her interview, Gail Bushrod talked with the college senior and candidate for the job.

Identify the problem: Did Gail talk with one person who was a senior and who was interviewing for the job, or with two people—one of whom was a senior and one of whom was interviewing for the job?

Here's the repaired sentence that's now parallel:

In conducting her interview, Gail Bushrod talked with both the college senior and the candidate for the job.

Sometimes you may deliberately repeat certain elements of your sentence, as in this example:

I promise to cut taxes, spending, and exorbitant salary raises.

That sentence is fine the way it is, but to add emphasis to the cuts, you might choose to write it this way:

I promise to cut taxes, to cut spending, and to cut exorbitant salary raises.

Parallelism Problem #7: Too Many Words

You don't need to repeat the same introductory word if it applies to all of the items in your list. Look at this problem sentence:

Bill hopes to see Randa on November 20, December 13, and on January 7.

Identify the problem:

Bill hopes to see Randa on [preposition before noun] November 20, [preposition missing] December 13, and on [preposition appears again] January 7.

Here's the repaired sentence that's now parallel:

Bill hopes to see Randa on November 20, December 13, and January 7.

The same preposition relates to each date, so there is no need to repeat it.

Parallelism Problem #8: Too Few Words

If different prepositions apply to items in a series, be sure to include all the prepositions. Look at this problem sentence:

The ants are on the living room floor, the dining room table, and the sink. (Yikes! Better get out the bug spray!)

Identify the problem:

The ants are on [use the preposition on *with this phrase] the floor, [use the preposition* on *with this phrase] the kitchen table, and [use the preposition* on *with this phrase, but the preposition should be* in*] the sink.*

Here's the repaired sentence that's now parallel:

The ants are on the living room floor, on the dining room table, and in the sink.

The beginning preposition *(on)* doesn't relate to each area, so you should repeat it in the second phrase and change it to *in* for the third phrase.

Parallelism Problem #9: Parallel Sentences

To add emphasis or smoothness, construct your sentences in a parallel way. Look at this example:

I was nervous and frightened, and I hid my emotions. My sister showed the world that she felt confident and carefree.

Identify the problem: Actually, there's no grammatical problem with the sentences, but they can certainly be improved by being written in a parallel manner.

Here are the repaired sentences that are now parallel:

I was nervous and frightened, and I hid my emotions. My sister was confident and carefree, and she showed the world how she felt.

Tips for Parallelism

If a lack of parallelism is often a problem in your writing, try the following tips:

- Look for *-ing* or *-ed* constructions.
- Look for constructions beginning with *it, that, to,* and *you.*
- Look for constructions beginning with the same preposition.
- Look at the voice (active or passive) used in the constructions.
- Check to see if one of the constructions is more important than the others; if so, place it last.

- If you've used a correlative conjunction, check to see if you have its partner (e.g., *either . . . or*).

If you have items in a series, write them down in a column. Look for common elements in two parts of the series, and then convert the other items so they'll be formed in the same way. Sometimes your ear is more reliable than your eye. Good writers read their material aloud and listen for words and phrases that aren't parallel.

Try the interactive quizzes on parallelism at these Web sites:

tinyurl.com/2ys764   *tinyurl.com/2e7ngz*
tinyurl.com/23kzv6

Logically Speaking

Making sure your sentences are inherently logical is one of the most important steps in becoming a good writer. You can be quite meticulous in crafting the grammar and punctuation of your sentences and very careful with your spelling and word usage, but if your material has errors in logic, all your hard work will have been for nothing. Lapses in logic can take several different forms. Some are instantly recognizable in a sentence, while others are a little more subtle and, thus, a little more dangerous. Don't let these errors sneak up on you.

Asking the Impossible: Faulty Predication

Faulty predication (also called illogical predication or—are you ready for this one?—selectional restriction violation) is one type of illogical writing. The term *faulty predication* means that your subject and verb don't make sense together—that is, the subject can't "be" or "do" the verb.

ALERT!

The illogical uses of *when* and *where* are two of the most common examples of faulty predication. Don't describe a noun or pronoun by using *when* or *where*. Be sure to check your sentence every time (that is, whenever and wherever) you use *when* or *where*.

Take a look at these sentences:

The new breath mint assures customers that it will last all day.
An economics class is when you study monetary and fiscal policy.
In tennis, "playing the net" is where you stand close to the net and hit balls before they bounce.
The reason Felicia Sanners was late was because she had a flat tire.

Each of these sentences has an example of faulty predication. Obviously, a breath mint is incapable of assuring anybody of anything; a class isn't *when* anything; playing the net isn't *where* anything; and a reason isn't *because* anything. Each of these sentences needs to be reworded, perhaps like this:

The makers of the new breath mint assure customers that the mint will last all day.
In an economics class you study monetary and fiscal policy.
In tennis, "playing the net" means you stand close to the net and hit balls before they bounce.
The reason Felicia Sanners was late was that she had a flat tire.

To check for faulty predication, ask yourself if it's possible for each subject to "do" or "be" the verb. If it's not possible, then change your wording.

A Doesn't Follow B: Faulty Coordination

Faulty coordination occurs if you join (combine or coordinate) two clauses in an illogical way:

Joey and Micah made their way to the head of the checkout line, yet Joey realized he had forgotten his wallet.

The word *yet* (the word that joins, combines, or coordinates the two clauses) is used incorrectly. The sentence could read:

Joey and Micah made their way to the head of the checkout line, but then Joey realized he had forgotten his wallet.

Another example of faulty coordination comes in sentences that contain independent clauses of unequal importance. The sentences are written in a way that makes the clauses seem equal, as in the following sentence:

David and Kathy paid $50,000 for their new car, and it has tinted glass.

The cost of the car is much more important than the fact that it has tinted glass (at least, it is to most people). To correct the problem, you could make the second clause subordinate to the first (making the second clause an adjective clause).

David and Kathy paid $50,000 for their new car, which has tinted glass.

Absolutely—Not!

One common problem with comparison occurs when you use absolute adjectives, which are words that—by their definition—can't be compared. Therefore, be sure not to use *more*, *most*, *quite*, *rather*, *somewhat*, *very*, and other qualifiers in front of them.

Round, for instance, is one of those words. Something is either round or it's not. Since one thing can't be rounder than something else, *round* is an absolute adjective. Other absolute adjectives include: blank, pure, complete, square, dead, straight, empty, true, eternal, and favorite.

Look at these examples:

The test paper I turned in was somewhat blank.

You can't have a paper that is somewhat blank; either it has something on it or it doesn't.

This is my most favorite restaurant.

Because *favorite* means "at the top of my list," one place can't be more favorite than someplace else.

Putting Apples with Oranges: Faulty Comparisons

Another problem with faulty comparison occurs if you compare two unlike people, places, or things:

The traffic mishaps in April were more numerous than May.

This sentence compares mishaps to May, which makes no sense. The sentence should be rewritten like this:

The traffic mishaps in April were more numerous than those in May.

Take a look at this one:

Jeff Eichholtz decided that the people in Crydonville are friendlier than Park City.

Here people are being compared to a city—obviously, an illogical comparison. The sentence needs to be reworded, perhaps like this:

Jeff Eichholtz came to the conclusion that the people in Crydonville are friendlier than the people in Park City.

Still another problem is an ambiguous comparison, which occurs if you write a statement that could be interpreted two different ways. Look at this sentence:

Dawn dislikes traveling alone more than Dave.

This is an ambiguous comparison because readers aren't sure what the word *more* applies to. Does Dawn dislike traveling alone more than she dislikes Dave, or does she dislike traveling more than Dave does?

Let's Not Be Hasty! Sweeping Generalizations

Sweeping (hasty) generalizations use all-encompassing words like *anyone, everyone, always, never, everything, all, only,* and *none,* and superlatives like *best, greatest, most, least.*

The country never recovers from an economic downturn in just six months.

Be careful with sentences with generalizations like this one. What happens to the writer's credibility if the country does, in fact, recover from a downturn in six months? You're far better off to write in terms of what happens *most of the time* than in terms of what *always* or *never* happens (not to mention that you're protected when you make a mistake). One rewording of the example is this:

The country almost never recovers from an economic downturn in just six months.

Here's another example of a sweeping generalization:

Everyone should strenuously exercise at least thirty minutes a day.

Everyone? Surely a newborn baby or someone who's recovering from surgery shouldn't strenuously exercise. If you reword the sentence, you can leave some room for exceptions or for debate. Here's a rewording that is more reasonable:

Everyone who is able should exercise at least thirty minutes a day.

I Don't Follow You: Non Sequiturs

A non sequitur is a problem in logic that states an effect that doesn't follow its cause. Put another way, in a non sequitur, the inference or conclusion that you assert doesn't logically follow from what you previously stated.

I turned in a paper; therefore, I'll pass the class.

As any teacher can tell you, the fact that you turned in a paper doesn't necessarily mean you'll pass the class. What if the paper is (a) not on the assigned topic? (b) too short or too long? (c) plagiarized? (d) three weeks late? (e) written on a kindergarten level? In other words, just because one thing happened, the other doesn't necessarily follow. Here are other examples of non sequiturs:

Charlie Buckman has bought products made by Commonwealth Foods for years. The new product, Dog Biscuits for Humans, is bound to be tasty.
Jack Spratt stole a box of paper clips from the office. He probably cheats on his taxes, too.

The Missing Link: Omitted Words

Another frequent mistake in logic is to omit *else* or *other* in sentences with comparisons. Read this sentence:

Aunt Lucy likes Louise more than she likes anyone in the family.

The way the sentence is written, Louise isn't in the family. The sentence needs to be reworded this way:

Aunt Lucy likes Louise more than she likes anyone else in the family.

Sometimes sentences need *than* or *as* in order to be logical:

Brent said he could play the guitar as well, if not better than, Jessie.

Taking out the phrase *if not better than* leaves *Brent said he could play the guitar as well Jessie*, a sentence that's obviously incomplete. The sentence should be written with the extra *as* to complete the phrase:

Brent said he could play the guitar as well as, if not better than, Jessie.

Without Rhyme or Reason: Additional Lapses in Logic

Another type of illogical writing to check for is commonly called *post hoc, ergo propter hoc*, which translates as *after this, so because of this* (also called coincidental correlation). Here the assumption is that because one thing follows another, the first caused the second.

Ashley washed her car in the morning, and the rain started in the afternoon.

The second event wasn't caused by the first: the rain wasn't caused by the car being washed (although, come to think of it, it does seem to rain every time you wash your car, doesn't it?).

If you use a false dilemma (an either/or fallacy), you state that only two alternatives exist, when there are actually more than two.

Whitney Becker can get to her appointment in one of two ways: she can either drive her car or she can walk.

Whitney Becker has other choices: she could call a cab, take the bus, or ask a friend for a ride, so she isn't limited to only two ways of getting to her appointment. If your argument has a red herring, then it dodges the real issue by citing an irrelevant concern as evidence.

The driver in front of me ran the red light and was speeding, so it's not right that I got a ticket for going 100 mph in a 50 mph zone.

The writer or speaker did something wrong; the fact that the driver ahead did something worse is irrelevant.

If you're guilty of circular reasoning, then your writing has what its name implies—reasoning that goes around in a circle, with nothing substantial in the middle. Here's an example:

The epidemic was dangerous because everyone in town felt unsafe and at risk.

That sentence has no insight because the writer gives no clarification in the second part about why the epidemic was dangerous; the fact that everyone felt unsafe and at risk doesn't explain the danger.

Checkpoint

Using parallelism, rewrite the following story starter:

Studying long hours, giving up fun-filled time with friends, and lots of coffee to drink were my habits when I was in school. My favorite classes were ancient Greek, quantum physics, advanced chemistry, and I also liked microbiology. At that time in my life, reading compelling subject matter was more important to me than to play cards with the rest of the gang. I wanted to get good grades, to retain my scholarship, and be working part-time at a job that would help my future career. I wanted to not only impress my instructors, I wanted to impress my boss. Because of this, I worked industriously and studied with diligence. I was constantly worried that my scholarship money would evaporate, that I'd lose my job, and that my future career would be hampered by one of my coworkers.

_____

_____

_____

Chapter 12

Shaping Strong Sentences

Fragments and run-ons can significantly weaken your writing, confusing your readers and preventing you from getting your point across. But don't let these problems scare you. By this time you've already mastered so many points of grammar and style that you'll probably find gaining the upper hand over fragments and run-ons to be a piece of cake!

A Few Words about Fragments

You've been told time and again not to use sentence fragments. Right? (Notice that fragment?) Generally speaking, you shouldn't use fragments because they can confuse your reader, and they sometimes don't get your point across.

How can you recognize fragments? The textbook definition says that a fragment is "a group of words that isn't a sentence." Okay, so what constitutes a sentence? Again, the textbook definition says a sentence is a group of words that (1) has a subject, (2) has a predicate (verb), and (3) expresses a complete thought.

FACT

Depending on when and where you went to school, you might be more familiar with the definition that says a sentence must form an independent clause. Actually, an independent clause must have a subject, predicate, and complete thought, so the definitions are the same.

If a string of words doesn't have all three of the qualifications (a subject, a verb, and an expression of a complete thought), then you have a fragment rather than a sentence. That's pretty straightforward, don't you think? Take a look at these two words:

Spot ran.

You have a subject *(Spot)*, a verb *(ran)*, and the words express a complete thought; in other words, you don't get confused when you read the two words by themselves. Since you have all the requirements (subject, verb, complete thought), you have a sentence.

Now, look at this group of words:

Although Christian Hazelwood had a new job in a modern office building.

This example is a subordinate clause that's punctuated as if it were a sentence. You have a subject *(Christian Hazelwood)* and a verb *(had)*, but what you don't have is a complete thought. The words serve only to introduce the main idea of the sentence. If someone said only those words to you, you'd be left hanging because you wouldn't know what the main idea was. (Although Christian Hazelwood had a new job—what? He took off for the Far East? He called in sick on his first day? He decided to elope with a billionaire and never have to work again?) The *although* that introduces the sentence means there should be something else to explain the first group of words.

A participial phrase often creates another common sentence fragment. Look at these examples:

> *Scared stiff by the intense wind and storm.*
> *Going to the beach with her family and friends.*

Neither of these groups of words has a main clause to identify who or what is being talked about. Who was scared stiff? Who was going to the beach? Obviously, something's missing.

If you're not sure if the words you've used constitute a sentence, first write them by themselves and then ask yourself if they could be understood without something else being added. If you're still not sure, let them get cold for a while and then reread them. If you're *still* not sure, call a friend and say those particular words and nothing else. You know you have a fragment if your friend says something along the lines of, "And then what?"

Another good way to see if you have a fragment is to take the word group and turn it into a yes-or-no question. If you answer yes to the question, you have a sentence; if you answer no (or if the question makes no sense), you have a fragment. Look at these examples:

> *Jordan Hill quickly ran back to the shelter of the mansion.*
> *Did Jordan Hill quickly run back to the shelter of the mansion? Yes, he did.*
> *Therefore, you have a sentence.*
> *Scared stiff by the intense wind and storm.*

Did scared stiff by the intense wind and storm? No, that doesn't make sense. You have a fragment.

Read the following paragraph and see if you can spot the fragments:

> *The lone woman trudged up the muddy riverbank. Determined that she would make the best of a bad situation. Because of her family's recent run of bad luck.*

She knew that she had to contribute to the family's finances. That's why she had accepted a teaching position. In this town that was new to her. Impatiently waiting for someone to show her where she was to live. She surveyed the streets and rundown buildings of the little village. Little did she know the problems that she would face in the "wilderness," as she had mentally thought of her new home. First, the schoolhouse wasn't ready. Even though she had written that she wanted to begin classes on the twenty-fourth. The day after her arrival.

Did you spot all the fragments? Take a look at:

Determined that she would make the best of a bad situation.
Because of her family's recent run of bad luck.
In this town that was new to her.
Impatiently waiting for someone to show her where she was to live.
Even though she had written that she wanted to begin classes on the twenty-fourth.
The day after her arrival.

If you had those words alone on a piece of paper, would anybody know what you meant? No—those words don't form complete thoughts.

Now, how can you correct these fragments? Usually the fragment should be connected to the sentence immediately before or after it—whichever sentence the fragment refers to. (A word of caution: Just be sure that the newly created sentence makes sense.)

The first fragment *(Determined that she would make the best of a bad situation)* can be corrected by hooking it on to the sentence right before it. The corrected sentence should read:

The lone woman trudged up the muddy riverbank, determined that she would make the best of a bad situation.

You could also put the fragment at the beginning of a sentence:

Determined that she would make the best of a bad situation, the lone woman trudged up the muddy riverbank.

Or you could put the fragment inside the sentence:

The lone woman, determined that she would make the best of a bad situation, trudged up the muddy riverbank.

Each of these three new sentences makes sense.

Now, look at the second fragment: *Because of her family's recent run of bad luck.* What about their run of bad luck? Again, if you said those words—and only those words—to someone, you'd get a blank stare; you didn't give the reason behind the *because.* To correct this fragment, you could tack the fragment onto the beginning or middle of the sentence that follows it in the original paragraph:

> *Because of her family's recent run of bad luck, Elizabeth knew that she had to contribute to the family's finances.*
> *Elizabeth knew that, because of her family's recent run of bad luck, she had to contribute to the family's finances.*

By slightly changing some wording (without changing the meaning), you could also add this fragment to the end of the sentence:

> *Elizabeth knew that she had to contribute to her family's finances because of her parents' recent run of bad luck.*

Here's another example of possibilities for rewording a sentence when you incorporate a fragment. Take this fragment and its related sentence:

> *Impatiently waiting for someone to show her where she was to live. Elizabeth surveyed the village.*

You might reword the fragment and sentence and combine them this way:

> *Elizabeth surveyed the village as she waited impatiently for someone to show her where she was to live.*

Another way you might revise is to create an appositive phrase. Take this combination of a sentence and two fragments:

> *The schoolhouse wasn't ready. Even though Elizabeth Blackwell had written that she wanted to begin classes on the twenty-fourth. The day after her arrival.*

It can be rewritten to read:

The schoolhouse wasn't ready even though Elizabeth Blackwell had written that she wanted to begin classes on the twenty-fourth, the day after her arrival.

Here, *the day after her arrival* functions as an appositive phrase.

Acceptable Uses of Fragments

Formal writing generally doesn't permit you to use fragments; however, using fragments in casual writing is okay—if they don't confuse your reader. Remember that using fragments (even sparingly) depends on your audience, the restrictions of your instructor or company, and your personal writing style.

Remember that you may use fragments if you're quoting someone; in fact, you *must* use fragments if that's what the speaker used.

You might use fragments in short stories or novels (you've started your Great American Novel, haven't you?). A rule of thumb is that you shouldn't use them too often and you certainly shouldn't use them in any way that would puzzle your readers.

Rarely—if ever—should you use a fragment in a news story in a magazine or newspaper. If, however, you're writing an editorial, a fragment might be just what you need to get your point across.

Do we need the new tax that's on the ballot? Without a doubt. Will it pass? Probably not.

Both *Without a doubt* and *Probably not* are fragments. But look at how much punch you'd lose if you'd worded that passage and had used complete sentences instead of fragments.

Do we need the new tax that's on the ballot? Without a doubt we do. Will it pass? No, it probably will not.

Fragments are also acceptable in bulleted or numbered lists. Take a look at the following example:

Acceptable uses of a fragment include the following:

- when you're quoting someone
- in a bulleted or numbered list
- to make a quick point—but only when the construction isn't confusing to readers

Taken individually, each of the bullets is a fragment, but its meaning is clear. In the type of writing that you do, if you're permitted (or even encouraged) to include bulleted lists, then using fragments is fine.

FACT

You'll often see fragments as titles, captions, or headings; that's generally acceptable because space restrictions usually won't allow complete sentences. Fragments are also frequently used in advertising. Since fragments are short, readers probably remember them more easily than they would complete sentences.

Sometimes you'll see a fragment intentionally used for emphasis or wry humor. Look at the title of this section and you'll see words that were deliberately constructed as fragments. Also, take a look at this example:

> *Charlotte Critser quickly told the prospective employer she would never accept a job in a city more than a hundred miles from her hometown. Never. Under no circumstances. For no amount of money. Well, maybe for a new car, an expense account, and double her current salary.*

Reining In Run-on Sentences

Another mistake in sentence construction is a run-on sentence. The term *run-on* simply means that your sentence has at least two complete thoughts (two independent clauses, if your mind thinks that way), but it lacks the necessary punctuation between the thoughts. This punctuation is needed for readers to know when one thought stops and another begins. Consider the following sentence:

> *The punctuation code gives your readers a signal about where one thought stops and another begins if you don't use some code your readers will be confused.*

Say what? Instead of having the needed punctuation between *begins* and *if*, the sentence, well, "runs on" and its meaning is unclear. (A fairly simple concept, wouldn't you say?)

It's Time to Take a Break: Fused Sentences and Comma Splices

One type of run-on, called a fused sentence, occurs when two or more sentences are written (fused) together without a punctuation mark to show readers where the break occurs. Take a look at this sentence:

> *For our annual picnic, Chris Doss and Brad Cummings brought hamburgers we brought potato salad.*

This sentence has two separate thoughts:

> *For our annual picnic, Chris Doss and Brad Cummings brought hamburgers*

and

> *we brought potato salad.*

This sentence needs some punctuation to tell readers where one thought ends and another begins. You may do this in one of three ways:

- by creating two separate sentences *(For our annual picnic, Chris Doss and Brad Cummings brought hamburgers. We brought potato salad.)*
- by inserting a semicolon *(For our annual picnic, Chris Doss and Brad Cummings brought hamburgers; we brought potato salad.)*

- by inserting a comma and one of seven conjunctions—*but, or, yet, so, for, and, nor* (remember *boysfan?*) *(For our annual picnic, Chris Doss and Brad Cummings brought hamburgers, and we brought potato salad.)*

Remember that you must have two (or more) complete thoughts in order to correct a run-on sentence. Ask yourself if each group of words could stand alone (that is, could be a sentence by itself). If one group of words doesn't make sense as a sentence, then you don't have a complete thought.

Another type of run-on is a comma splice (comma fault), a sentence that has two complete thoughts that are joined (spliced together) by just a comma. The problem with a comma splice is that the comma should be replaced by something else—a different punctuation mark, additional words, or both. Take a look at this sentence:

Rachel Johnson wanted to go to the ball game, her friend Kelly Estes wanted to see the new movie.

On either side of the comma, you have a complete thought. The punctuation code says that you need something stronger than just a comma to help readers understand that a thought has been completed.

You have several choices to correct the sentence. You could create two separate sentences by using a period:

Rachel Johnson wanted to go to the ball game. Her friend Kelly Estes wanted to see the new movie.

Another option is to separate the two complete thoughts with a semicolon:

Rachel Johnson wanted to go to the ball game; her friend Kelly Estes wanted to see the new movie.

A third choice is to separate the two complete thoughts with a semicolon and a connecting word or phrase:

Rachel Johnson wanted to go to the ball game; however, her friend Kelly Estes wanted to see the new movie.

Or you could join the two sentences by leaving in the comma but adding one of the seven *boysfan* conjunctions (*but, or, yet, so, for, and, nor*). Of course, you may use the conjunctions only if the sentence makes sense. You may have:

Rachel Johnson wanted to go to the ball game, but her friend Kelly Estes wanted to see the new movie.

FACT

A comma splice frequently occurs with two quoted sentences, as in this example:

"We're going to the theater at seven," Katrina Rose said "I'd better get dressed right now."

Katrina stated two separate sentences, so you should use either a period (preferable in this case) or a semicolon after *said*.

Another way you can correct either a fused sentence or a comma splice is to reword the sentence so that one part becomes subordinate (that is, it can't stand alone as a complete thought). Let's look at the first example:

For our annual picnic, Chris Doss and Brad Cummings brought hamburgers we brought potato salad.

You might reword this in a number of ways:

While Chris Doss and Brad Cummings brought hamburgers for our annual picnic, we brought potato salad.

or

Whereas Chris Doss and Brad Cummings brought hamburgers for our annual picnic, we brought potato salad.

Yes, this one sounds really stuffy, and you probably wouldn't use it because of its style—but it does make sense.

Now look at the second example:

Rachel Johnson wanted to go to the ball game, her friend Kelly Estes wanted to see the new movie.

You could rewrite it in this way:

Although Rachel Johnson wanted to go to the ball game, her friend Kelly Estes wanted to see the new movie.

or

While Rachel Johnson wanted to go to the ball game, her friend Kelly Estes wanted to see the new movie.

In each of these examples the first part of the rewritten sentence (the part before the comma) couldn't stand alone as a sentence.

E-LINK

Try the interactive quizzes on sentence fragments, run-ons, and comma splices at these Web sites:

tinyurl.com/3xnkp9	*tinyurl.com/2u5u85*
tinyurl.com/36xnyf	*tinyurl.com/2oak5j*
tinyurl.com/38m7mz	*tinyurl.com/33c5dc*
tinyurl.com/2kptlf	*tinyurl.com/383wt5*
tinyurl.com/32qujw	*tinyurl.com/3xjwdd*

In closing, keep in mind that a sentence doesn't become a run-on merely because of its length. Take a look at this sentence:

At eleven-thirty one Saturday night not long ago, while young Steve Anthren was absentmindedly driving his dilapidated 1953 gray-and-white Chrysler sedan down a lonely, one-lane gravel road that looked as if it hadn't been traversed in many a year, he suddenly glanced in the rearview mirror and was alarmed to see two blinking lights coming from what he supposed was a vehicle of some sort or another; instead of immediately panicking and screaming bloody murder, however, Steve decided that perhaps this signaled a visit from someone from outer space, an alien who would be friendly and would take him to worlds that he had only dreamed of in all of the twenty years of his friendless life.

Although it is basically a nightmare to read (at 117 words, it should be broken into several sentences), it's properly punctuated and isn't a run-on. On either side of the semicolon there's just one complete thought.

Transitional Words and Phrases

Good writers rely on the use of transitional words and phrases. Transitional words and phrases show your readers the association between thoughts, sentences, or paragraphs; plus, they help make your writing smoother.

Sometimes sentences and paragraphs have perfectly constructed grammar, punctuation, and usage, but they lack transitional words or phrases. Material written that way seems awkward and stiff, as in this example:

The blind date was a disaster. It was a complete debacle. I was intrigued by what my "friend" Sarah had told me about Bill; she had said he was charming and was open to meeting someone new. He had recently seen me at a party and had wanted to meet me. Sarah said Bill was just my type. She said he was an avid reader; we would have lots to talk about. He liked playing tennis; that was a plus for me.

There's nothing wrong with the grammar, punctuation, or spelling in that paragraph, but it's choppy and boring. Now read the same paragraph after transitional words and phrases (underlined) have been added:

The blind date was <u>more than</u> a disaster. <u>Actually</u>, it was <u>clearly</u> a complete debacle. <u>At first</u>, I was <u>somewhat</u> intrigued by what my "friend" Sarah had told me about Bill; <u>namely</u>, she had said he was <u>quite</u> charming and <u>also</u> was open to meeting someone new. <u>In fact</u>, he had recently seen me <u>in the distance</u> at a party and had wanted to meet me. <u>Besides</u>, Sarah said, Bill was just my type. She said he was <u>quite</u> an avid reader <u>for one thing</u>; <u>therefore</u>, we would have *lots to talk about. In addition, he liked playing tennis; that was certainly a plus for me.*

Much better, isn't it? By including the transitions, the movement from one idea to another is much smoother, and the language of the paragraph has some life in it.

As important as transitions are in sentences, they're equally important between paragraphs. (Do you see how that transition sentence connects the idea of the preceding paragraph with the idea of this one?) These transitions help you move smoothly from one major concept to the next one.

The following is an excerpt from a piece that compares an essay titled "Why Would You . . . ?" to a personal experience of the writer. Read the two paragraphs and pay particular attention to the first sentence of the second paragraph, the transitional sentence.

In Conrad Allen's essay "Why Would You . . . ?" the author recounts how he had been humiliated in elementary school. Allen had been infatuated with Mandy Grayson, a pretty, pigtailed little girl in his class. One Valentine's Day, Allen gave Mandy a card with Manndy perfectly printed—if incorrectly spelled—on the envelope. After she tore open the card, Mandy glanced at it and, much to Conrad's dismay, let it drop on the floor. In a voice loud enough for all the class to hear, she said to Conrad, "Why would you give me a card? You're too dumb and ugly." Allen writes that he first felt his face turn red in embarrassment, and then he felt complete humiliation as the whole class turned around to stare at him to see his reaction. All he could do was stand frozen in front of Mandy, trying in vain to hold back his shame and his tears.

Like Allen, I felt shame when I was young. When I was in the fifth grade, my family was undergoing some difficult times. At that age, I was close friends with a group of four other girls; in fact, we called ourselves the "Live Five." Because we all had the same teacher, we were able to spend recess and lunchtime together, and we frequently spent the night at each other's houses as well. At one of the sleepovers at my house, the Live Five vowed to stay up all night. Big mistake. In our efforts to keep each other awake, we disturbed my father. That night happened to be one of the many when he was drunk, and he came down to the basement and began cursing and screaming at all of my friends. Not only did he say horrible things to me, but he also yelled at each of my friends and called them terrible names. The shame of that night continues with me today whenever I see one of the Live Five.

Wow, get out the tissues! You probably noticed that the sentence at the beginning of the second paragraph provides a connection between the ideas of the first paragraph and second paragraph. The first two words *(Like Allen)* signal that the main idea of the first paragraph will be continued and that a comparison will be made. Plus, the rest of the sentence *(I felt shame in school)* gives a clue about the topic of the second paragraph. If the transition sentence weren't there, and the second paragraph began *When I was in the fifth grade . . .* , the second paragraph would seem disjointed from the first, and readers would be confused.

Remember that transitional phrases are usually enclosed in commas, unless they're necessary to the meaning of a sentence.

As you can see from these examples (that's another transitional phrase—but you picked up on that, didn't you?), you should add transitions whenever possible to provide necessary links between thoughts and paragraphs. By using them, your writing becomes much more unified and articulate.

Classifying the Connectors

Transitional words and phrases can be divided into categories, grouped according to their use. The following should give you lots of ideas for adding transitional elements to your writing:

- **addition/sequence:** *additionally, afterward, again, also, another . . . , besides, finally, first . . . second . . . third, further, furthermore, in addition, in the first place, initially, last, later, likewise, meanwhile, moreover, next, other, overall, still, too*

- **concession:** *admittedly, although it's true that, certainly, conceding that, granted that, in fact, it may appear that, naturally, no doubt, of course, surely, undoubtedly, without a doubt*

- **contrast:** *after all, alternatively, although, and yet, at the same time, but, conversely, despite, even so, even though, for all that, however, in contrast, in spite of, instead, nevertheless, nonetheless, nor, notwithstanding, on the contrary, on the other hand, or, otherwise, regardless, still, though, yet*

- **examples, clarification, emphasis:** *after all, an instance of this, as an illustration, by all means, certainly, clearly, definitely, e.g., even, for example, for instance, for one thing, i.e., importantly, indeed, in fact, in other words, in particular, in short, more than that, namely, of course, of major concern, once again, specifically, somewhat, such as, that is, that is to say, the following example, this can be seen in, thus, to clarify, to demonstrate, to illustrate, to repeat, to rephrase, to put another way, truly, undoubtedly, without a doubt*

- **place or direction:** *above, adjacent to, at that point, below, beyond, close by, closer to, elsewhere, far, farther on, here, in the back, in the distance, in the front, near, nearby, neighboring on, next to, on the other side, opposite to, overhead, there, to the left, to the right, to the side, under, underneath, wherever*

- **purpose/cause and effect:** *accordingly, as a consequence, as a result, because, consequently, due to, for that reason, for this purpose, hence, in order that, on account of, since, so, so that, then, therefore, thereupon, thus, to do this, to this end, with this in mind, with this objective*

- **qualification:** *almost, although, always, frequently, habitually, maybe, nearly, never, oftentimes, often, perhaps, probably, time and again*

- **result:** *accordingly, and so, as a result, as an outcome, consequently, hence, so, then, therefore, thereupon, thus*

- **similarity:** *again, also, and, as well as, besides, by the same token, for example, furthermore, in a like manner, in a similar way, in the same way, like, likewise, moreover, once more, similarly, so*

- **summary or conclusion:** *after all, all in all, as a result, as has been noted, as I have said, as we have seen, as mentioned earlier, as stated, clearly, finally, in any event, in brief, in conclusion, in other words, in* *particular, in short, in simpler terms, in summary, on the whole, that is, therefore, to conclude, to summarize*

- **time:** *after a bit, after a few days, after a while, afterward, again, also, and then, as long as, as soon as, at first, at last, at length, at that time, at the same time, before, during, earlier, eventually, finally, first, following, formerly, further, hence, initially, immediately, in a few days, in the first place, in the future, in the meantime, in the past, last, lately, later, meanwhile, next, now, on (a certain day), once, presently, previously, recently, second, shortly, simultaneously, since, so far, soon, still, subsequently, then, thereafter, this time, today, tomorrow, until, until now, when, whenever*

The Biggest Bugbears

Need a little advice (or should that be *advise?*) about when to use certain words? Are you feeling alright (or *all right?*) about your ability to distinguish between (or is that *among?*) alumni, alumnae, alumnus, and *alumna?* Could you use an angel (or an *angle?*) on your shoulder to give you some guidance? Are you anxious—or are you *eager?*—to overcome your brain freeze about when to use particular words?

Not to worry! This section contains an extensive list of words that are commonly misused or confused. Also included are a number of mnemonics to help you remember the differences when this book isn't handy (although you *should* carry it with you at all times!).

Here are the words that cause some of the greatest amounts of perplexity and befuddlement:

a, an: Use *a* before words that begin with a consonant sound (*a* pig, *a* computer); use *an* before words that begin with a vowel sound (*an* earring, *an* integer). The sound is what makes the difference. Write *a habit* because *habit* starts with the *h* sound after the article, but write *an honor* because the *h* in *honor* isn't pronounced (the first sound of *honor* is the vowel *o*).

What an honor and a privilege it is to meet a history expert like Prof. Maltby.

a lot, alot, allot: Okay, let's begin with the fact that there is no such word as *alot*. If you mean a great number of people or things, use *a lot*. Here's a mnemonic for this: "a whole lot" is two whole words. If you mean *that allocate*, use *allot*. A mnemonic for *allot* is *allo*cate = *all*ot.

Tomorrow night, the mayor will allot a lot of money for various municipal projects.

accept, except: *Accept* has several meanings, including *believe*, *take on*, *endure*, and *consent*; *except* means *excluding*. If your sentence can keep its meaning if you substitute *excluding*, use *except*.

Except for food for the volunteers, Doris wouldn't accept any donations.

adapt, adopt: To ad*a*pt is to ch*a*nge; to ad*o*pt is to take and make your *o*wn.

After Mary Elizabeth and Ron adopted the baby, they learned to adapt to having little sleep.

advice, advise: *Advise* is what you do when you give *advice*. Here's a mnemonic to help you remember: To adv*ise* you must be w*ise*. Good adv*ice* is to drive slowly on *ice*.

Grandpa tried to advise me when I was a youngster, but I wouldn't listen to his advice.

affect, effect: *Affect* is usually a verb (something that shows action), usually means *change* or *shape*, and—as a verb—has its accent on the first syllable. (There is a meaning of *affect* as a noun, but unless you're a psychologist you needn't worry about it.) *Effect* is almost always a noun meaning *result* or *outcome*, *appearance* or *impression* (*effect* has a rare use as a verb, when it means *to achieve* or *cause*). One mnemonic to help you remember is this: Caus*e* and *e*ffect (that is, if you want the word that is to be used in this phrase, you want *effect*—the word that begins with the last letter of *cause*).

The effect of the announcement of impending war won't affect Adam's decision to join the military.

aggravate, annoy: If you mean *pester* or *irritate*, you want *annoy*. Aggravate means *exaggerate* or *make worse*.

Steven was annoyed when his boss aggravated the situation by talking to the press.

aid, aide: If you help, you *aid*; if you have a helper or supporter, you have an aide.

The aid from my aide is invaluable.

aisle, isle, I'll: An *aisle* is in a theater; an *isle* is an island (a shortened form of the word); *I'll* is short for *I will*.

I'll walk down the aisle to meet my groom; then we'll honeymoon on a desert isle.

all ready, already: If you mean all is ready, use *all ready*; if you mean in the past, use *already*.

I already told you we're all ready to go out to dinner!

all right, alright: *All right* is always two words, although you often see the incorrect spelling *alright*. You wouldn't say something is *aleft* or *alwrong*, would you? (Please say you wouldn't!)

Is it all right if we eat in tonight?

all together, altogether: *All together* means *simultaneously* or *all at once*; *altogether* means *entirely* or *wholly*. If you can substitute *entirely* or *wholly* in the sentence and the meaning doesn't change, you need the form of the word that is entirely, wholly one word.

You're altogether wrong about the six friends going all together to the dance; each is going separately.

alumni, alumnae, alumnus, alumna: You can thank the Romans for this confusion; Latin has separate words for masculine, feminine, singular, and plural forms. Here's the rundown: One male graduate is an *alumnus*; one female graduate is an *alumna*; several female graduates are *alumnae*; and several male graduates or several male and female graduates are *alumni*. You can see why the short form *alum* is often used informally; when you use it, you don't have to look up the right form of the word.

Although Mary Jo and her sisters are alumnae from Wellesley, Mary Jo is the alumna who receives the most attention; her brothers Martin and Xavier are alumni of Harvard, but Martin is a more famous alumnus than Xavier.

FACT

Other often-confused Latin singulars and plurals are these:

Singular	Plural
criterion	criteria
datum	data
minutia	minutiae
stimulus	stimuli
syllabus	syllabuses/syllabi

allusion, illusion: An *allusion* is a reference; an *illusion* is a false impression. If you want a word that means mistaken idea, you want *illusion*.

Kay told Jerry that she was under the illusion he'd be her Prince Charming; Jerry didn't understand the allusion.

altar, alter: If you change something, you alter it; you worship before an *altar*.

We'll alter the position of the altar so the congregation can see the new carvings.

among, between: Think division. If only two people are dividing something, use *between*; if more than two people are involved, use *among*. Here's a mnemonic: be*tw*een for *tw*o and among for a group.

The money was divided between Sarah and Bob; the land was divided among Billy, Henry, and Lillian.

angel, angle: An *angel* has wings; the degre*e* of an angl*e* is often studied.

The angel's wings are set at ninety-degree angles from its body.

anxious, eager: These two words are often confused. If you're *anxious*, you're nervous or concerned; if you're *eager*, you're enthusiastic.

I had been anxious about my medical test results, but when they proved negative I was eager to kick up my heels.

anybody, any body: *Anybody* means *any one person* (and is usually interchangeable with *anyone*). *Any body* refers (pardon the graphic reference) to one dead person.

Anybody can help to search for any body that might not have been found in the wreckage.

appraise, apprise: To ap*praise* is to give value to something (to see how much *praise* it needs); to app*ris*e is to *i*nform.

The auctioneer called to apprise our family about how he would appraise various items for us.

bad, badly: When you're writing about how you feel, use *bad*. However, if you're writing about how you did something or performed or reacted to something, use *badly* (twisted your ankle *badly*; played *badly* in the game).

Gregg felt bad he had scored so badly on the test.

bazaar, bizarre: The first is a marketplace; the second means *strange*, *weird*, or *peculiar*.

The most bizarre purchase that came from the bazaar was a pair of sandals without any soles.

bear, bare: A b*ear* can t*ear* off your *ear*; if you're bar*e*, you're nud*e*.

The bare bathers were disturbed when the grizzly bear arrived.

besides, beside: If you want the one that means *in addition to*, you want the one that has an additional *s* (*besides*); *beside* means *by the side of.*

Besides her groom, the bride wanted her dad beside her in the photo.

breath, breathe: You take a *breath*; you inhal*e* and *e*xhal*e* when you breath*e*.

In the cold of the winter, it was hard for me to breathe when taking a breath outside.

cavalry, Calvary: The *cavalry* are soldiers on horseback (the word isn't capitalized unless it begins a sentence); Ca*l*vary is the hi*ll* where Christ was crucified (and is always capitalized).

The cavalry wasn't in attendance for the march up Calvary.

can, may: If you *can* do something, you're physically able to do it. If you *may* do it, you have permission to do it.

You can use "ain't" in a sentence, but you may not.

cannot, am not, is not, are not, and all other "nots": For some strange reason, *cannot* is written as one word. All other words that have *not* with them are written as two words. Go figure.

capital, capitol: The *capitol* is the building in which the legislative body meets. If you mean the one in Washington, D.C., use a capital *C*; if you mean the one in your state, use a lowercase *c*. Remember that the building (the one spelled with an *o*) usually has a dome. Use *capital* with all other meanings.

The capital spent by the legislators at the capitol is appalling.

carat, caret, carrot, karat: A *carat* is a weight for a stone (a diamond, for instance); *carat* is also an alternate spelling of *karat*, which is a measurement of how much gold is in an alloy (as in the abbreviation 18k; the *k* is for *karat*). A *caret* is this proofreading mark: ^ (meaning that you should insert something at that point). Finally, a *carrot* is the orange vegetable your mother told you to eat.

Set in an eighteen-karat gold band, the five-carat diamond was shaped like a carrot.

censor, censure: To censor is to take out the bad material; to *censure* is to place blame (don't cen*sure* someone unless you're *sure*).

The full Senate voted not to censure the senator for trying to censor the e-mail that came to other congressional employees.

cite, sight, site: Your *sight* is your vision or a view (you use your *sight* to look at a beautiful *sight*); to *cite* is to make reference to a specific source; a *site* is a location, such as on the Internet.

The colors on the Web site you cited in your paper were a sight to behold.

climactic, climatic: *Climactic* refers to a climax, a pinnacle; *climatic* is related to the weather (the climate).

Last year's weather featured many climatic oddities, but the climactic point came when snow arrived in June.

coarse, course: If something is *coarse*, it's rough; *oars* are c*oars*e. A c*ours*e is a r*out*e, a class, or part of the idiomatic phrase "of course."

The racecourse led the runners over coarse terrain.

complement, compliment: If something completes another thing, it *complements* it (*comple*te = *comple*ment). If you receive praise, you've gotten a *compliment* (*I* like to receive a compl*i*ment).

The jewelry will complement the outfit the star will wear, and she will surely receive many compliments on her attire.

conscience, conscious: Your *conscience* tells you whether something is right or wrong; if you're *conscious*, you're awake and aware.

On the witness stand, Marie said she wasn't conscious of the fact that her conscience told her not to steal the ashtray from the hotel room.

continual, continuous: *Continuous* actions go on uninterrupted; *continual* actions are intermittent.

The continual rains lasted for ten days; because of that, the Blacksons had a continuous problem with water in their basement.

core, corps, corpse: A *core* is a center or main section; a *corps* is a group or organization; a *corpse* is a dead body.

At the core of the Marine Corps lieutenant's sleeplessness was his discovery of a corpse while on a training mission.

council, counsel: A *council* is an official group, a committee; to *counsel* is to give advice (the stock broker coun*sel*ed me to *sell*).

The town council decided to counsel the youth group on the proper way to ask for funds.

desert, dessert: A *desert* is a dry, arid place or (usually used in the plural form) a deserved reward or punishment *(just deserts)*. The verb that means *to leave* is also *desert*. The food that is *so* *s*weet is a de*s*sert.

While lost in the desert, Rex craved a dessert of apple pie à la mode.

device, devise: A *device* is a machine or tool; to *devise* means *to invent* or *concoct something*.

To devise, you must be wise. Will this device work on ice?

discreet, discrete: *Discreet* means *cautious, careful,* or *guarded in conduct* (be discr*ee*t about whom you m*ee*t). *Discrete* means *separate* or *disconnected.*

The dancer's discreet movements were discrete from those performed by the rest of the chorus.

dual, duel: The first means *two* (*dual* purposes); the second is a fight or contest (the lover's jealousy was f*uel* for the d*uel*).

The dual reasons for the duel were revenge and money.

elicit, illicit: To *e*licit something is to *ex*tract it, to bring it out; something *ill*icit is *ill*egal.

The telephone scam artist engaged in the illicit practice of trying to elicit credit card information.

emigrate, immigrate: To *e*migrate is to *ex*it a country; to *i*mmigrate is to come *i*nto a country.

Ten people were trying to emigrate from the tyranny of their country and immigrate to the United States.

eminent, imminent: Someone well known is *e*minent; something that might take place *imm*ediately is *imm*inent.

Our meeting with the eminent scientist is imminent.

ensure, insure: To *ensure* is to *make certain of something*; *insure* is only for business purposes (to *insure* a car).

To ensure that we continue to insure your house, send payment immediately.

everyday, every day: *Everyday* means *routine* or *daily* (*everyday* low cost); *every day* means *every single day* (low prices *every day*). Use *single* words if you mean every *single* day.

The everyday inexpensive prices of the store meant that more shoppers came every day.

faze, phase: To *faze* is to *intimidate* or *disturb*. As a noun, a *phase* is *a period of time*; as a verb, it means *to establish gradually*.

I wasn't fazed by his wish to phase out our relationship.

fewer, less: Use *fewer* to describe plural words; use le*ss* to describe singular words.

The new product has fewer calories but less fat.

figuratively, literally: *Literally* means *precisely as described*; *figuratively* means *in a symbolic or metaphoric way.*

When Pauline called, she asked if I was off my rocker; I thought she meant figuratively and wondered why she thought I had gone crazy. However, she intended to be taken literally, as she wondered if I was still sitting outside in my rocker.

flaunt, flout: If you *flaunt* something, you show it off (*flaunt* your new jewelry); to *flout* is to jeer at someone or something in a contemptible way, or to intentionally disobey (*flout* the laws).

In an attempt to flaunt his new car to the girls on the other side of the road, James decided to flout the law and not stop at the red light.

forego, forgo: If you mean something that has gone be*fore*, use *fore*go (a *foregone* conclusion); if you want the word that means *to do without something*, use *forgo* (the one that is without the *e*).

It's a foregone conclusion that Meg and Marion will forgo sweets when they're dieting.

foreword, forward: The word that means *the opening information in a book* is *foreword* (it comes be*fore* the first important *word* of the book); for any other meaning, use *forward.*

To gain insight into the author's intent, you should read the foreword before you proceed forward in the book.

foul, fowl: The animal is a *fowl*; the action on the basketball court is a *foul*; a bad odor smells *foul.*

The foul smell came from the fowl that had been slaughtered.

good, well: *Good* is an adjective; it doesn't mean in *a high-quality manner*, or *correctly.* If you want either of those meanings you need an adverb, so you want *well.*

You did well on the test; your grade should be good.

graduated, graduated from: A school *graduates* you; you *graduate from* a school.

The year Tiya Hudson graduated from college, the school graduated 5,000 students.

grisly, grizzly: A horrible or gruesome sight is *grisly*; the North American bear is a *grizzly*.

A grisly scene was left after the attack by the grizzly bear.

heal, heel: *To heal* means *to cure* or *patch up* (to *heal* a wound); among other verb definitions, *to heel* is *to tilt to one side*, *to give money to*, or *to urge along*; a *well-heeled* person has a *considerable amount of money*.

You might need ointment to heal the blisters you get from trying to right the sails when the ship heels in the wind.

hear, here: You h*ear* with your *ear*. *Here* is the opposite of t*here*.

Did you hear that Aunt Helen is here?

hopefully: If you mean *I hope*, or *it's hoped*, then that's what you should write. *Hopefully* means *confidently* or *with anticipation*.

The director waited hopefully for the Oscar nominations to be announced.

imply, infer: Both of these have to do with words not said aloud. A s*p*eaker im*p*lies something; a liste*n*er i*n*fers something.

Rufus thought the boss had implied that she would be back for an inspection next week, but Ruth didn't infer that.

in, into: *In* means with*in*; *into* means from the outside *to* the *in*side.

Go into the house, look in my purse, and bring me money.

its, it's: *It's* means only *it is* (before *it's* too late); *its* means *belonging to it* (I gave the dog *its* food and water).

It's a shame the dog lost its bone.

lead, led: If you want the word that means *was in charge of* or *guided*, use *led*; otherwise, use *lead*.

The company, led by one of the richest people in the world, announced that its CEO was retiring; today a newcomer will lead it.

loose, lose: *Loose* (which rhymes with *noose*) means *not tight*. *Lose* is the opposite of *find* or *win*.

Will I lose my belt if it's too loose?

may of, might of, must of, should of, would of, could of: In speech, we slur these phrases so that they all sound as if they end in *of*, but in fact all of them end in *have*. Their correct forms are *may have*, *might have*, *must have*, *should have*, *would have*, and *could have*.

I must have thought you would have been able to find the room without any directions.

moral, morale: If something is *moral*, it's *right* or *ethical* (that's the adjective form); if something has a *moral*, it has a *message* or a *meaning* (that's the noun form). Your moral*e* is your *e*steem.

The moral high road that the politician took boosted the morale of the entire staff.

myself, itself, yourself, himself, herself, themselves, ourselves, yourselves: None of these pronouns should ever be used without the antecedent that corresponds to it. You might write:

I myself would like to go for a drive.
But you shouldn't write, "Mike took Pat and myself for a drive."

nauseated, nauseous: *Nauseous* is often misused; it means *disgusting* or *sickening*; *nauseated* means *sick to your stomach* (you can get nause*ated* from something you *ate*).

The nauseous fumes caused the workers to become nauseated.

pacific, specific: *P*acific means *p*eaceful; *specific* means *precise or individualized.*

To be specific, the pacific view from Hickory Mountain is what calms me the most.

passed, past: *Passed* is a verb; *past* is an adjective (p*ast* often means l*ast*) or noun meaning *the preceding time.*

In the past, twenty parades have passed down this street.

peace, piece: Pe*a*ce is the opposite of w*a*r; a *piece* is a part or portion (a p*ie*ce of *pie*).

The father bargained with his small children, "Give me an hour's peace, and I'll get you a piece of cake."

persecute, prosecute: To *persecute* is to *oppress or bully*; to *prosecute* is to *bring legal action.*

We warned our neighbors that we would prosecute if they continued to persecute their dog.

pore, pour: If you *read something carefully*, you *pore* over it. If you make a liquid go *out* of a container, you p*ou*r it.

After Harry accidentally poured ink on the new floor, he pored over several books to find out how to clean the stain.

prophecy, prophesy: You have a forecast or a prediction if you have a prophe*c*y. *Prophesy* is pronounced with the last syllable sounding like *sigh*, and you might sigh when you *prophesy* something dismal.

Last week the audience heard the medium prophesy about forthcoming bad weather; the prophecy has yet to come true.

principle, principal: *Principle* means *law* or *belief. Principal* means *major* or *head*; it also means *money that earns interest in a bank.* The princi*pal* is the head person in a school; he or she is your *pal* and makes princi*pal* decisions.

That is the most important principle our principal believes.

quiet, quite: *Quiet* is *calm* or *silence*; *quite* means *to a certain extent*. Be sure to check the ending of the word you use; that's where mistakes are made. Think: I hope my pet is qui*et*.

Are you quite sure that you were quiet in the library?

real, really: *Real* means *actual* or *true*; *really* means *in truth* or *in reality*. Except in the most casual tone in writing, neither *real* nor *really* should be used in the sense of *very* (that's a *real* good song on the radio; I'm *really* glad you listened to that station).

When Debbie and Phillip realized they were lost, the real importance of carrying a compass hit them.

respectfully, respectively: If you're *full* of respect for someone and want to show it, you do it respect*fully*. *Respectively* means *in the order stated*.

Upon hearing the news, I respectfully called Bob and Janie, respectively.

role, roll: A *role* is a *position or part* (in a production); a *roll* is a *piece of bread* on the dinner table; to *roll* is to *rotate*.

The role of the acrobat will be played by someone who can perform a backward roll.

set, sit: If you plac*e* something, you s*e*t it. If you're in an upr*i*ght pos*i*tion (like in a chair), you s*i*t. In addition, *set* is transitive (it must have an object); *sit* is intransitive (it doesn't have an object).

Please set the table before you sit down.

stationery, stationary: If you mean something that lacks any motion, use *stationary*; if you mean something you write a lett*er* on, use station*ery*.

The stationery had a picture of people riding stationary bicycles.

supposed (to): Often the *-d* is incorrectly omitted from *supposed to* (meaning *expected to* or *designed to*).

In this job, you're supposed to be able to write short, clear, and effective memos.

than, then: If you mean *next* or *therefore* or *at that time*, you want *then*. If you want the word that shows a comparison, use th*a*n.

For a while, Mary ran more quickly than I; then she dropped her pace.

that, which: For clauses that don't need commas (restrictive clauses), use *that*. For nonrestrictive clauses, which need commas, use *which*.

The local dog kennels, which are nearby, are the ones that have been featured in the news lately.

there, their, they're: If you want the opposite of *here*, use t*here*; if you mean they a*re*, you want they*'re*; if you mean belonging to *the*m, use *the*ir.

There are employees who think they're going to get their 10 percent raises tomorrow.

to, too, two: If you mean something *additional*, it's the one with the *additional o (too)*; *two* is the *number after one*; *to* means *in the direction of something*.

Did our supervisor ask the two new employees to go to Detroit and Chicago, too?

troop, troupe: Both are groups of people, but *troupe* refers to actors only. The troupe of actors performed for the troop of Brownies.

try and, try to: Almost always the mistake comes in writing *try and* when you need to use *try to*.

The lady said she would try to get the dress in my size; I hoped she would try and keep looking.

weather, whether: If you mean conditions of the climate, use *weather*. (Can you stand to *eat* in the h*eat* of this bad w*eat*her?) If you mean *which*, *whichever*, or *if it's true that*, use *whether*.

It's now mid-April, and the weather can't decide whether it's spring or winter.

when, where: If you're writing a definition, don't use either of these words. For instance, don't write "A charley horse is when you get a cramp in your leg"; instead, write something like: "A charley horse is the result of a cramp in your leg."

A bank is a place in which you can make a deposit or withdrawal.

who, which, that: Don't use *which* when you're writing about people. Some style guides have the same restriction for *that* and some don't, so be sure to check.

The inspector, who gives the orders that we must obey, said that the law, which had never been enforced, would result in higher costs.

FACT

No Such Puppy: These are considered nonstandard words and phrases (in other words, ones you shouldn't use): *anyways, can't hardly, can't help but, can't scarcely, everywheres, hisself, irregardless, nowheres, off of, theirselves, theirself*—and the number one nonstandard word: *ain't.*

whose, who's: *Whose* means *belonging to whom*; *who's* is short for *who is* (the apostrophe means the *i* has been omitted).

After the sock hop, who's going to determine whose shoes these are?

woman, women: One *man*, two *men*. One wo*man*, two wo*men*. It's that simple.

The local woman asked the two visiting women if they'd like a tour of the town.

your, you're: If you mean *belonging to you*, use *your* (this is *our* car; that is y*our* car); if you mean *you are*, use *you're* (remember that the apostrophe means the *a* has been omitted).

If you're in the sun in Florida, be sure to put sunscreen on your nose.

Try the interactive quizzes on confusable words and phrases at these Web sites:

tinyurl.com/33fqp8   tinyurl.com/2zvnnf
tinyurl.com/33l9a2   tinyurl.com/2rqggp
tinyurl.com/2jrtjg

Checkpoint

Look at this story starter and determine which word in parentheses is the correct form to use in each case:

I (use, used) to be better at saying no. I was (suppose, supposed) to be writing a report, but (to, too, two) friends called and asked if I wanted to go spelunking, (which, witch) they had to explain meant exploring in caves.

Agreeing to go along with my friends, (who, which, that) weren't experienced spelunkers, was my first mistake. When we got to the cave, (there, their, they're) was a huge rock blocking the entrance. At first the rock (seamed, seemed) to be (stationery, stationary), but using all the strength we had we were finally able to move it (slow, slowly) and get inside. It was (than, then) that I should have left and gone home, but I didn't know (weather, whether) my friends would be disappointed in me if I left them. My (sole, soul) reason for staying was to keep face with them, and so the three of us formed a little spelunking (troop, troupe) and set off to explore.

Staying in the cave was my second mistake. When we were fairly deep inside, I became fascinated with a (stalactite, stalagmite) (that, which) was shaped like a (throne, thrown) and decided to take a break and (sit, set) on it for a while. At that point, I realized I was hungry and decided to (try and, try to) convince my friends that we should stop and eat the lunches we had brought.

Chapter 13

In Plain English, Please

Clichés, redundancies, and wordiness can really clutter your writing. Also, they might distract and annoy your readers and, perhaps worst of all, they can completely obscure your message. You can more easily avoid them by becoming more aware of their use in everyday life. The lists included in this chapter will also help.

Steering Clear of Clichés

A cliché is a worn-out expression, one you've heard over and over, or time and time again, or a thousand times before (do you get the picture?). It may have been clever or had a special meaning the first time you heard it, but by now you've come across it so many times that it's lost its pizzazz and so doesn't add any spice to your writing.

FACT

Many clichés are also similes (comparisons using *like* or *as*). You're probably familiar with the following expressions:

happy as a lark	*slippery as an eel*	*pretty as a picture*
fit as a fiddle	*blind as a bat*	*snug as a bug in a rug*
dumb as a post	*high as a kite*	*sharp as a tack*

As a rule, you should avoid using clichés because they're unoriginal, stale, and monotonous. Your readers won't think your work is the least bit creative if all they see is cliché-ridden writing.

Most likely, you're familiar with hundreds of clichés. If you read the first part of a phrase and you can fill in its ending, then your phrase is probably a cliché.

Take a look at the first parts of these phrases:	
put all your eggs _____	there's more there than meets _____
read the handwriting _____	costs an arm _____
every cloud has _____	that's the way the_____

You know the ending for each of those, don't you? That's how you know they're clichés. If, however, English isn't your native language, you may not be familiar with these clichés. Take a look at the following chart:

Here are the complete phrases:	
put all your eggs in one basket	there's more there than meets the eye
read the handwriting on the wall	costs an arm and a leg
every cloud has a silver lining	that's the way the cookie crumbles

When you're getting ideas or writing your first draft, sometimes you'll think of a cliché. Go ahead and write it down. But when you revise your work, get out your eraser (or press the Delete key) pronto and get rid of that cliché.

If you can't think of an original way to reword your cliché, try "translating" it in a literal way. Say, for instance, that you've written:

It was plain as the nose on his face that Corey wouldn't stick his neck out for anybody else.

In that sentence, you're dealing with two clichés *(plain as the nose on his face* and *stick his neck out).* To make the sentence cliché-free, you could change it to:

Plainly, Corey wouldn't take a risk for anybody else.

Is there any time that using a cliché is permissible? Sure. The style for using an occasional cliché is relaxed or casual, so keep in mind that clichés have no place in academic writing. But if your style allows you to use a cliché in a humorous way, go ahead and add one occasionally. For instance, you might be writing about nobility in Europe. With a casual tone, you might use this expanded cliché as your title: "Putting Up Your Dukes (and Earls)."

It is permissible to use clichés in academic writing if you are quoting someone. You must quote the dialogue exactly in such a case.

The trick is to let your reader know that you're using a cliché intentionally. If you're in a pinch (yes, that's a cliché), write something along the lines of "Even though I knew the cliché 'Little pitchers have big ears,'" and then go on to elaborate as to how the cliché fits in with your topic.

No Need to Repeat Yourself!

"I've said it before and I'll say it again."

"I've said it before, but now I'll reiterate."

"I've said it before and I'd like to repeat myself."

We've all heard words like these before—and, odds are, hearing people repeat themselves drives most of us crazy. When it comes to writing, using redundant words or phrases not only diminishes the value of your work, it's also a waste of your reader's time.

Take a look at the following commonly seen or often heard redundant phrases and read the explanations about why they're redundant. (Get ready to smack yourself on the head as you mutter, "I should have thought of that"—but comfort yourself with the thought that you're certainly not alone in using these phrases!) Then start cutting your own redundancies.

FACT

Cease and desist. Will and testament. Goods and chattels. Legal documents are rife with redundancies, and the reason goes back to 1066. Before William of Normandy conquered England, English law had commonly been written in Latin and Old English. When William took control of England, Norman French gained stature. However, many people weren't fluent in all three languages. Since lawyers wanted to be certain their documents and proceedings were written precisely and were understood by everyone, they developed phrases that incorporated words with synonyms in Latin, Old English, and Norman French.

Redundant Phrase	Explanation
advance planning	Planning must be done in advance. Delete *advance*.
A.M. in the morning	A.M. means *morning*. Delete *in the morning*.
and also	Use one word or the other, but not both.
as an added bonus	If something is a bonus, it must be added. Delete *added*.
ask the question	You can't ask anything except a question; delete *the question*.
ATM machine	The *M* in *ATM* stands for *machine*. Delete *machine*.
basic essentials	If they're the essentials, they have to be basic. Delete *basic*.
cash money	Is cash ever anything but money? Delete *cash*.
close proximity	You can't have far proximity, can you? Delete *close*.
closed fist	A fist must be closed. Delete *closed*.
combined together	Things that are combined must be together. Delete *together*.
completely unanimous	Something cannot be partially unanimous. Delete *completely*.
continue on	Can you continue off? Delete *on*.
cooperate together	You can't cooperate apart. Delete *together*.
each and every	The words mean the same thing; delete one.
end result	Can you have a result that's not in the end? Delete *end*.
estimated at about	*Estimated* means *about*. Delete *at about*.

exactly the same	If something is the same, it must be exact. Delete *the same*.
excised out	You can't excise in, can you? Delete *out*.
foreign imports	Material that's imported must be foreign. Delete *foreign*.
free gift (free gratis)	If it's a gift or is gratis, it's free. Delete *free*.
green in color	As opposed to green in what? Delete *in color*.
HIV virus	The *V* in *HIV* stands for *virus*. Delete *virus*.
honest truth	If something isn't the truth, it isn't honest. Delete *honest*.
important essentials	If items are essential, surely they're important. Delete *important*.
large in size	The word *large* denotes size. Delete *in size*.
mutual cooperation	Cooperation has to be mutual. Delete *mutual*.
my own personal opinion	*My opinion* means it's your own and it's personal. Delete *own personal*.
overused cliché	If a phrase isn't overused, it's not a cliché. Delete *overused*.
past memory	You can't have a future memory, can you? Delete *past*.
PIN number	The *N* in *PIN* stands for *number*. Delete *number*.
P.M. at night	P.M. means night. Delete *at night*.
return back	Here again, it's hard to return forward. Delete *back*.
roast beef with au jus	The *au* means *with*; delete *with*.

safe haven	By definition, a haven is a safe place. Delete *safe*.
sudden impulse	An impulse is sudden, or it's not an impulse. Delete *sudden*.
sum total	If you have a sum, you have a total. Delete one word or the other.
totally monopolize	A monopoly is total, isn't it? Delete *totally*.
true fact	By definition, a fact must be true. Delete *true*.
valuable asset	If something is an asset, then it has value. Delete *valuable*.

When Less Is More

Wordiness is the first cousin of redundant writing. If you use six words when two will do, your writing becomes bloated and loses its effectiveness. Wordiness takes up your readers' valuable time, and it can make your writing seem pompous.

Still have your eraser handy or your finger on the delete key? Take a look at the following list of common wordy expressions; then get to work putting your words on a diet. For even more common wordy expressions and their suggested substitutes, see Appendix C.

Wordy Phrase	Suggested Substitute
a small number of	a few
being of the opinion that	I believe (think)
cannot be avoided	must, should
due to the fact that	since, because
excessive number of	too many
for the purpose of	to, for
give consideration to	consider
has a tendency to	often

last but not least	finally
make an examination of	examine
none at all	none
present time	present, now
the majority of	most
until such time as	until
with regard to	concerning, about

E-LINK

Try the interactive quizzes on eliminating wordiness at these Web sites:

tinyurl.com/lrqdr   *tinyurl.com/2owum2*

Close, but No Cigar: Misused Phrases

In a recent informal survey, copyeditors and English teachers from around the world were asked about mistakes they frequently see in print or speech. This chapter includes some of the results of that survey. Don't feel as if you have to hang your head in shame if you see your own mistakes reported here; the point is to learn from them (and to promise yourself you'll never make them again).

Sometimes people hear certain nifty or impressive phrases and then later use those same phrases in their own writing or speech. Problems arise when they either misheard the phrase or remembered it incorrectly. What they end up writing or saying is close to the original, but it's not quite right.

The result is often a humorous take on the correct phrase (like a "doggie-dog world" instead of a "dog-eat-dog world"), and sometimes it's just plain puzzling ("beckon call" instead of "beck and call").

The following are some of the more common mistakes of this variety, as reported by copyeditors and teachers. Have you made any of these mistakes? (Just nod silently. Now you'll know what to write next time.)

The Correct Phrase	What You'll Sometimes See or Hear
all it entails	all it in tails
all of a sudden	all of the sudden
amusing anecdotes	amusing antidotes
beck and call	beckon call
bated breath	baited breath
begging the question	bagging the question
beside the point	besides the point
by accident	on accident
can't fathom it	can't phantom it
down the pike	down the pipe
dyed in the wool	died in the wool
en route to a party	in route (or) in root to a party
far be it from me	far be it for me
for all intents and purposes	for all intensive purposes
free rein	free reign
got my dander up	got my dandruff up
got his just deserts	got his just desserts
had the wherewithal	had the where with all
home in on	hone in on
I couldn't care less	I could care less
I hope to be at work	hopefully, I'll be at work
in his sights	in his sites
in like Flynn	in like Flint
mind your *p*'s and *q*'s	mind your peas and cues
moot point	mute point
nip it in the bud	nip it in the butt

The Correct Phrase	What You'll Sometimes See or Hear
nuclear power	nucular power
one's surname	one's sir name
out of whack	out of wack
pored over a document	poured over a document
prostate cancer	prostrate cancer
recent poll	recent pole
shoo-in to win	shoe-in to win
supposedly	supposably
take it for granted	take it for granite
the die is cast	the dye is cast
toe the line	towed the line
tongue in cheek	tongue and cheek
tough row to hoe	tough road to hoe
up and at 'em	up and adam
whet my appetite	wet my appetite

Mirror, Mirror, on the Wall, Whose Mistakes Are Worst of All?

In their responses concerning blunders in written work, the copyeditors tended to focus on errors of grammar, spelling, and usage, while the teachers were inclined to concentrate on the specifics of writing. Following each "complaint" are some suggestions for eliminating these mistakes from your work.

Comments from the Copyeditors' Camp

Take a look at this list of errors that copyeditors say frequently arise in material they check.

Simple misspellings. If you're working on a computer, send your material through a spell check. Your computer won't catch all of your mistakes (you have to do *some* work yourself), but you'll be surprised at the number of mistakes it does find.

Omitted words or words put in the wrong place after cutting and pasting the text. If, through some great mystery, what you're sure you've written isn't what appears on the page, read, reread, and then (surprise!) reread your material—especially after you've cut and pasted.

Using the passive voice when the active voice would be appropriate—and would read better, too. Look through your completed material for sentences written in the passive voice. Unless there's a particular need for the passive voice, rewrite the sentence in the active voice. (Remember that in the active voice the subject performs the action of the verb.)

Improper use of apostrophes (especially plural versus possessive). Review Chapter 3 on the use of apostrophes. Look at each one you've written and ask yourself if you've used it correctly in a contraction or in showing possession. Pay particular attention to apostrophes used with *yours*, *his*, *hers*, *theirs*, *ours*, *its* (only *it's* ever takes an apostrophe, and only when you mean *it is*).

Use of they to refer to a singular word (e.g., the child . . . they/their). Study each *they* in your material and determine which noun it refers to (that is, look at its antecedent). If the noun (the antecedent) is singular, reword your sentence so that the noun is plural, or change *they* to a singular pronoun (*his* or *her*, *he* or *she*, *it*).

Gratuitous capitalization (sometimes dubbed "decorative capitalization"). Some writers think something is given greater importance or specificity if it's capitalized, even if it isn't a proper noun. Copyeditors say the problem is that writers think anyone or anything that is referred to with some precision seems to get capitalized: job titles (Caseworker, Commissioner, Director), agencies (the Department, the College), or particular fields or programs (Child Welfare, Food Stamps). If you see many capital letters in your writing, take a look at each capitalized word and see if a particular rule applies to it. If not, use lowercase for the word.

Comma complaints. A few of the transgressions that deal with commas are these:

- misplaced or omitted commas, often resulting in ambiguous sentences
- commas inserted between a month and year (September, 2008)

- commas dropped after parenthetical phrases (such as, "Barack Obama, Senator from Illinois said he . . .")
- commas misused with restrictive and nonrestrictive clauses (no commas before *which*; commas before *that* used unnecessarily)
- commas inserted between the subject and the verb (e.g., "The speeding car, was seen going through a red light")
- commas used too frequently, even in positions that no style guide would accept

If these mistakes look familiar, review the section on using commas (Chapter 3). Remember that commas are used for particular reasons, so make sure that you have a reason for each time you used a comma.

Number disagreements—either subject-predicate or antecedent-pronoun. Look for each verb and its subject (or each pronoun and its antecedent); then check to see if *both* of them are singular or *both* of them are plural. If you have a discrepancy, reword your sentence.

Omission of a colon after the greeting in a business letter. If you're writing a business letter, put a colon after your greeting; if you're writing any other kind of letter, use a comma.

And the most common error: mistakes in word choice. If you look through the following list of common mistakes and you recognize ones you often make, look up the correct usage and then develop mnemonics to help you remember. The most common mistakes in word choice are these:

- using *which* for *that* and vice versa
- using *affect* for *effect* and vice versa
- confusing *they're*, *their*, and *there*
- confusing *your* with *you're*
- overusing *utilize* (a coined word for this phenomenon: *abutilize*)
- using *between you and I* instead of *between you and me*
- using *compare to* when *compare with* is correct
- using *convince someone to* (rather than *persuade someone to*)
- using *its* for *it's* and vice versa (by far the most common mistake)

Testimony from Teachers in the Trenches

English teachers identified these common problems in writing assignments:

Difficulty grasping the concept of a topic sentence. A topic sentence is the main sentence of the paragraph, one that all other sentences support or elaborate on. Determine your paragraph's topic sentence; then read every other sentence separately and ask yourself if it elaborates on the topic sentence. If it doesn't, eighty-six it.

Trouble focusing on the subject at hand. Go back through your paper and read each sentence separately. Ask yourself if each sentence deals with the topic sentence of its paragraph and also if each sentence relates to your thesis sentence. If you've strayed away from either your topic or your thesis, delete or reword the sentence.

No transition from paragraph to paragraph in language or thought. Review the section on transitional words and expressions (Chapter 12). As you reread your work, locate where you move from one point to another or from one example to another; then use appropriate transitional words or phrases to make a meaningful connection.

Inconsistency in verb tense (especially present and past tense). Go back and determine which tense you've used. Unless you have a reason for a tense change, reword the sentences that change tense.

Reliance on the computer spell check for proofreading. Although spell checkers are helpful, all they can do is offer suggestions about what you *may* have intended to spell. Using a dictionary, look at the suggested word's definition to be sure that what the checker suggests is in fact the word you intended to write.

Comma splices. For example: "I went to the store, I bought a jug of milk and a six-pack of cola." Review each comma in your work.

Sentence fragments. Read each sentence separately and ask yourself if the words in that sentence make sense when you read them alone. If they don't, your "sentence" is a fragment.

Confusion of homophones. Homophones are words that sound alike but have different meanings and perhaps different spellings, like *to*, *too*, and *two*; *they're*, *their*, and *there*; *here*, and *hear*. If these mistakes with homophones are creeping into your writing, then review the section on word usage in

Chapter 12. Look up the correct usage of the homophones you often misuse, and then develop your own mnemonics to remember them.

No sense of who the audience is. Be sure you're clear about who your intended audience is (that is, to whom or for whom you're writing). Then make sure that each sentence addresses that audience. Common problems arise in the tone used (for instance, don't use language or reasoning that insults people if you're trying to persuade them to your line of thinking) and in addressing someone who isn't part of the audience (for instance, writing "When you take freshman English . . . " when the audience—in this case, the instructor—isn't taking freshman English).

Colloquial usages that are inconsistent with the rest of the writing or inappropriate for the type of writing. Look through your writing for slang words or idiomatic phrases. Unless your work calls for a relaxed or conversational tone (and your instructor or supervisor agrees that tone is necessary), reword your piece and use more formal language.

No sentence variation (writing only noun-verb-complement sentences). Review the section on types of sentences in Chapter 8. Reword some of your sentences so they begin with phrases or dependent clauses. Also try combining two related sentences into one to create less monotonous sentences.

Not following directions. Realize that you're not making up the rules for the assignment, and that—strange as it may seem—your teacher or supervisor probably has a reason for every direction that he or she has given. Keep the directions in mind as you write a rough draft, and then reread them after you've completed your assignment. If you've "violated" any of the directions, rewrite those parts.

Use of generalities, instead of specifics. Your paper must detail any general statements you make. One way to generate details or supporting evidence is to ask *who? what? when? where? why?* and *how?* questions about your topic or thesis sentence.

Use of "non-sentences" that have lots of fluff but little substance. (For example, "Language is important to everyday life and society.") Look for generalizations, clichés, and platitudes in your work. Reword your sentences to be more specific, to be less hackneyed, or to give more details.

Point of view that changes (sometimes first person, sometimes third) or is inappropriate (usually second person). Check each sentence of your manuscript and determine its point of view. If you've changed from one point of view to another without a reason, reword your sentences. Also, check to see if using first or second point of view is permitted (third person is the only point of view allowed in many formats of academic writing).

Checkpoint

Complete the following clichés that have to do with sports and politics:

Sports Clichés

1. about the rookie who looks promising: You'll be hearing _____.

2. about players who can shoot from far out: They can really shoot _____.

3. about a perfect basket: Nothing but _____.

Political clichés

1. when a challenger is running: It's time for _____.
2. about criticizing what the other side has been saying: This is turning into _____.
3. about a scandal that's leaked before a pivotal point in the race: You have to question _____.

Chapter 14

Putting Pen to Paper

If you're like lots of writers, you may find that getting your ideas on paper is one of the hardest parts of preparing your masterpiece for the eyes of the rest of the world. This chapter is meant to help you better contend with this often painful stage of the writing process by providing you with some ideas to help organize your thoughts.

14

Practical and Profitable Preliminaries

Beginning a writing assignment is what's called prewriting—the first phase, in which you think and plan, gather ideas and information, and consider various formats to organize your writing. Prewriting occurs before you put your pen to paper.

So at this prewriting stage of the game, how do you get ideas? Well, you could try the method used by one of the world's most prolific writers, Agatha Christie, who used to sit in her bathtub and munch on apples while plotting her bestsellers. What? You say apple eating doesn't appeal (pun intended) to you? Don't worry; this chapter has plenty of other suggestions.

Just remember that one method of prewriting may not work for you all the time. If it doesn't, try another one. Use whichever technique (or combination of techniques) that helps you think clearly and keep track of your ideas. And keep in mind that you're not being graded for the way you jot down your ideas; you can be as sloppy and (gasp!) ungrammatical as you like, as long as you're able to decipher your work later on.

Keep in mind that you'll probably come up with a number of ideas that you'll eventually discard. That doesn't matter. What does matter at first is getting your thoughts on paper. After you do that, you can go back and decide which ones are keepers.

One way to generate ideas is to keep a journal. If you know for a while beforehand that you want to—or have to—write about a particular subject, try keeping a journal about your topic. Whenever ideas come to you, jot them down in your journal. Don't worry about writing in complete sentences; just write enough so that you'll know later what you meant. When the time comes for writing your first draft, you'll already have a number of ideas, so you can go back to them and decide which are the best to use.

A Free and Easy Format: Freewriting

Freewriting is one of the most effective methods of cultivating ideas. Begin by writing your topic at the top of the page. At first, your topic may be so general that you might not have a clear idea about what direction you want to take. That's not important at this point. All you're going to do in freewriting is just (surprise!) write. Write anything related to your topic—words, phrases, or complete sentences, whatever scraps of thought come to mind. Give yourself a time limit of about ten minutes (at this stage, you'd probably be wasting time with anything longer than that).

Because you've got only ten minutes, you should *not:*

- be concerned with spelling or punctuation
- go to the time or trouble of grouping your ideas
- bother erasing anything
- worry even if you digress from your topic
- stop if you're in the middle of a thought and you can't think of a specific word. Just write *???* or *XXX* or some other shorthand; then go on and get the rest of the thought on paper. The same holds true if you have the first part of a good idea and you can't think of how to end it. Just use your "I'll-come-back-to-this-later" shorthand and forge ahead.

If you're stumped for something to write, keep your pen moving on the paper or your fingers moving on the keyboard. You can even write something like "I don't know anything more about this topic. I don't think I can come up with another thought." Just keep writing and chances are, in spite of yourself, you'll discover a new idea. At the end of your time allotment, stop. Look over your work. From the resulting splinters of writing, you'll see some good ideas and some that you're probably ready to toss. Decide what best fits with the direction that your work takes, and cross out what doesn't. Then go back to the ideas that seem workable and underline the key parts of them.

Now you've got a start. You can repeat the process to expand on the ideas that you like. Since you're working in ten-minute sessions, the assignment may not seem as overwhelming as it first did. Also, you won't suffer from "brain strain" and you might find that you're quite productive when you use these short writing segments.

Making a List and Checking It Twice: Brainstorming

In brainstorming—a first cousin to freewriting—you also list whatever comes to mind about your topic; you jot down words or phrases as they pop into your head; and you don't worry about spelling, punctuation, usage, or grouping ideas.

Unlike freewriting, though, you have no time restrictions. If you're interrupted in your list making, you just return to it later. In fact, sometimes there's an advantage to brainstorming in short shifts (maybe your brain can take just so many storms at a time?). Whatever length of time you have, use each stint of your brainstorming sessions to write as much as you can think of about your topic.

Here's an example: Suppose that a writer is angry with a company and wants to write a complaint letter to its customer relations department. His or her brainstorming list may look something like this:

telemarketers
rude questions
IMPUDENCE!
2hrs. = three unasked-for calls
why treat potential customers like this
put me on don't call list imediately
is this way company feels about customers????
told caller wasn't interested all three times he called
caller said in smart-aleck way they'd call back and get information
asked about way I pay bills—none of their business—invasion of priv'cy
won't do business w/ company now, but had been considering switching to it

As you can see, the thoughts are random, jotted down as they popped into the writer's head. There's no order as yet, and the writer didn't bother with spelling, punctuation, or writing style. (Can you tell that the writer was still very angry about the calls?)

Nevertheless, this brainstormed list gives a good start. The ideas are there, and with some organization, details, and surface corrections, the letter will be ready to send.

If you find that you don't have much luck making a written list while brainstorming, you might want to consider using a tape recorder to act as your pen and paper. Just switch it on and begin talking about your topic, saying anything that comes into your mind. Since your mind often works faster than you can write, you may get more ideas recorded this way. After you've gotten your ideas on tape, go back and transcribe them so that you can begin to get them organized.

If you don't have a mechanical tape recorder handy, turn to one of the human kind. Talk to a friend, an instructor, or a supervisor, and have him or her jot down what you're saying. Your human "recorder" might ask some questions that send you in a different direction or might prod you into giving explanations or details that you hadn't realized you needed.

Just Pretend You're Jimmy Olsen: Questioning

Get out your press card, your stubby pencil, and your pocket notebook—you've just become an ace reporter. Asking the reporter's fundamental six *w* and *h* questions *(who? what? when? where? why? how?)* is another method to develop ideas. The twist is that you're interviewing yourself.

Suppose you've been given a very general topic like "relate a terrible dining experience you once had." In thinking back to a particularly horrible experience, you could ask yourself questions like these:

Who was involved? (you and your date Pat)

What happened at first? (you were on a first date with someone you barely knew)

What happened before the horrible part of the evening? (since you didn't know each other well, you were just trying to find things to talk about)

What started the "horrible" part of the evening? (you both became sick while still sitting at the table)

What happened next? (the manager of the restaurant noticed that you were ill and came to the table to offer to help)

When did this happen? (on a summer evening in 2007)

Where did this happen? (at Sally's Scrumptious Shrimp Shack, in Seattle)

Why did this happen? (you had eaten seafood that hadn't been cooked long enough)

How did this happen? (you both felt yourselves turning green and having upset stomachs)

How did the evening end at the restaurant? (the manager gave you a complimentary dinner and a gift certificate to return another time)

How did the evening end after leaving the restaurant? (you both wound up in the emergency room at the hospital)

What could you have done differently? (you could have been more suspicious when you thought the food smelled bad)

What lessons did you learn? (if it smells funny, don't put it in your mouth)

Who was at fault? (mostly it was the restaurant's fault for serving ill-prepared food)

How could the night have been any better? (in almost every way, with no bad food and no trip to the hospital)

What was the silver lining in the experience? (you did get to become good friends with your date)

Because you expanded on the basic *who? what? when? where? why? how?* questions, you've compiled lots of details to paint a more descriptive picture of what happened that night.

To broaden the way you look at your topic, you might also ask questions that approach it from various points of view. For instance, if you're writing about a recent concert you attended, write down your own reflections and then put yourself in the place of the performers you heard. What might have been their reaction to the goings-on that night? What about the stagehands? the parking attendants? the ushers? Thinking about the experiences that others had will often take your mind in a different direction and will help you generate new ideas.

Lines and Boxes and Words—Oh, My!

Still stumped at getting started? Maybe your brain works better with drawings than with just words alone. If you think this may be the case, try the prewriting strategy called *clustering*, or *mapping*. In clustering, you draw boxes and lines to connect your thoughts. You can use clustering to begin your writing, or you can use it to help generate ideas for any subsections that have you stumped. Begin by drawing a box in the middle of your paper and writing your topic inside it.

Then start thinking of random words or phrases associated with your topic. As you think of something, write it in a separate box and connect it to the main idea with a line.

As you think of ideas that are offshoots of the new boxes, draw other boxes, write the new information in them, and then connect them.

Don't worry about your clusters being messy and don't be concerned if you can't think of anything associated with some of the circles. If you get stumped, try asking yourself one of the *who? what? when? where? why? how?* questions.

As with other techniques for getting ideas, with clustering you'll probably end up with some material that you won't include in your final paper. That's fine. At this point, you're just getting ideas down.

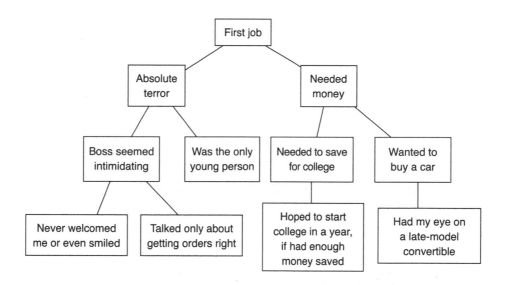

Out in the Open: The Outline

You might find that your work becomes easier if you create an outline, a kind of blueprint that helps you both organize your thoughts in a logical pattern and see the relationships between your main ideas and supporting ideas. You can use outlining as a prewriting method in itself, or you can use it as a way of organizing the ideas you generated in freewriting, brainstorming, questioning, clustering, or any other technique.

Outlines can be either formal or informal. If you write a formal outline, you must use a prescribed style. You must:

- designate your main points with Roman numerals
- designate your subordinate points with capital letters, Arabic numerals, and lowercase letters
- alternate between using numbers and letters
- have at least two entries in each category (that is, you must have at least two Roman numerals, two capital letters under each Roman numeral, and so on)
- have a parallel grammatical structure in your entries (for instance, if the first Roman numeral is a noun, the other Roman numerals must be nouns)

Is all of this confusing? It won't be when you examine the sample of the formal outline that follows. The topic is comparing and contrasting watching a movie in a theater and watching a movie at home.

If the formal outline style seems a bit overwhelming, think of it this way: After you write down your main points, then you just fill in the subcategories with details or examples.

Contrast and Compare Watching a Movie in a Theater and at Home

A number of differences and similarities exist between watching a movie in a theater and watching a movie at home.

I. Differences
  A. Home
    1. Greater freedom
      a. More comfort
        (1) Can watch wearing pajamas, if I choose
        (2) Have choice of seating at home
          (a) Can sit in favorite easy chair
          (b) Can lie on floor or couch
      b. More choice of times to watch
        (1) Can stop to talk if phone rings
        (2) Can stop for bathroom breaks

      (3) Can stop if want to get food or drink

      (4) Can finish watching movie another time

   2. Fewer restrictions about food or drink

     a. Less expensive at home

     b. Open choice of food or drink

 B. Movie theater

   1. Much larger screen at movies

   2. Better popcorn at movies

   3. Earlier date for availability to be seen

   4. Better sound system

   5. Larger seating capacity, if needed for large group of friends

   6. Better "maid service" (someone else picks up the discarded candy wrappers, etc.)

II. Similarities

 A. (Follow the same format to fill in details about the similarities between watching a movie at a theater and at home)

   1. ....

     a. ....

       (1) ....

       (2) ....

         (a) ....

         (b) ....

     b. ....

   2. ....

 B. ....

Looking at the organization in this formal outline, you'll see that each main entry begins with a Roman numeral. Next are the indented capital-letter entries *(Home* and *Movie Theater)* under each Roman numeral, and both are written in a parallel way (in this case, as nouns). Then come indented entries written with Arabic numbers; each of these begins with a comparative adjective *(Greater, Fewer, Larger, Better, Earlier)*. As you can see, the entries go on—lowercase letters, then numbers inside parentheses, then lowercase letters inside parentheses—and each subcategory has a parallel grammatical layout.

If you're writing an informal outline, begin by writing your topic (main idea) and your thesis statement (the main point you're trying to make about your topic) at the top of your paper. These give you a good reference and help you keep your work focused. Some writers find creating an outline after they've finished their first draft to be helpful. In looking over the outline, they see how well—or not so well—their ideas connect.

E-LINK

More information on freewriting, brainstorming, clustering, and outlining is available at these Web sites:

tinyurl.com/3bwmme   tinyurl.com/2mluvu
tinyurl.com/3dsmqc   tinyurl.com/364cjs

If you're outlining from a list or cluster you've already created, take a look at what seem to be your major points. Fill these in as the main categories of your outline, leaving a number of lines in between them. After that, go back and fill in details or examples about each of the main points. If you have additional points about the examples or details, write them under the appropriate category (again, make sure you indent a little with each new subcategory). If you indent the same amount each time you write a subcategory, you'll be able to see the various sections more easily.

Delineating the Details of Your First Draft

After you have your ideas in some form (an outline or a cluster or a list—whichever kind of prewriting you chose), it's time to take those ideas and write your first draft. (Did you notice the adjective *first?*) The object of this next stage of writing isn't to have something that's ready to turn in to your teacher, your supervisor, or your editor but rather just to get all of your ideas down on paper in complete sentences. Even if you're writing a personal journal, the piece you develop in this stage probably won't be in its final form. All of that will come later.

Start by taking a look at your ideas—whether they're complete sentences or just random words and phrases—and organize them into groups. Decide which ideas are more important than others and which give details or examples of the main ideas. Keep in mind that you might not use all of your initial ideas. If something in your original list or cluster seems superfluous or if it goes in a separate direction from the rest of your piece, just cross it out; you can always include it later if you change your mind.

Once you get your information organized, begin writing in complete sentences and paragraphs.

In this phase, some writers prefer to begin thinking about mechanics, usage, and spelling, and others prefer to worry about the fine-tuning later. Do whatever works for you. Right now your main concerns are (1) your purpose in writing, (2) the audience for whom you're writing, and (3) the format or type of writing that's required.

And Your Point Is? Defining Your Purpose

Writing usually proves a point, answers a question, gives instructions, provides reflection, or presents entertainment. Before you begin writing, decide what your particular purpose for this piece is (this may have been decided for you by your teacher or supervisor) and keep this purpose in mind as you write.

Is this piece one of the following:
narrative (telling a story)
expository (explaining or giving information)
descriptive (providing a written picture of someone, someplace, or something)
informative or explanatory (giving data or some other type of information)
expressive (detailing your thoughts or emotions)
persuasive or argumentative (attempting to influence others to come around to your way of thinking)
analytical (examining material presented to you)

Remember that you can improve most academic-related nonfiction (such as descriptive, narrative, expository, persuasive, or analytical writing) by using lots of specific examples or supporting details. Take a look at this sentence, written for an essay about an ideal vacation spot:

England is a good place to visit.

That sentence doesn't exactly make you want to pack your bags, does it? However, with a few details added, it becomes a workable sentence:

From the jam-packed boulevards of cosmopolitan London, to the barely-wide-enough cobblestone paths of ancient York, to the right-for-rambling lanes of Lake District villages, olde England crooks its finger and beckons me.

Now you have examples of why England is so enticing (the three regions) as well as specific details about those areas, and all of this gives readers a much clearer picture of why you want to travel there.

Not only is it important that you know your purpose, you must also communicate your purpose to your reader—preferably in your first few sentences. For example, if you had read the revised sentence about visiting England, you'd expect that the rest of the work would be about what a fascinating place England is to visit. In other words, from reading the first sentence you'd expect that the author's purpose was to inform you about England's various charms or to persuade you to visit England on your next vacation.

This sentence is your thesis sentence (thesis statement). If you use a thesis statement, your readers should be able to easily identify it. Also, they should know after reading it what's in store in the rest of the piece.

If your writing format requires a thesis statement, here's an additional point to keep in mind: Every sentence of your work has to be connected to the thesis statement in some way. When writers, especially student writers, are giving examples, they often find themselves drifting away from the thesis. After you've finished your work, look at each separate sentence or idea and ask yourself if it's somehow related to your thesis statement. If it isn't, cross it out.

Keeping a large copy of your thesis statement on a piece of paper close to your desk may also be useful. Referring to this copy will help you stay focused on your purpose and stick to your main idea.

Even for writing that doesn't require a thesis statement, you might find that writing a one-sentence statement of your purpose helps center your thoughts. You won't necessarily include this in the final version of your work, but referring to it will keep you from straying from your main point(s).

Playing to the House: Anticipating Your Audience

Picture a group of comedians performing in a retirement village. Then picture the same group appearing on late-night TV. Because of the difference in the two audiences, the comedians would probably use different material and they'd probably present it in a different way.

What's that got to do with you? Just like a performer, you need to be aware of your audience, the person or group for whom you're writing. If the piece is for yourself, then you can approach your subject matter any way you want. However, if it's for a specific person or group, you should keep certain things in mind, like the tone, vocabulary level, subject matter, and style that's appropriate for your audience.

If you're writing a letter of complaint, for instance, you might use a far more aggressive tone—and maybe even a different level of vocabulary—than if you're writing for yourself, your business, or your instructor. Also, depending on what you're writing, your style could be formal, informal, or even very casual. A good idea is to put yourself in your reader's place and ask yourself what style of writing you'd expect to read.

In considering your audience, think about these questions:

- Does the age of your audience dictate you should write on a particular level? (Usually it doesn't, unless you're writing for children.)
- Will your audience expect extra information in your work, like quotations, citations, tables, or graphs? (These might be needed in an academic or business paper.)
- Are you writing for people from a specific location? Do you need to explain any geographic considerations or cultural differences?
- Are your readers people of a specific gender, or do they have a particular political or religious preference? If this is the case, be sure to keep this in mind and don't step on toes—unless, of course, your purpose is to be argumentative.

- What's the occupation of your audience? For instance, are you writing for your teacher, your supervisor, the readers of the local newspaper, the quality control department of your company?
- What need does your audience have for what you're writing? Will the information clarify the purpose of a particular meeting? help you get a good grade? decrease civic problems? track a lost package?
- What information does your audience already have? (There's no use in defining terms that your audience would be familiar with.)
- What might your audience not be aware of? For example, they may not be aware of the plot of a literary work that you're critiquing, may not know the names of participants at a work meeting, may not be informed about why the city would be wasting money on a proposed project, may not know when a package was ordered and to whom it was to be shipped.

As you write, keep in mind that you don't want to insult your audience by either using inappropriate humor or being patronizing or pretentious, so adjust your tone and your vocabulary accordingly.

Remember that conveying sarcasm and irony is very difficult in any type of writing, and neither of those has a place in most academic or business writing.

Writing à la Mode: Adhering to a Particular Style

The next part of your work is deciding the style or format to use. If you have an assignment from school or work, the style may have been decided for you. For example, for school you might be assigned to write a three-page essay critiquing a recent tax proposal, or at your business you may need to write a summary of the main points of a meeting you attended.

If a particular style is required, adhere to it. Generally speaking, teachers and supervisors don't appreciate it if you create a style on your own; they expect you to present material in the way they have directed. If you're uncertain about how to write in a particular style or format, look at successful past material and model your work after it.

If, for instance, you're told to write the definitive essay about the pros and cons of front-wheel drive, and the format you're to use is a five-paragraph essay, your essay shouldn't exceed five paragraphs, even if you find it next to impossible to squeeze in all your ideas. Or if your boss says that your analysis of a new product should contain bulleted lists rather than complete sentences, use the bulleted lists, odd as you may think they look.

Also, don't forget the minor details of a mandatory format. For instance, check to see if you're required to use a title, page numbers, headings, citations and other references, and a table of contents. If these are required, find out if they must be written in a specific way.

More information on purpose, audience, and style is available at these Web sites:

tinyurl.com/2t9pzl   *tinyurl.com/2orywz*
tinyurl.com/2oalc3

You may not like the format that's required, or you may not think it allows you to express yourself in the best way. Use it anyway. Later on, you'll have plenty of time to write the way you want to—when a grade or salary isn't at stake.

Relax and Leave Your Writing Alone—For Now

After you've finished writing your first draft you can relax—for a while.

You'll have plenty of time to improve your material, so don't worry about it being perfect right now. In the next step you'll polish your work by editing and revising, but at this stage of the game you should just take a moment to enjoy the fact that you've made it this far.

Checkpoint

Select one of the following topics and use either freewriting, brainstorming, clustering (mapping), questioning, or outlining to generate ideas. Then choose a different topic and a different technique.

- Coffee or Tea or Cola?
- Pros and Cons of Working on a Computer
- Our Company Versus the Competition
- Examples of "Slacking Off"
- Ethics in the Workplace (or in the Family) (or in College)

Chapter 15

The Final Dress Rehearsal

Now, it's time to fine-tune your work by revising it. This chapter will help you in this process by detailing a variety of organizational, grammatical, and content-related issues to check in your draft. By employing these pointers, you'll get the most out of the time you invest.

15

Rereading, Revising, and Rewriting

Revising is much more than just looking for misspelled words and an errant comma or two. Rather, it entails looking at the big picture (organization, purpose, vocabulary, tone, etc.) as well as the little brush strokes of punctuation, usage, and spelling. Keep in mind that making these improvements takes time, and you can usually count on writing more than one revision. In fact, in most cases you're smart to allow time for four or five revisions. I hope you haven't passed out from the shock of that idea. The truth is, though, if you want your writing to be the best it can be, you need to devote a great deal of time to the editing process. If it helps and if you can afford the extra time, give yourself breaks of a day or two in between your various revisions.

Looking at the Big Picture

A good place to begin revising is by looking back at your subject and your purpose in writing. What were you supposed to do in this piece? If, for instance, you were supposed to argue against capital punishment, did you maintain that argument throughout your paper or did you slip into an "on the other hand" approach and start giving arguments for the opposing side? If you wrote a summary of a meeting that took place in your job, did you emphasize all the points of the meeting or did you insert a recommendation for something that wasn't discussed?

If you find your writing has a tendency to wander, try this trick: circle the main idea of each paragraph, and then go back and ask yourself if each sentence relates to that idea.

How about your introduction—is it clear enough? Does it contain enough information to lead your readers to your main points? Is your conclusion effective? Does it stray from the topic or your thesis statement? One helpful trick is to read your introduction and your conclusion (skipping the parts in between), and ask yourself if both are saying the same thing. If not, you need to revise.

Look closely at the bulk of your writing.

✓ If your piece of writing requires a thesis, do you state it clearly?

✓ Do you make sure that each of your supporting points relates to your thesis?

✓ Are all of your other sentences focused on your thesis?

✓ Have you checked that each sentence relates to the point of the individual paragraph it's in?

✓ Have you presented all of your information coherently?

✓ Have you given enough examples, facts, or details to support each of your points?

✓ If you gave examples in your work, did you explain why each example is significant? Do your examples follow each other in a logical order? Would rearranging them (for example, in chronological or emphatic order) make them clearer or more forceful?

✓ Would adding anything strengthen your work?

✓ Will your audience be familiar with all the terms you used? If not, you may need to add extra explanatory information.

Take a look at the organization of your paragraphs.

✓ Would your points be more emphatic or clearer if your paragraphs were organized differently?

✓ If you moved or eliminated any of them, would your work be easier to understand? If you think a problem may be in the way your material flows, try cutting and pasting paragraphs into different positions.

Consider the tone you've used throughout the piece.

✓ Is it suitable for your audience?

✓ Have you gone overboard and ended up presenting your material in a manner that's too personal or too emotional?

✓ Have you used any language that's inappropriate either for your audience or the genre of writing?

✓ Did you adhere to the formatting or style that was mandated?

✓ Did you format your material to use prescribed margin sizes, font style, point size, or spacing requirements?

✓ Were you mandated to use a particular style to identify yourself, your class, your department, or your company?

✓ Are your pages numbered in the right places? in the right way?

✓ If you have included any tables or graphs, have you labeled them well enough that your readers will have no problem interpreting them?

✓ Do any of them need information in addition to captions?

✓ Have you included a title that communicates the concepts of your paper?

✓ If your paper is about a literary work, have you stated the author's first and last names and the title of the work?

✓ After you cited the author the first time, have you used only his or her last name in later references?

✓ Have you used the citation or documentation methods required for your paper?

✓ Have you checked to see that any paraphrasing you included was in fact paraphrasing and not a direct quote?

If you're using citations, make sure you place quotation marks, periods, and commas in the right places, and that you follow the assigned order for listing author, publisher, publication date and location, and other required material. Instructors often say a major problem in formal papers is that students aren't meticulous about following the assigned rules for citations.

Particulars to Ponder in the Perusal of Your Piece

Analyze each individual sentence. Have you varied your sentence structure and the length of your sentences? Do many sentences begin in the same way (for example, look for several sentences that start with "The company . . . " or "The main character . . . ")?

Sentence Structure

Check to see if a number of your sentences are composed in a subject-verb-complement format. If you have too much repetition, vary your sentence structure (create more compound or compound-complex sentences), change your sentence length, or alter the rhythm of your words. Do whatever it takes to keep monotony out of your writing. Finally, look to see if several of your sentences have nearly the same number of words; if so, try combining some of them.

Do you need to put any of your sentences on a diet? Have you over-explained anything? Look for wording that can be more concise. If you can use fewer words and convey the same meaning, by all means do so. Examine each sentence and ask yourself if your wording could be more precise, more vivid, or more explanatory.

Pronouns

Note the types of pronouns you use in your paper. Red flag any first- or second-person pronouns *(I, me, we, you, us)*. Is using them in writing acceptable in your class or workplace? Is it appropriate? While you're looking at pronouns, check to see that you have maintained a consistent point of view with them.

Transitions

Study how you change course in your writing.

- ✔ Have you used transitional words and phrases to your best advantage?
- ✔ Have you used enough transitions so that your work reads smoothly?
- ✔ Do your transitions guide your readers from one thought to the next? From one paragraph to the next? Have you used them in the correct way?
- ✔ Do you see any related thoughts or sentences that would become stronger if you inserted a transitional word or phrase?

Voice

Except for certain scientific material, you should write using the active voice whenever possible. If you have a number of sentences that contain *be* verbs (*is*, *are*, *was*, *were*, and so on), change the structure of your sentence. For instance, you could change:

> *The downtown area is enhanced by the new streetlights. (passive voice)*

to

> *The new streetlights enhance the downtown area. (active voice)*

Along the same lines, look for sentences that begin with expletives like *it*, *this*, or *there*; these sentences often become more forceful when you reword them. If you've written, for instance:

> *There are six changes that should be made in the method of production of the widget.*

you can make the sentence stronger by changing it to:

> *Six changes should be made in the production method of the widget.*

Word Choice

Can you use any synonyms to make your meaning clearer or to make your work read more smoothly? Don't hesitate to consult a dictionary or thesaurus. (If you're using a word processor, you probably have quick access to a built-in thesaurus.) If you can, substitute synonyms for repeated words or phrases.

Has any slang or jargon crept into your work? Ask yourself if using it is appropriate, and reword as necessary. Also look for any clichés and change them to more original thoughts.

Some instructors (and perhaps some companies) dictate that certain words not be used (generally these are overused words like *great* and *very*). If that applies to you, have you checked through to see if you have deleted those particular words or phrases? The find function on word processing software can show you if any prohibited words or phrases appear in your work, and the thesaurus can help you to find replacements.

Jettisoning Gender-Based Generalities

One hot spot you want to make sure you avoid in your written work is the use of sexist language. If you've mentioned particular jobs by name, for example, make sure your wording isn't exclusively all-male or all-female. The following list of substitutions might help you to avoid sexist language:

Sexist Term	Substitution
chairman/chairwoman	chair, chairperson, presiding officer
coed	student
congressman/congresswoman	congressional representative, legislator
forefathers	ancestors
foreman	supervisor
layman	layperson, nonspecialist
man/men	person/people, individual(s)
man hours	work hours
mankind	men and women, humankind, the human race, humanity
man-made	synthetic, manufactured
manpower	workforce
one-man show	one-person show
policeman	police officer
saleslady/salesman/saleswoman	sales clerk, salesperson, sales representative

In years gone by, the rule was to use the masculine pronouns *he*, *him*, or *his* to refer to any noun that could be masculine or feminine. ("Every employee must check his voice mail.") Today that rule is obsolete; the generally accepted rule is to use both the masculine and feminine forms. ("Every employee must check his or her voice mail.")

E-LINK

Look at these Web sites and try the online exercises about gender-based language:

tinyurl.com/yqf5z7   *tinyurl.com/yv7knm*

In an effort to avoid sexist language, however, you may find yourself using too many dual constructions (*he or she*, *his or hers*, and *him or her*), which can make your writing boring and cumbersome. To avoid having to use too many of these constructions, you might:

- Change your wording to plural pronouns.

    Original: *Each supervisor should greet all of his or her employees by name.*

    Revised: *Supervisors should greet all their employees by name.*

- Substitute a noun

    Original: *Tell him to change the sexist language.*

    Revised: *Tell the writer to change the sexist language.*

- Alternate using a male and a female pronoun in long constructions where you must use a singular form
- Reword your sentences to use the first or second person (providing this is permitted)

    Original: *If a driver loses a number of points on his license, he must attend driving school.*

    Revised: *If you lose a number of points on your license, you must attend driving school.*

    Alternate revised: *If we lose a number of points on our license, we must attend driving school.*

The Revising Process

After you've checked your paper for all these points, you'll probably need to rewrite parts of it. Jump right in and do it. Then reread the revision section and apply it to your rewritten version. (Remember that warning that more than one revision would be necessary?)

If you're writing on a computer, use a spell checker to catch mistakes you don't see. Remember, though, that a spell checker won't catch words that are spelled correctly but that aren't the words you intended. To get around that problem, you need to use your own eagle eye for checking.

A computer's grammar checker is another story; use it with a grain of salt. If you send your manuscript through a grammar checker, be aware that you may disagree with what the computer tells you—and you may be right. If you're unsure about a grammar question, consult the corresponding section of this book or other grammar handbooks.

The Proof Is in the Reading

Hurray! You're almost home free. You've checked your content, your organization, and your sentence structure, and you're satisfied that everything you've written is brilliant (you're sure about that, aren't you?). Now you're ready to do some serious proofreading to find those little nitpicky errors that can transform a masterpiece into a laughter piece.

FACT

Some writers find doing separate "read-throughs" to be helpful—one looking at spelling, one at punctuation, one at tense, and so on.

The hints that follow will help to slow down your eyes so that they don't go faster than your brain. In other words, you read what you *actually* wrote rather than what you *think* you wrote. These strategies should help you to find mistakes more easily:

To begin with, try reading your paper out loud; this may help you to catch any word you out. (Oops! Reread the preceding sentence. Did you read it correctly the first time?) When you read silently, you often read what you *think* you've written. When you read out loud, however, you must read more slowly, so you'll often catch grammatical and spelling mistakes you'd miss in silent reading. Also, reading out loud helps you hear the rhythm of your words. In revising your paper, you looked for sentences that have similar construction, but by reading your work out loud you may hear similarities your eye didn't catch. If you have time, tape-record yourself as you read your paper, then listen to the tape the next day to see if your thoughts flow smoothly.

As you read your paper, touch each word with a pencil. (An added bonus of this tip is that you'll already have your pencil in hand if you find a mistake.) Try using a ruler or piece of paper to cover the lines below what you're reading. This helps you to focus on each line. If you're pressed for time and you have to edit and proofread from a computer rather than on paper, pretend you're back in primary school. Move your finger across the screen as you read each word separately.

Another tip is to read backward. Start at the end and read the last sentence, then the sentence before that, and so on until you reach the beginning. When you read out of order, you'll spot errors more easily.

Think about errors that you're prone to make, and take extra time to look for them. For instance, if you have trouble with sentence fragments, go back through your work and closely examine each sentence. Read each one as a separate thought and ask yourself if it makes sense by itself, without the sentences on either side of it. If you often make mistakes with comma usage, check each comma to make sure you know the reason why you've used it. Remember that a comma splice (that is, putting a comma where you need a stronger punctuation mark) is a frequent mistake. If each thought on either side of a comma could be a separate sentence, then change your comma to a semicolon or break the sentence into two separate sentences.

Use the search or find function on your computer to look for spelling errors that you tend to make. For instance, if you often misuse *its* and *it's*, search for each usage of the words. Keep this book open to the page that explains *it's* and *its*, and then check each word separately to be sure you used it correctly.

Even though you've put your work through a spell checker, also check spelling yourself. You know that a spell checker will detect only words that aren't in the dictionary. If you intended to type *not* and instead you typed *nor*, the spell checker won't know the difference. A good idea is to make one pass through your copy looking for spelling errors alone. Pay particular attention to words that you frequently mistype and for words that are common spelling errors, like *to, two,* and *too,* and *their, they're,* and *there.*

Save scrap paper to print out drafts of what you've written. Although it may seem like a waste to print out something you can easily read on screen, it's much easier to spot changes on a printed document.

Check your tense usage. If you began your piece using the past tense, for example, make sure you wrote the rest in the past tense (not including any quoted material, of course). Instructors say that unnecessary tense change is one of the most common problems in papers.

If you have time, let your paper get "cold." Give yourself an hour or two—or overnight, if possible—and then come back to it. Odds are you'll see what you wrote in a fresh light, and you'll make further revisions.

Let someone else—more than one person, if possible—proofread and respond to your paper (this is known as peer editing). Ask the other readers to be as critical as possible and to look for any kind of error—in spelling, punctuation, usage, mechanics, organization, clarity, even in the value of your ideas. Although you may not agree with the other person's editing suggestions, chances are if he or she had trouble reading or understanding your material, you should do some extra revision. Repeat your editing and proofreading process as many times as necessary.

When Really Bad Is Really Good

You've been working so hard on your drafting, revising, and proofreading that you're probably just about due for a good laugh. Here are some examples of really bad writing culled from the Bulwer-Lytton Fiction Contest, which challenges writers to compose the *worst* possible opening sentence. The contest, which began in 1982, was named for Victorian novelist Edward George Earle Bulwer-Lytton (that's Baron Lytton of Knebworth to you), who began his novel *Paul Clifford* with one of the most famous (infamous?) lines in English literature: "It was a dark and stormy night."

In your revision, remember George Orwell's five important rules of writing from his "Politics and the English Language":

1. Never use a metaphor, simile, or other figure of speech which you are used to seeing in print.
2. Never use a long word where a short one will do.
3. If it's possible to cut a word out, always cut it out.
4. Never use the passive where you can use the active.
5. Never use a foreign phrase, a scientific word, or a jargon word if you can think of an everyday English equivalent.

If you'd like to read more about the contest, see the "Lyttony" of winners at *www.bulwer-lytton.com/lyttony.htm*.

Recent winning entries have included the following:

Detective Bart Lasiter was in his office studying the light from his one small window falling on his super burrito when the door swung open to reveal a woman whose body said you've had your last burrito for a while, whose face said angels did exist, and whose eyes said she could make you dig your own grave and lick the shovel clean.

—Jim Guigli, Carmichael, California (2006 winner)

....

As he stared at her ample bosom, he daydreamed of the dual Stromberg car-
buretors in his vintage Triumph Spitfire, highly functional yet pleasingly formed,
perched prominently on top of the intake manifold, aching for experienced

hands, the small knurled caps of the oil dampeners begging to be inspected and adjusted as described in chapter seven of the shop manual.

—Dan McKay, Fargo, North Dakota (2005 winner)

....

She resolved to end the love affair with Ramon tonight . . . summarily, like Martha Stewart ripping the sand vein out of a shrimp's tail . . . though the term "love affair" now struck her as a ridiculous euphemism . . . not unlike "sand vein," which is after all an intestine, not a vein . . . and that tarry substance inside certainly isn't sand . . . and that brought her back to Ramon.
—Dave Zobel, Manhattan Beach, California (2004 winner)

....

They had but one last remaining night together, so they embraced each other as tightly as that two-flavor entwined string cheese that is orange and yellowish-white, the orange probably being a bland Cheddar and the white . . . Mozzarella, although it could possibly be Provolone or just plain American, as it really doesn't taste distinctly dissimilar from the orange, yet they would have you believe it does by coloring it differently.

—Mariann Simms, Wetumpka, Alabama (2003 winner)

....

On reflection, Angela perceived that her relationship with Tom had always been rocky, not quite a roller-coaster ride but more like when the toilet-paper roll gets a little squashed so it hangs crooked and every time you pull some off you can hear the rest going bumpity-bumpity in its holder until you go nuts and push it back into shape, a degree of annoyance that Angela had now almost attained.

—Rephah Berg, Oakland California (2002 winner)

....

FACT

The Lytton ancestral residence, Knebworth House in Herfortshire, England, has been in the family since 1490. Today visitors come to Knebworth for tours of the home and for open-air concerts held on the grounds. The estate was chosen to be Wayne Manor for some of the *Batman* movies and has also been featured in *The Shooting Party, Wilde, Jane Eyre, The Canterville Ghost*, and *Haunted Honeymoon*.

Checkpoint

Rewrite the following sentences, making the designated changes. Check your answers in Appendix D.

Rewrite these sentences to be in active voice:

1. The four-year-old child was bitten by her neighbors' cat.
2. The medical test results were read by the doctor's assistant.

Rewrite these sentences to eliminate the beginning *There*:

3. There are three different ways that Julia approaches this problem.
4. There is my new guitar beside the chair.

Rewrite these sentences to eliminate gender-biased wording:

5. Within five minutes of the accident, six policemen arrived on the scene.
6. Our forefathers certainly do not get the credit they deserve.
7. In the last fifteen years, many man-made materials have come under scrutiny.

Chapter 16

Maximizing Your Means of Expression

If you're confused about a writing assignment that you've been given—whether for a class or for work—or if you just want to try your hand at different styles, take a look at the various types of writing in this chapter. You'll find descriptions of a number of styles, from short essays to abstracts and process papers.

Short Takes

Let's start out with the short papers. You may be asked to condense all your knowledge on a subject into a pithy essay or abstract, or even into a single paragraph. It's okay. Take a deep breath. You can do it, and here's how.

All in One: A Single Paragraph

Let's start out small. If you must get your thoughts across in only a single paragraph, you should pay attention to the central thought of your paragraph and the details that support that thought. The most important part of a single paragraph is its topic sentence, which contains the paragraph's main idea. The topic sentence is often (but not always) the first sentence. All the other sentences in the paragraph should support the topic sentence in some way. If they don't, cut them.

Some one-paragraph compositions also end with a summary sentence that restates, reviews, or emphasizes the main idea of the paragraph (using different words, of course).

Some writers who have been confused about the organization of a single paragraph have found this military analogy helpful: A paragraph has a topic sentence as its general; all the rest of the sentences "report to" the topic sentence. If a sentence goes AWOL (if it strays from the main idea of the paragraph), it should be court-martialed (or crossed out).

Some writers have trouble understanding how to show support of a main idea. If you're one of them, think about ways that you can:

- *elaborate* on your topic sentence
- *explain* or *clarify* your topic sentence
- *give details* about your topic sentence
- *provide factual information or proof* about your topic sentence
- *help define* your topic sentence

A good topic sentence lets your readers know what to expect from the rest of the paragraph. Read this topic sentence:

While April is the favorite time of year of many people, I dread it because my allergies are aggravated by blooming plants, I'm under a lot of tension to get my taxes finished by the fifteenth, and I have to attend seven birthday parties for various family members.

After you read this topic sentence, you know that the rest of the paragraph will give you more details about the allergies, the tax-related tension, and the birthday parties.

Don't forget to use transitional words or phrases within your paragraph. These help show your reader the connection between the various ideas you state or points you make.

Room for Expansion: The Five-Paragraph Essay

After single paragraphs, beginning writers often proceed to five-paragraph essays. These works follow a prescribed form (could you guess that it has five paragraphs?) of an introductory paragraph, three body paragraphs, and a concluding paragraph.

Just as a topic sentence is the main focus of a single paragraph, five-paragraph essays are centered around a thesis statement (or thesis sentence), the central view or argument of the whole essay. Your thesis statement may be either argumentative or informative, depending on the direction you take in your body paragraphs, and it should be a summary of what the rest of your essay will contain. By your thesis statement alone, readers should know either the direction of the rest of your essay or the individual points you'll make.

Make sure your thesis statement is narrow enough to cover a five-paragraph essay. For example:

The United States should increase its aid to Jamaica, Bosnia, and Namibia.

This statement is much too broad because you'd need far more than five paragraphs (maybe five books?) to explain why additional aid is needed for those countries.

Your introductory paragraph should contain your thesis and also give a clear indication as to what your body paragraphs will be about. Some instructors or style guides mandate that your thesis statement be the first or last sentence of your introductory paragraph; some will allow it to be in any position in your first paragraph. Whichever format you follow, be sure that your first paragraph contains more than just your thesis statement; it should also include sentences that develop on or build up to your thesis statement.

Your body paragraphs give more elaborate support for your thesis statement. Each of your body paragraphs should contain a topic sentence (a sentence that tells what that particular paragraph is about) that must be directly related to your thesis statement. In other words, one subtopic (one individual point) can be developed in each of your three body paragraphs. Some writers find that they stay more focused if they list these three subtopics in their thesis statement. Read this example:

> *I will no longer fly Zebra Airlines because its online reservation system isn't reliable, its support staff isn't helpful, and its departures and landings are rarely on time.*

From the thesis statement alone, readers know the first body paragraph will elaborate on the complaint about the reservation system, the second body paragraph will elaborate on the problems with the support staff, and the third body paragraph will elaborate on the unreliability of the schedules.

If you arrange the information in your body paragraphs in chronological order, be sure that you word your thesis statement chronologically. Or if you arrange your body paragraphs so that the most important or most emphatic reason or example comes last, word your thesis statement in the same way. Some instructors or style guides specify that you write a certain minimum number of sentences in each paragraph of the essay; some leave this up to the individual writer. Be sure you're aware of any requirements that apply to your essay.

As with every kind of writing, including transitions in your five-paragraph essay is extremely important. Each of your body paragraphs should have some sort of word or phrase that ties together what you said in the preceding paragraph with the subtopic you're beginning in that paragraph.

ALERT!

One common problem in essays is body paragraphs that don't pertain to the thesis statement. To remedy this problem, (1) reread the thesis statement, (2) read each body paragraph separately, and (3) ask if what's written in each paragraph directly relates to the thesis statement. If the paragraph doesn't relate, you've veered away from your focus and you need to revise that paragraph.

Your concluding paragraph is a summary of what you've stated in your body paragraphs (of course, with different wording). The information in your concluding paragraph gives you the opportunity to recap what you stated in the preceding paragraphs and give additional emphasis to your individual points. You should be careful not to introduce any new material in your concluding paragraph.

Some writers find that restating (again, in different words) their thesis statement is a straightforward way to begin their concluding paragraph. If you're having trouble writing your concluding paragraph, try starting out with the phrase *In conclusion* or *To summarize.* Don't keep the phrase after you finish your paragraph, as readers find phrases like these to be trite. But using one of the phrases in writing your first draft may be enough to help you get started.

Some writers find that composing a five-paragraph essay is easier when they see an outline for it and then fill in the parts.

OUTLINE OF A FIVE-PARAGRAPH ESSAY

1. *Introductory Paragraph*

Has the thesis sentence (check if it must be in a specific place in this paragraph)

Has sentences that follow or lead up to the thesis sentence

2. *Body Paragraph #1*

Has a transitional word or phrase connecting the preceding paragraph and this one

Begins with a topic sentence

Has other sentences that support, elaborate on, or give specific evidence for the topic sentence

Has transitional words or phrases throughout the paragraph

3. Body Paragraph #2

Has a transitional word or phrase connecting the preceding paragraph and this one

Begins with a topic sentence

Has other sentences that support, elaborate on, or give specific evidence for the topic sentence

Has transitional words or phrases throughout the paragraph

4. Body Paragraph #3

Has a transitional word or phrase connecting the preceding paragraph and this one

Begins with a topic sentence

Has other sentences that support, elaborate on, or give specific evidence for the topic sentence

Has transitional words or phrases throughout the paragraph

5. Conclusion

Has several sentences

Has transitional words or phrases

Might contain a summary

Might contain general closing remarks

Might restate the idea of the thesis sentence

Summing It All Up: The Abstract

Don't worry—there's actually nothing at all abstract about writing an abstract. In an abstract (usually written in just one paragraph), you summarize the methodology, essential sections, and main points (or conclusion) of research or a manuscript. By examining your abstract alone, readers should be able to determine what information the complete manuscript contains.

Different instructors, publications, and companies use different styles for abstracts, so ask about particular requirements. General points concerning abstracts include these:

- The purpose of an abstract is to summarize a longer work (commonly a literary, scientific, or historic work, although it might be something in another field) and any methods the work described or conclusions it reached.
- If you have a specific word limit, be sure to write as close as possible to that limit without going over it. Abstracts that exceed a specified word limit will often be rejected because they can't fit in certain databases or summary formats.
- Be sure you emphasize the primary discoveries and major conclusions of the work and include the key words of the research or work (that is what will be used in databases).
- Your wording should be as concise as possible and all irrelevant details should be omitted.

Have someone who is experienced in writing abstracts take a look at yours before you submit it. They will be able to catch any missteps you don't see yourself.

Business and Technical Writing

Because they cover such wide fields, business and technical writing often have many individual fine points. The company you're writing for may have particular styles that you're expected to use. In general, however, in business and technical writing, you should concentrate on five areas: audience, clarity, conciseness, tone, and correctness.

First, keep in mind who's going to receive your information (who your audience is). If you're writing for the general public, you'll probably need to take a different slant than if you're writing to a business associate. Your audience may also determine the tone that you'll use. Sometimes—for instance, when you're conveying technical information to beginners—you'll need to use a basic "here-are-the-instructions" tone. Other times—for example, in business dealings—you'll need to be more formal (but not so formal that you offend your audience by seeming pompous or cold).

Whether you're conveying information to your audience or selling services, you want your message to have an impact. To that end, make sure your writing is clear and concise. Use vocabulary your audience will be familiar with. Now isn't the time to impress readers with twenty-dollar words; readers will simply turn away from the piece (or, worse, they'll toss it in the trash). If you must introduce a word or concept that's unfamiliar to your audience, be sure to explain it in plain language.

Flowery descriptions and bloated language simply don't have a place in business and technical writing. Be as succinct as possible in getting your point across.

After you've written your piece as clearly as possible, go back through it and see if you have any places it can be shortened. Your audience will read and remember a short piece more easily than they will a long one.

Let's say you've written a perfect piece. You know your audience, and you can tell you've picked the right words to convey your message. You've checked to be sure you've written as clearly and concisely as possible. What could possibly go wrong?

Know madder how good you're peace is if it ain't spelled an punctuated proper oar if you yews words wrong youll loose your readers. After you've written your piece, be sure to check—and recheck and recheck—your spelling, punctuation, and word usage. You sure don't want something you wrote to be the latest joke around the water cooler.

If X, Then Y: The Cause-and-Effect Essay

In a cause-and-effect essay, you examine the relationships between how certain events bring about or lead to other events. Depending on the depth of your topic, you need to determine if you have several causes you need to explore, if some causes may have more importance than others, or if some causes have more immediate or long-term effects than others.

For instance, if you're looking at the causes of U.S. involvement in World War II, you'd write about the immediate cause (the bombing of Pearl Harbor) as well as causes that had been building up for some time (growing hostilities between the United States and Germany and the United States and Japan, increasing bonds between the United States and the Allies, and so on).

In a cause-and-effect essay, some writers find thinking in these terms to be helpful:

- If X happens, why does Y occur?
- Because X happened, why did Y occur?
- If Y happens, what will X have done?
- When Y happened, what X was a cause?

Be sure that there is actually a relationship between X and Y. For instance, suppose you buy a new car and then two days later the dealership lowers the price on the model you bought. The dealership's sale had nothing to do with your previous purchase of the car, so there was no cause-and-effect relationship.

When writing a cause-and-effect essay, the following transition words and phrases can come in handy: *accordingly, as a consequence, as a result, because, consequently, for this purpose, for that reason, hence, in order that, so, so that, then, therefore, thereupon, thus, to do this, to this end, with this in mind, with this objective.*

Learning to Look Beyond the Obvious

In a comparison-and-contrast paper, you record the similarities and the differences of people, places, events, and so on. Be sure you omit any statements of the obvious (e.g., Mercury and Mars are both planets that revolve around the sun) because they will undermine the effectiveness of your paper. Comparing and contrasting two people—or places or works—that have many similarities makes for an interesting or informative piece only if you look beyond what's readily apparent and describe or examine similarities and differences that your readers may not have been aware of or have thought about.

If an assignment calls only for comparison, make sure you don't contrast—or vice versa. On the other hand, if the assignment calls for both, be sure you do in fact include both and give each approximately the same amount of space.

When you're writing a comparison-and-contrast paper, these transition words and phrases of contrast can be useful: *after all, alternatively, although, and yet, at the same time, but, conversely, despite, even so, even though, for all that, however, in contrast, in spite of, instead, nevertheless, nonetheless, nor, notwithstanding, on the contrary, on the other hand, otherwise, regardless, still, though,* and *yet.*

Transition words and phrases of similarity include *again, also, and, as well as, besides, by the same token, for example, furthermore, in a like manner, in a similar way, in the same way, like, likewise, moreover, once more, similarly,* and *so.*

The Abridged Version: The Précis

Although you may already have had some type of experience with several of the writing styles mentioned thus far, you may not be familiar with the précis (pray-cee, from the French word for *precise*). A précis is a clear and logical summary or abridgement of another author's work. Your précis should include the substance or general ideas put forth in the original work, but you must use your own words.

In writing a précis, you must:

- identify the author's tone and point of view
- include the key words and major points of the original work
- include any valuable data that illustrates or supports the original work
- disregard any introductory or supplementary information
- use your own voice (you don't have to copy the original author's tone or voice)
- refrain from giving your opinion of the author, the work, or the ideas presented.

Still confused? Think of a newspaper headline; it's a type of précis in that it summarizes the content, focus, and tone of a longer piece.

In general, your précis should be no more than one-third the length of the original work you're summarizing. Remember that requirements (both of length and of format) vary with instructors, publishers, and companies, so be sure to check with them about what they specify.

The Process Paper

A process paper is a kind of how-to or explanation paper that details a particular process by giving step-by-step directions or by describing certain changes or operations. Remember that you must write a process paper in chronological order; if you write it out of sequence, you defeat the purpose of your paper.

When you begin a process paper, you should be able to define your audience because they'll determine what kind of language you'll use and how much detail you'll go into. For instance, in a process paper about how to change a tire, you'd write in a less detailed manner if your readers are mechanics than if they're a group of beginning drivers.

If you're writing for a general audience, you need to explain anything that might be confusing or unfamiliar. Think about how you would explain the process to children. Then reread your material and add a simple explanation of any words or concepts with which children wouldn't be familiar (without being patronizing, of course). In addition, be precise when you give measurements. While you may be comfortable in writing "Use a little compost in the mixture," your readers may think that "a little" is a tablespoon, when you actually meant a gallon.

Your readers will have an easier time following your directions if you explain the "whys" behind the directions. So, instead of writing:

When pots are on top of the stove, turn their handles to the side.

Elaborate by giving the reason:

When your pots are on top of the stove, turn their handles to the side so that you'll be less likely to accidentally bump into them, knock them over, and burn yourself.

Remember that transition words and phrases help your reader see the chronological flow of the steps *(next, after that, finally)* as well as the placement of materials *(above, beside that, to the right)*.

FACT

Instead of just picturing the activity as they're writing about it, many writers actually perform the activity and tape-record the various steps of what they're doing. Doing this helps them gather all the steps correctly, completely, and chronologically.

Be sure to check with your instructor, publisher, or company about any mandates regarding:

- point of view (usually a process paper is written in second person)
- use of bulleted lists (for instance, in listing the materials to have on hand before beginning)
- use of illustrations, diagrams, or photos (if they're allowed, be sure to include any that enhance the written part of your work—and therefore make your instructions easier to understand)

Digging Up the Details: The Research Paper

In a research paper, you investigate a topic (often one that's been approved by an instructor or publisher) through consulting various sources, interpreting what the sources relate, developing ideas or conclusions, and citing the sources in your paper. A research paper might be one of the longest and (dare I say it?) most work-intensive pieces you'll ever have to write.

Research papers fall into two categories: analytical papers, which provide evidence that investigates and evaluates issues, or argumentative papers, which provide evidence to support your point of view and convince readers that you're right. Research papers can be written in many formats, and entire books are available to detail various styles. Before you jump into your topic, be sure you know whether you're supposed to use a specific documentation style. The two most popular are the Modern Language Association (MLA) style, detailed in the *MLA Handbook for Writers of Research Papers*, and the American Psychological Association (APA) style, detailed in the *Publication Manual of the American Psychological Association*. Other books that you may be directed to use include:

- *The American Medical Association Manual of Style: A Guide for Authors and Editors*, by C. L. Iverson, A. Flanagin, P. B. Fontanarosa, et al. (Baltimore, MD: Williams & Wilkins, 1998).
- *The Chicago Manual of Style: The Essential Guide for Writers, Editors, and Publishers*, University of Chicago Press Staff, editor. (Chicago, IL: University of Chicago Press, 2003).
- *Effective Writing: Improving Scientific, Technical, and Business Communication*, by Christopher Turk and John Kirkman. (New York, NY: E. & F.N. Spon, 1989).
- *Form and Style: Research Papers, Reports, Theses*, by Carole Slade. (Boston, MA: Houghton Mifflin Company, 2003).
- *Good Style: Writing for Science and Technology*, by John Kirkman. (New York, NY: Routledge, 2006).
- *A Manual for Writers of Term Papers, Theses, and Dissertations*, by Kate L. Turabian. (Chicago, IL: University of Chicago Press, 1966).
- *Scientific Style and Format: The CBE Manual for Authors, Editors, and Publishers*, by Edward J. Huth. (New York, NY: Cambridge University Press, 1994).

Often, there's more to a research paper than meets the eye. Be sure you're aware of timelines about material you must turn in before your actual paper is due. Some instructors give grades on different phases of writing a research paper, such as:

- identification of your topic
- a preliminary proposal of your paper
- your notes (sometimes required to be on cards of a specific size)
- an outline of your paper
- various drafts of your paper
- identification of bibliographic information and footnote style

Common problems for research papers:

Topics that are too broad (for instance, "Jupiter: The Fifth Planet" or "Why Americans Enjoy the Cinema")

Papers that don't adhere to specified page limits or word limits

Papers that don't follow the directions about font size, font style, spacing, and margin size

Papers that contain plagiarized material

Citations that aren't written in the prescribed manner. In checking references and citations, make sure you have included all the information that is necessary, correctly placed the information, and correctly punctuated the information.

Checkpoint

The following paragraph has a sentence that should be cut because it strays from the topic sentence. Determine which sentence it is and check your answer in Appendix D.

In my new job, I've learned a number of interesting facts. First, I've learned that being on time is quite important to my boss. Once I came in just five minutes late, and I'd already had a call asking about a file. I was late because I hadn't felt well the night before and I'd forgotten to set the alarm clock. Another thing that is new to me is that my coworkers, for the most part, seem interested in hearing about the projects I'm working on. Several of them continually ask for updates, and that is unlike anything I've experienced in previous jobs. Finally, I've learned that I need to bring change for the vending machines, as they're often out of change and I can't get the soda that I want in the afternoon.

Chapter 17

Getting Personal

Sometimes your writing can take a personal slant. For instance, you may need to support an argument, present a critical analysis, keep a journal, offer a description, relate an event from your life, give an opinion through a review, or send an e-mail with personal or business information. If you need help in any of those areas, this is the chapter to consult.

Taking a Stand: The Argument Essay

In an argument essay, you take a stand on a particular issue and expand your point of view with supporting evidence. To construct an argument, ask yourself what your main point is, and then decide why that particular point is important. For instance, would a segment of society benefit if your stance were taken? Would certain problems be eradicated? Would money be saved?

Keep in mind that you must pursue some line of thought that's open to question, or else you don't have an argument. In other words, you wouldn't write something like:

Cotton candy is mostly made out of sugar.

That's a simple statement of fact—there's nothing to argue. However, if you wrote that people should eat more cotton candy, you'd have the basis for debate, and you could proceed with an argument.

Before you begin, think about the evidence you can give to support your point. If you can't think of (or find through research) several reasons why your point is important, then you should abandon that particular idea because you won't be able to support it well in your essay.

FACT

According to Aristotle, argument has three types of appeal:

Ethos—the appeal of the character and credibility of the speaker or writer (establish your credentials or the credentials of those whose research you cite)

Pathos—the appeal to the emotion of your audience (ask yourself what feelings you want your audience to have)

Logos—the logical appeal through facts or reasons (present enough evidence so your readers will be convinced yours is the only sound conclusion)

The strength of argument essays lies not only in the evidence provided by writers to support their point but also in their ability to anticipate opposing arguments and to objectively disprove them.

Requirements for an argument vary with individual instructors, with various academic disciplines, and with different publications. Be sure you understand specific requirements regarding the format you must use and the type or amount of support or proof you must give.

Advancing an Assessment: The Critical Analysis

In a critical analysis, you examine and assess a work from a number of points of view. Requirements often vary by instructor or company, but you should always include the following:

- enough background information to familiarize readers with the piece you're analyzing (including the name of the author or artist)
- a description of the way the piece was written
- the general thesis behind the piece or a synopsis of the work

Since details and the proper use of quotations and citations are important in a critical analysis, you should take care to follow classroom or company directions explicitly.

Considering the following list of questions may be helpful when composing a critical analysis.

- What is important biographical data about the author or artist?
- What are the purpose, tone, and format of the piece?
- How can the work be interpreted? (Remember, you're not writing a summary of the work but rather an interpretation of its meaning.)
- Is any information in the work inaccurate or incomplete?
- In what ways was the work successful? How did the author or artist achieve the success?
- In what ways was the work unsuccessful? How did the author or artist fail?

- What could the author or artist have done to be more successful?
- Is the piece you're analyzing fair? If not, what's your evidence that it's biased or subjective?
- Do any historical, psychological, geographical, gender, racial, cultural, or religious considerations have an impact on the work?

If you're writing a critical analysis of a literary work, consider points such as theme, symbolism, imagery, figurative language, setting, and characterization. Avoid using the first-person point of view in a critical analysis unless you have permission. In most instances, your like or dislike of a work wouldn't be considered a suitable subject (but you probably already figured that out).

In order to get the ball rolling, you might begin this way:

I think the Anna Ohlrogge piece "Trials of a Country Farmer" succeeds on a number of levels.

But when you're revising, cross out "I think that" and then begin your sentence.

Dear Diary: The Journal

Your journal material might be very intimate or very detached—or anything in between. Maybe you use a journal just to record snippets of thoughts about work, or quotations that you find appealing or inspirational, or even the foods you eat every day—or maybe you choose to write about more personal experiences of your private life.

FACT

Londoner Samuel Pepys (pronounced *Peeps*) is perhaps the most famous English-language diarist. He kept his diary from 1660 to 1669, and it was published after his death. To get ideas for your own work, read Pepys' diary or the diaries of other famous people.

If you're required to keep a journal, you may be given specific topics to reflect upon. In this case, be sure you understand whether your journal entries will be shared with others, and don't write anything you feel is too intimate (you don't want the whole world to know your personal business!).

Painting Word Pictures: The Essay of Description

To be successful, an essay of description relies on imagery. Your readers depend on your words alone in order to see, hear, smell, taste, or feel your subject. For example:

> *The unexpected spring storm sent sharp pellets of rain onto Ryan Miller's face, forcing him to swallow the droplets as he panicked and screamed for help.*

In this sentence, readers can see, feel, and taste the rain, can hear the scream, and can therefore get a good picture of the narrator's predicament.

FACT

Onomatopoetic words (words that sound like the meaning they express) help convey imagery and impact. The *murmur* of the wind helps readers hear the sound the wind makes; the *swish* of a basketball helps readers see and hear a game's excitement; the *splatter* of raindrops shows readers their sound and sight.

Use description for a number of reasons. In a short story or novel, description of a setting helps readers feel closer to the characters or the plot because they can see and appreciate the environment. In a nonfiction work, description helps readers know how a finished product should look (or feel, taste, smell, or sound).

In writing a description, ask yourself, "What dominant impressions do I want to convey?" Do you want readers to appreciate the beauty and scent of the spring flowers you saw on a recent walk? Or do you want to convey the various smells and tastes that you remember from your grandmother's kitchen at Thanksgiving dinner? Or perhaps you want to express the unsightliness and rancid smell of a local landfill you've visited.

In these examples, you'll convey subjective images, so you're allowed to use words that may otherwise be seen as biased. However, if you're describing something objectively (such as a particular building, giving its height, occupancy, history, and so on), don't use words that give a particular bias to your subject.

Works of description rely on details, so be generous with them. Since description relates to as many of the senses as possible, use adjectives and adverbs liberally. In addition, take a look at the verbs you use and see if you can substitute ones that are more descriptive or precise. Instead of writing, "Lemour Elianor walked into the room," for example, give readers a better look at how the man entered. Did he tiptoe into the room? bound? slink? prance? Each of those verbs gives a better picture of what happened. Now add adjectives and adverbs. Did the well-dressed man scurry into the room breathlessly? Did the always-late man tiptoe into the room hesitantly?

While you should choose your descriptive words carefully, don't overuse them. Keep in mind that every noun doesn't need an adjective (much less two or three) and every verb doesn't need an adverb.

The Autobiographical Narrative

In an autobiographical (personal) narrative, you're telling a story about a noteworthy experience in your life. This type of assignment, usually written in the first person, revolves around a single incident that made an impact in your life or taught you an important lesson that you can convey to your readers. Pay particular attention to your characters, plot, setting, and climax. In addition, be sure to include descriptions of the tension—the events that create the interest in your work.

Concentrate on an angle that's not only important to you but also is valuable enough to be shared. The story of your exhilaration the first time you were behind the wheel of a car may be something you'd like to remember, but it alone would probably be boring for your readers. However, if you learned some valuable lesson that your readers can relate to (such as how to talk your way out of a speeding ticket) or an amusing anecdote that readers can be entertained by (such as how you met a movie star by accidentally crashing into his or her car on the freeway), then you have something you can develop into an autobiographical narrative.

Adding concrete details will explain and enhance your plot, setting, and characters. Details also help you re-create the incident so your readers will stay involved in your story.

An Opportune Occasion to Offer an Opinion

You have many ways to write a review, but every way has this in common: you give your opinion about something, and you also support or explain your opinion. Whether you're reviewing a scholarly book, a recent movie, or your tour of the Outer Hebrides, making a statement like "It was cool" without giving your readers any information as to why it was cool sure doesn't give them any reason to read further. Because you're writing a critical evaluation, you have to cite the noteworthy and the flawed aspects of your subject, and you also have to explain what made them receive high or low marks.

In writing a review—as in writing of any kind—keep your audience in mind. If you're reviewing a new restaurant, for instance, would your audience be familiar with the type of food the restaurant specialized in? You'd probably need to give more explanation to a general newspaper audience than you would to readers of, say, *Great Gourmet Goodies in America* magazine.

FACT

To get more ideas of how to write your review, consult magazines, journals, or scholarly papers that focus on your topic. As you read, note the various features the writer addressed and think about incorporating those features in your work.

Your instructor, your company, or the publication you're writing for may mandate specific issues to address in your review. Above all else, be sure you address those issues.

If a rating system is allowed, create one that's both clever and applicable to your subject matter (for example, a calendar to show how long readers should wait—or not wait—to read a particular book).

Egads! E-mail

E-mail generally falls into one of two categories—business or pleasure—and while each has several different rules, they also both have common ground.

First, remember your audience (have you heard that often enough?) and adjust your tone and style for your recipients. If you're telling your children about your upcoming birthday party, you'll probably use different language than you would if you're sending the same information to your friends or your boss.

Keep in mind "netiquette," a blended word meaning "etiquette for the Internet." This means that, under no circumstances, should you criticize someone in your post ("flaming"); write all your post in capital letters ("shouting"); send unsolicited advertising ("spamming"); write something long or inappropriate in the subject line; send an e-mail to those for whom the e-mail is irrelevant; send attachments without asking permission; or forward messages that are hoaxes or urban legends (try *snopes.com* to check the truth or fiction of a message).

In this time of rampant computer viruses, beware of forwarding or opening posts that have a questionable origin. With one quick click of a button, you can open a virus-ridden attachment and wipe out years of work.

Private and Personal—or Not?

Perhaps the most important thought to keep in mind about personal e-mail is that anything sent as a private post can easily become public. All a recipient has to do is forward an e-mail, and it can quickly become fodder for the whole world to read.

Another area to think about—albeit a far less important consideration—is whether to use abbreviations, such as acronyms or other shorthand (e.g., typing @TEOTD to mean "at the end of the day"). Again, your audience is your key. You'll probably be fine using some of these in chatty e-mail with friends, but they usually don't have a place in an e-mail to your grandmother.

E-LINK   For a list of acronyms and other shorthand commonly used online, see

tinyurl.com/25w2j   *tinyurl.com/ampun*

While writing in all capital letters is a no-no, a trend in personal e-mail is to write in all lowercase letters. This may be fine between friends who are accustomed to writing (and reading) this way, but it may be off-putting to others. When in doubt, use that shift key when it's appropriate.

One problem with e-mail messages is that they're usually short and often hastily written, so their tone can sometimes be questionable. Because of this, you can add emoticons (a word blended from *emotion* and *icons*) to clarify the tone (often to show humor, sadness, disbelief, or sarcasm). Emoticons are stick drawings you make with punctuation, letters, or numbers on your keyboard, like this

:-) smiling; agreeing with something

^5 high five

:* kiss

Just remember your audience when you use emoticons so you'll be sure your readers will know what you're trying to convey.

Getting Down to Business

Of course, business e-mail is far more professional than personal e-mail. Since, as the old saying goes, time is money, keep your message concise, direct, and clear. Take awhile to think about why you're writing and what you want to accomplish (maybe this is a mental rough draft). This information will eventually go in the first part of your e-mail.

Begin your e-mail with concise information in your subject line. Something like "Bring new notebook to meeting" or "Do you have Johnson file?"

will let your reader know what to expect in the body of your post. If you don't have any details to add to the information in the subject line, you can just copy and paste the same message in the body (some people who read lots of e-mails say they first look at the body rather than the subject).

In academic or literary writing, authors will often lead a reader up to a climax in a paragraph (that is, they'll place their topic sentence at the end of the paragraph). Don't do this in business e-mail. The sooner you can let your reader know what your post involves, the better—so get to your point in your first sentence or two.

Resist any urge to be flowery in your message. You're not writing the Great American Novel here. Keep your paragraphs short, and skip lines between paragraphs so that your material will be easier to read. Reading from a computer screen is often more difficult and time-consuming than reading from a hard copy.

E-mail recipients tend to read their messages quickly, so if you have several points to tackle, use numbered or bulleted lists so your reader will note all the points that require attention. If your points are quite detailed, dividing them into separate messages might be better. This also makes responding to your points easier.

For a list of emoticons commonly used in e-mail, see

tinyurl.com/ph3rl   *tinyurl.com/3gb6*
tinyurl.com/2qcc8

Use correct spelling, capitalization, grammar, and mechanics—that is, use what you learned in the beginning of this book. Almost all companies look for certain grammatical standards in business correspondence.

Whenever possible, use the active voice ("We will deliver the shipment on May 15" rather than "The shipment will be delivered on May 15"). Posts written that way give the impression that you and your company are more involved and concerned than if they had been written in the passive voice.

Always give personal or business information (your name, your company's name and address, your business telephone or fax number) to those with whom you're not in frequent contact.

As often as possible, avoid sending attachments. In addition to their potential danger as carriers of viruses, downloading them takes valuable time. Unless your recipient knows to expect an attachment, put your material in the body of the message.

Make sure that your e-mail spell checker is turned on and that you go back and proofread your post before you send it. You don't want to type an order for six billion parts when you intended to order six million instead (the spell checker wouldn't have realized this was a mistake).

After you've finished your post, reread it to see if your tone comes across too harshly or too abruptly—or in any other way that might be offensive. If so, change your wording.

Checkpoint

Rewrite these sentences to make the verbs more descriptive or precise. Possible answers are in Appendix D.

1. The car went up the hill.
2. Alfred is going around the corner.
3 Bobbie said that she was leaving.

Chapter 18

Literary Terms You Need to Know

You say you don't know a *dactyl* from a *pterodactyl*? You think maybe a *round character* needs to go on a diet? You're unsure about whether *irony* is a vitamin supplement you're supposed to take? If you're bamboozled, befuddled, bewildered and baffled (cross out three of those so the sentence won't be redundant) about literary terms, this is the section to examine.

Echoing Your English Teachers: The Basics

You may remember these literary terms—they're among the ones most emphasized in high school and college English classes. In fact, you probably use many of them without thinking of their specific definitions. If you've said you're so hungry you could eat a horse—that's both hyperbole and a cliché. If you've described two outcomes as having the "same difference," you've used an oxymoron. Look at the list and see which others you recognize.

alliteration	the repetition of beginning sounds in words (e.g., *sweet Sue* or *March Madness*)
antonym	a word that is the opposite of another (e.g., *happy* is an antonym of *sad*)
cliché	an overused expression (e.g., *over the hill* and *always been there for me*)
euphemism	the use of a gentler word or phrase in place of something explicit or harsh (e.g., "buy the farm" instead of "die")
hyperbole	conscious exaggeration to make a point (e.g., "Sandy is as skinny as a rail")
metaphor	a comparison without using *like* or *as*; (e.g., "The prisoner's icy eyes stared at me"; eyes are compared to ice, with no *like* or *as*)
onomatopoeia	words or phrases that sound like what they mean (e.g., *buzz* and *kerplunk*)
oxymoron	a phrase in which seemingly incompatible or contradictory terms are combined (e.g., *definite maybe*)
palindrome	a word or phrase that is spelled the same backwards and forwards (e.g., *kayak* and *a Toyota*)
parody	a work that makes fun of or imitates the style of another work, either affectionately or harshly
personification	giving human qualities to places or things that aren't human (e.g., "The sun smiled on my wedding day")
simile	the comparison of two unlike persons or objects, using the word *like* or *as* (e.g., "overcooked meat as dry as the Sahara")

symbol	something that represents something else
synonym	a word that means the same or nearly the same as another word

As you write, look for places you can use these literary terms. You can add spice to your fiction writing by including more personification, alliteration, onomatopoeia, metaphors, or similes. Alternately, look for clichés; reword them to show more originality.

Beyond the Basics

Some of these may be familiar to you, depending on how much you remember from earlier English or speech classes. The following terms apply to prose, poetry, and drama. If you're writing for a technical or business purpose, you probably want to hold off on using them.

allegory	a literary work with a meaning other than its literal meaning (e.g., *Animal Farm* was an allegory of life in Soviet Russia)
allusion	a reference to a well-known person, place, or thing (e.g., in "I'm no Scrooge, but $100 is too much for Jack's present," the allusion is to Scrooge, the stingy character in *A Christmas Carol*)
anagram	words or phrases spelled with the same letters as other words or phrases. "Grab okra, Mom" is an anagram for "grammar book."

Create your own anagrams by using the Internet Anagram Solver at *wordsmith.org/anagram/*.

You can also create words and phases from the letters assigned to your phone number by using *phonespell.org/*.

analogy	a comparison showing a similarity in two or more persons or things that wouldn't ordinarily be thought similar (e.g.,

the instructor in my first computer class was a Daniel Boone, leading me through unchartered territory)

aphorism	a short statement of a truth (e.g., Benjamin Franklin's "Lost time is never found again")
assonance	repetition of similar vowel sounds successive or proximate words, as in the phrase "live wire"
comic relief	intentional use of humor in a literary work in order to relieve tension
connotation	emotions a word brings to mind (e.g., *Mother* has a connotation that includes nurturing and protection. See *denotation*.)
consonance	repetition of consonant sounds in words (e.g., *strong* and *thing*)
denotation	the dictionary definition of a word (See *connotation*.)
denouement	resolution at the end of prose or drama
epithet	a term used in place of the proper name in order to give more description; "Windy City" is an epithet for Chicago.
imagery	use of words or phrases that appeal to any of the five senses
irony	the opposite of what is expected to happen or to be said
malapropism	the unintentional misuse or distortion of a word or phrase (e.g., *polo bears* instead of *polar bears*)

FACT

Mrs. Malaprop, a character noted for her misuse of words, appeared in R. B. Sheridan's 1775 *The Rivals*. Her name, in turn, is derived from the French phrase *mal à propos*, meaning *inappropriate*.

metonymy	use of a word or phrase that's substituted for another with which it's closely related (e.g., in "The pen is mightier than the sword," *pen* represents any written matter; *sword* represents any hostile action)

mood	the tone or emotional thrust an author deliberately imparts in characters or scenes
Oedipus complex	a complex that addresses a male's desire for the exclusive love of his mother
paradox	a statement that seems to be impossible or contradictory but also seems to be true (e.g., "The more I learn, the less I know.")
pseudonym	a false name a writer chooses to use instead of his or her own
satire	writing that ridicules its subject, usually to try to change some situation or person
setting	the time and place of a story, novel, drama, or poem
spoonerism	words or phrases in which letters or syllables are switched (e.g., *shake a tower* instead of *take a shower*)

FACT

Spoonerisms are named after Oxford University's Reverend William A. Spooner (1844–1930), a man so famous for his verbal slips of the tongue that this type of mistake came to be named after him.

synecdoche	a figure of speech in which a part represents a whole (e.g., "I like your new wheels"; *wheels* is a synecdoche for the whole car)

In Praise of Prose

By definition, prose is any writing that's not in verse form (that is, it isn't poetry). Strictly speaking, prose includes, for instance, a dictionary or a math textbook. In literary terms, however, prose deals with anecdotes, short stories, novellas, novels, or speeches.

antagonist	the opponent to the main character (the protagonist)
autobiography	a lengthy work based on the life of the author
biography	a work detailing the events in the life of a real person, written by someone else

characterization	the creation of believable, well-rounded characters, and the way in which an author reveals characters' individualities
climax	the highest point of action in a story
coming-of-age	a type of novel or story in which the main character develops into adulthood
conflict	the struggle characters face
dialogue	conversation between two characters
dystopian novel	a novel in which the attempt to create a perfect society fails (e.g., Aldous Huxley's *Brave New World*)
flashback	a literary device in which readers or viewers understand that a scene happens before the current time portrayed
flat character	a (usually minor) character who doesn't change during the story
first person	a style of writing that gives the thoughts of the speaker
first person	a point of view in which the speaker, a character in the story or poem, tells the events from his or her perspective
foreshadowing	the use of hints about what will come
man v. man	conflict between two or more characters
man v. nature	conflict between a character and nature
man v. self	conflict within a character
novel	a lengthy work of fiction that contains one or more major plots and several subplots
novella	a work of fiction that's longer than a short story but shorter than a novel
parable	a short story that teaches a lesson in morality
plot	the pattern of events in a story, novel, or drama
point of view	the standpoint from which a story is told
protagonist	the main character, usually but not always the "good guy"
round character	a character who grows or changes

second person	a method of writing that addresses readers as *you* (e.g., you drive on the right)

FACT

The second person also includes *y'all* (a blend of *you* and *all*) and the archaic *thou* and *thy*.

theme	a recurring message throughout a literary or dramatic work
third person	a style of writing giving the thoughts of someone other than the speaker (I) or readers (you)
tragedy	a drama or literary work that ends with the main character failing in valiant efforts
tragic hero	a character who should be great but has some sort of flaw that causes failure
understatement	an intentional restraint or lack of emphasis in writing, often for a humorous intention
utopian novel	a novel that depicts a society without any problems

Understanding literary terms helps you understand literature itself more fully. If, for example, you understand that a work you're reading is a parable, then you can decide if the idea it's suggesting is one you agree with. Or if you know to look for foreshadowing in a novel, then your understanding of the direction of the plot might be enhanced.

Or suppose you're right in the middle of your first novel; if so, understanding what a tragic hero is might just be what you need in order to change your protagonist from a flat character to a round character and make your work the next Great American Novel.

A key to using any type of literary term in your writing is appropriateness. Your company, for example, may insist that you write in first person, so be sure you adhere to that; on the other hand, in educational settings you may be told that only writing in the third person is acceptable. Check your work to see that you've used only third person.

Praising Points of Poetry

People have enjoyed poetry for thousands of years. *The Epic of Gilgamesh*, written in Samaria about 2000 B.C.E., is the oldest surviving poetry. Poetry in English has a far shorter history. It was first written down during the Anglo-Saxon period (the mid-400s C.E. to 1066) but probably predates that in the form of oral tradition.

ballad	a poem that tells a story and usually has a repeated refrain
caesura	a pause or break in a line of poetry
couplet	two consecutive rhyming lines
epic	an extended narrative poem, written in lofty language, celebrating a hero's feats
elegy	poetry that mourns someone or something
eye rhyme	words that are spelled as if they should rhyme (e.g., *though* and *tough*)
feminine rhyme	rhyme that matches at least two syllables at the end of the lines (e.g., *hand painted* and *acquainted*)
free verse	poetry with neither a regular rhythmic pattern nor a regular rhyme scheme
haiku	an unrhymed seventeen-syllable poem of Japanese origin, usually consisting of three lines
internal rhyme	rhyme within a line of poetry
limerick	a witty (and often bawdy) poem of five anapestic lines and an *aabba* rhyme scheme
masculine rhyme	a rhyme of single syllables at the end of words
ode	a lengthy lyric poem having a serious nature and expressing a lofty idea
rhyme scheme	the pattern of rhyme in a poem
scanning (scansion)	establishing the type of foot used in a poem as well as the sequence of different feet

sonnet	a fourteen-line poem, usually written in iambic pentameter, with a particular rhyme scheme
stanza	two or more lines of a poem, grouped together for length, metrical form, rhyme scheme, or meaning

Here's something that may be a surprise to you: poetry doesn't have to rhyme. A line of a poem can have one word or many, can have a particular beat or none at all, can rhyme within itself or with another line or not at all. The looks, the moods, the messages of poems—all are as numerous as their creators.

So what makes a group of words a poem? That question has been debated for thousands of years. An exact definition of poetry is difficult; suffice it to say that poetry comes from any creative expression shown through sound, language choice, and emotion. In the words of Robert Frost, a complete poem is one in which "emotion has found its thought and the thought has found the words."

Poetry—The Beat and the Feet

Historically, poetry was written using a particular meter—a certain beat of stressed and unstressed syllables and also a specific number of feet in a line. Each combination of stressed and unstressed syllables has a separate name, as does each number of feet in a line. To further complicate matters, some groupings of beat and feet have specific names.

anapest	a metric foot having two unstressed syllables followed by a stressed syllable
blank verse	unrhymed poetry written in iambic pentameter
dactyl	a metric foot having a stressed syllable followed by two unstressed syllables
dimeter	a line of poetry; it has two feet
foot	a basic meter, consisting of two or three stressed and unstressed syllables
heptameter	a line in poetry; it has seven feet
heroic couplet	in poetry and drama, two lines of rhyming iambic pentameter

hexameter	a line in poetry; it has six feet
iamb	a metric foot having an unstressed syllable followed by a stressed syllable
meter	a pattern of rhythm that results from an intentional arrangement of stressed and unstressed syllables
monometer	a line in poetry; it has one foot
nonameter	a line in poetry; it has nine feet
octameter	a line in poetry; it has eight feet
pentameter	a line in poetry; it has five feet
pyrrhic	a metric foot having two unstressed syllables
quatrain	a stanza of poetry consisting of four lines
scansion	the breakdown of the meter in a poem
spondee	a metric foot having two long syllables
tetrameter	a line of poetry; it has four metrical feet
trimeter	a line of poetry; it has three metrical feet
trochee	a metric foot having a stressed syllable followed by an unstressed syllable

A examination of meter is important in studying and writing poetry. Does the meter of your poem successfully affect the intended sound and mood? Does the poem adhere to the same meter, or does it change or allow variances? If the poem carries the same meter, does that make it seem monotonous? If the poem varies its meter, do the variances have a purpose? Does the rhythm created by the words lend itself to what you as a reader expect, or what you as a poet intend?

In both reading and writing poetry, some feel it is helpful to read a poem aloud several times to get the right feel for the meter and therefore get a better grasp of its meaning. Try doing that with the poem you're examining or creating and see if you can answer the previous questions.

Oh! The Drama of It All!

Drama, a blend of both literature and performing art, has its roots in ancient times. Civilizations all over the world developed their own forms of drama, and each has its unique characteristics. In Western civilization, the oldest extant plays come from ancient Greece, and those dramas later influenced the playwrights of ancient Rome. Later, in medieval times, Europe developed three main types of dramas—mystery plays (which were based on the Bible), miracle plays (which were based on lives of saints), and morality plays (which taught a lesson).

From these evolved English Renaissance theater, with grand performances presented by players associated with leading noblemen, and with themes far more secular. By the 1800s, drama had developed into elaborate productions, with costumes and scenery far more sophisticated than previously seen.

Drama of the twentieth and twenty-first centuries has dealt with more realism than that of previous eras but has also seen a surge of various forms of experimental theater.

ad-lib	to make up lines that aren't in the script
aside	words (usually humorous) a character says aloud onstage to let the audience (but not the other characters) know what he or she is thinking
dramatis personae	a list of characters in a play
deus ex machina	an unlikely event or improbable person that resolves the conflict in the nick of time

FACT

Deus ex machina translates from Latin as "god from the machine." Early Greek and Roman playwrights sometimes lowered to the stage a machine carrying an actor who was playing a god. Using magic powers, this god would then resolve an onstage crisis.

foil	a character whose actions contrast or parallel the protagonist, thus emphasizing the protagonist's characteristics
monologue	an extended speech by one character
soliloquy	a speech given by a character alone onstage; the audience realizes the character is voicing his or her thoughts
stage direction	comments about how a playwright intended the dialogue, setting, and action to be carried out
stock character	a type of character that the audience recognizes immediately
theater of the absurd	plays and style in which realism is abandoned and illusory moods are commonplace

Checkpoint

Look at the literary terms in the following table and determine which are used in the numbered examples. Check your answers in Appendix D.

alliteration   allusion   assonance   cliché   consonance
hyperbole   metaphor   onomatopoeia   simile   understatement

1. This little snack will do nicely," I said as the four plates of food were presented to me. _U_
2. "I've found my Romeo," Patricia sighed to her friend Susie. _al_
3. click, crackle, whoosh _O_
4. We'll leave no stone unturned in our search for the robber. _cl_
5. The newly wet grass sparkled like emeralds. _Sim_
6. Many men marched home. _Con_
7. I spent a couple of weeks in that dull city one day. _hy_
8. Peter Piper picked a peck of pickled peppers. _al_
9. Pop culture is the drug of the country. _M_
10. . . . the bird that chirped and slurped _as_

Chapter 19

Latin—Alive and Kicking!

No one can deny that Latin isn't what it used to be—the language of the Roman Republic and later the Roman Empire, as well as the preferred language of medieval scholars and the Catholic Church. Nowadays, though, Latin is no longer a native language in any country; in fact, probably the only place you'll hear "Salve" (a common Latin greeting) is in a scholarly setting. But that doesn't mean that Latin is dead; in fact, it's all around us.

19

It's Everywhere! Everyday Latin

At 11 A.M. I was already running late. I needed to get my job application in the mail before 1 P.M., so I knew I had to get started. When I opened the application, however, I was puzzled to see "BONA FORTUNA" on the top of it. Sending the phrase through Google, I discovered that it meant "Good luck" in Latin. "Latin?" I thought. "Nobody uses Latin. It's been dead for hundreds of years."

I put the Latin mystery out of my mind and began working, copying my curriculum vitae, and noting that I had graduated summa cum laude in A.D. 2008. For references, I listed Dr. Richard Payne, professor emeritus at my alma mater.

Then came a number of surprising questions, e.g., "What was the topic of the best paper you have written?" (my answer: "Antebellum Alter Egos of Famous Americans"); "What caveats have you heard about working for us?" (my answer: My university magnum opus won't be fully appreciated); "What do you see yourself doing c. 2012 (e.g., will your life be status quo or will you have a different job)?" (my answer: I'll have proven myself invaluable to the company; ergo, I will have been promoted).

Glancing at the clock, I discovered my time was almost up. "My goodness! Tempus fugit," I said to myself as I signed the application and stuffed it into the envelope. Even as I dropped the envelope into the mailbox, I was still scratching my head, trying to figure out the strange greeting in Latin, the dead language.

The writer in the previous anecdote seems puzzled by the introduction of a "dead language," but then he or she writes at least fifteen Latin words, phrases, and abbreviations in contemporary use: A.M., P.M., curriculum vitae, summa cum laude, A.D., emeritus, alma mater, e.g., antebellum, alter egos, caveats, magnum opus, i.e., ergo, tempus fugit.

a.d. (*Anno Domini*)	year of our Lord; used to designate a time after Christ was born
ad hoc	for a specific purpose or situation
ad infinitum	to infinity, without end
ad nauseum	to a nauseating extent
ad valorem	according to the value; usually used in conjunction to a tax

addendum	something to be added, usually to written material
alea iacta est	the die is cast, spoken by Julius Caesar when he decided to cross the Rubicon (49 B.C.)
A.M.	in the morning
antebellum	before the war; in the United States, commonly used to refer to the time before the Civil War (1861–65)
bona fide	in good faith; not counterfeit
cave canem	beware of the dog
caveat emptor	let the buyer beware
de facto	in reality, actually
e.g.	for example
etc. (et cetera)	and others, and so forth (I'll get paper, pens, tape, etc.)
ex officio	by virtue of his or her office
fait accompli	a deed already accomplished
i.e. (id est)	that is, in other words
ipso facto	by the fact itself
lb. (*Libra*)	scales; today, lb. is the abbreviation for pound(s)
mea culpa	through my fault; an acknowledgement of responsibility
non sequitur	it doesn't follow
per annum	by the year; for each year
per capita	for each person
per diem	by the day; for each day
per se	in itself, by itself
quid pro quo	something done in return
sine qua non	something indispensable
status quo	the existing condition or situation
sub rosa	confidentially
vice versa	with the order reversed

Because Latin no longer has any native speakers, some call it a "dead language" (more about that later). But maybe a better description would be that it's an "ancestral language."

Latin, you see, is *parens* (Latin for *parent*) to a number of modern languages, which are collectively called "Romance languages." Don't think, though, that they have this moniker because they evoke passion and love; the real reason is that they descend from the language of Rome. As the influence of the Holy Roman Empire spread across Europe, so did its language—Latin. Then, as the power of the empire decreased, dialects began and over many years, separate languages arose. These became Romance languages that we know today as French, Spanish, Italian, Portuguese, and Romanian.

(In case you're wondering, in spite of English having so much Latin in it, it's basically a Germanic tongue. But we'll leave that for another chapter.)

Ex Obscuritate in Lucem (*From Ignorance to Learning*)

If you read or write academic works, you'll no doubt encounter far more Latin than you would in everyday use. In addition to the often-seen *e.g.* and *i.e.*, you'll need to know about *cf.*, *ibid.*, *c.*, *et seq.*, *n.b.*, and *op. cit*—and those are just some of the abbreviations.

Diverse academic disciplines use Latin terms—from math to philosophy to history to writing. The following list is comprehensive enough to help you in many academic disciplines.

a posteriori	from the latter; reasoning that flows from particulars to general principles; inductive reasoning (antonym of *a priori*)
a priori	from the former; reasoning that flows from the known or assumed; deductive reasoning (antonym of *a posteriori*)
alma mater	nourishing mother; used to designate the college or university from which a person has graduated
alter ego	the other I; a secret identity; a separate personality

alumnus	one male graduate is an **alumnus**; one female graduate is an **alumna**; all male graduates are **alumni**; all female graduates are **alumnae**; male and female graduates are **alumni**
cf. (*confer*)	compare; look at the material just stated and compare it with other material cited immediately after the *cf.*
circa (**c.** or **ca.**)	around, about, approximately
cogito ergo sum	I think, therefore I am; an argument written in 1637 by French philosopher René Descartes to prove his existence
colloquium	a type of academic lecture usually offered to a wide audience
cum laude	used to designate those who graduate with distinction
dixi	I have spoken
emeritus	retired (professor, clergy person, other dignitary)
ergo	therefore, consequently
errata	errors; a list of errata from a previous edition of a work is often listed in a current edition
et al. (*et alii*)	and others (The paper was written by Fowler et al.)
Et tu, Brute?	Even you, Brutus?; a line spoken by the title character in Shakespeare's *Julius Caesar* as he's stabbed by his friend Brutus; now the term is used whenever a person is betrayed by a friend
ex libris	from the books; commonly found in bookplates, followed by a person's name; now means that the book comes from a person's library
ibid. (*ibidem*)	the material being cited comes from the same place as the previous citation
inter alia	among other things
magna cum laude	used to designate those who graduate with high distinction
magnum opus	a great work; especially an artist's masterpiece
n.b. (*nota bene*)	note well; used to call a reader's attention to something
post hoc, ergo propter hoc	after this, therefore because of this; a common fallacy in reasoning

q.e.d. (*quod erat demonstrandum*)	that which was to have been proved (placed at the end of mathematic proofs)
q.a.f. (*quod erat faciendum*)	that which was to have been shown (used to mark the end of a mathematical solution or calculation)
q.v. (*quod vide*)	a scholarly way of directing readers to a reference
symposium	an academic conference
sic	thus, just so; indicates a writer realizes that original material he or she is quoting contains an error (often a spelling error)
summa cum laude	used to designate those who graduate with highest distinction
tabula rasa	blank slate; refers to the argument that people learn only through experiences
viz (*videlicet*)	namely, used to introduce examples, lists, etc.; no period is placed at the end

Many colleges and universities have Latin mottoes. Among them are *In Veritatis Amore* (In the Love of Truth, Bellarmine University), *Lux et Veritas* (Light and Truth, Indiana University), *Vincit Omnia Veritas* (Truth Conquers All, Compton Community College), and *Et Facta Est Lux* (And the Light Was Created, Morehouse College). You can find others by clicking on links at *tinyurl.com/msgdw.*

In addition to these actual schools, you can impress your younger friends by working *Draco Dormiens Nunquam Titillandus (Never Tickle a Sleeping Dragon)* into your conversation. That's the motto of Hogwart's School of Witchcraft and Wizardry, Harry Potter's alma mater.

Ignorantia Juris Non Excusat (Ignorance of the Law Is No Excuse)

If you watch TV courtroom or police dramas, you've probably heard any number of somber-sounding legal terms being flung about (lawyers are famous for that). But you may have been confused by their meaning. *In cam-*

era—does that mean inside an actual camera? *In loco parentis*—a child's parents have gone batty? *Pro bono*—something's being done for the lead singer of U2?

You probably guessed that none of those explanations is correct. The phrases are all Latin, and when they're translated into English, the Latin words have an informative meaning—sometimes one that's used only with application to the law.

E-LINK

You can read the latest news—translated into Latin—at *tinyurl.com/h33db*; alternately, you can listen to the news broadcast in Latin (broadcast from Finland, of all places!) at *tinyurl.com/ytpkjq*.

Twenty-first century law still extensively uses Latin phrases. A number of the most frequently used legal terms of Latin origin (and the vast majority of the foreign-language legal terms do come from Latin) are explained in the following table.

affidavit	a signed statement made under oath and witnessed by an official such as a notary public
amicus curiae	a third party who is allowed to submit a legal brief
corpus delicti	the evidence that a crime has been committed (e.g., the body of a murder victim)
cui bono	who will benefit
de jure	by right, of right, according to law
et uxor	and (his) wife
ex curia	out of court
ex lege	as a matter of law
ex parte	done by or for one side or party only
ex post facto	coming after the fact; usually used with a law applied retroactively

habeas corpus	you may have the body; most commonly used in relation to prisoners' rights to know the charges against them
in flagrante delicto	while the crime is blazing; caught in the act of committing a crime (often euphemistically used to refer to a couple caught in a sexual act)
in loco parentis	in the place of a parent; without going through legal adoption, a person assumes parental rights and duties
in prope persona	in one's own person (without a lawyer)
mala fide	in bad faith
mutatis mutandis	after making the necessary changes
ne bis in idem	a person may not be punished twice for the same thing
nolo contendere	a plea in a criminal case in which the defendant answers the charges but doesn't admit or dispute guilt
non compos mentis	not of sane mind
obiter dictum	a judge's comment that has no bearing on the case outcome
onus probandi	burden of proof
pendente lite	while the case is pending
prima facie	at first sight
pro bono	for the good; used to describe work done with no cost
pro forma	as a matter of form; done in advance to stipulate a form or describe items
sine die	indefinitely
stare decisis	let the decision stand

Try the online quiz for legal Latin terms at *tinyurl.com/3cosc9*.

sui generis	of its own type
ultra vires	outside one's jurisdiction

Feeling a Little Under the Weather?
Latin in Medicine

Perhaps the most significant Latin phrase that deals with medicine—a phrase that you may see predominantly displayed in your doctor's office—is *Primum non nocere* (Above all, do no harm). This fundamental precept reminds doctors to consider potential injury that may occur as a result of outside intervention. Medical decisions carry a dual edge: the potential benefit and the potential harm. The physician is being reminded that not harming the patient is of paramount importance.

Another Latin aphorism you may see is this one: *Ars longa, vita brevis* (Art is long, life is short). This is a Latin translation of a phrase by Hippocrates, a physician so influential that he earned the title "Father of Medicine." What Hippocrates meant by "art" was "medicine," so he was saying that learning the craft of medicine takes a lifetime.

E-LINK

Want to impress your friends and give today's weather in Latin? Take a look at *tinyurl.com/iyx*.

Need more Latin medical quotes? In his *Aeneid*, the famous Roman poet Virgil wrote this: "Aegrescit medendo" (The disease worsens with treatment). "Plus a medico quam a morbo periculi" (More danger from the doctor than from the disease) was the pronouncement in Robert Burton's 1621 *Anatomy of Melancholy*. Bet you won't see either of those on your doctor's walls.

a.c. (*ante cibum*)	before meals
ad lib. (*ad libitum*)	use as much as one desires; freely
a.p. (*ante prandium*)	used in prescriptions to mean before a meal
b.i.d. (*bis in die*)	used to designate medicine taken twice a day
h.s. (*hora somni*)	used to designate medicine that should be taken at bedtime

in utero	in the womb
in vitro	in a synthetic atmosphere outside a living organism
p.c. (*post cibum*)	after meals
p.o. (*per os*)	orally
post mortem	occurring or done after death
postpartum	relating to the period immediately after childbirth
p.r.n. (*pro re nata*)	take as often as needed
q.a.d. (*quoque alternis die*)	used to designate medicine taken every other day
q.d. (*quater die*)	used to designate medicine taken every day
q.h. (*quaque hor*)	used to designate medicine taken every hour
q.i.d. (*quater in die*)	used to designate medicine taken four times a day
q.l. (*quantum libet*)	as much as (the patient) wishes
stat (form of *statim*)	immediately
t.i.d. (*ter in die*)	used to designate medicine taken three times a day
t.i.w.	used to designate medicine taken three times a week

As you read before, Latin isn't a living language; that is, it's no longer spoken by large numbers of people, and it isn't the official language of any large country. But don't pity the demise of Latin. The fact that it isn't living is a benefit in legal and medical circles.

What's the benefit? Living languages change in short periods of time. That won't happen in Latin because it's a "dead" language. The specific meanings of Latin terms will be the same in a hundred years as they were 200 years ago—a real advantage for those in the legal and medical professions.

Sacred Settings: Latin in Church

When Christianity was in its infancy, those who spread its message spoke Greek, not Latin. In fact, Latin was not used in the Roman Church services until around the middle of the third century, by which time it had become the vernacular of Rome. Since Church officials wanted to be in touch with the common people, conducting services in the language they spoke made sense. Latin remained the official language of the Catholic Church until the Second Vatican Council granted parishes permission to say Mass in the local language in the 1960s.

As time went on, not only did Latin gain a stronghold as the language of not only the common people, but also—after the fall of the Roman Empire—Latin became the language of educated people. As a result, many important religious works were written in Latin or translated into it. It's from these that we have many of the Latin religious terms that are important today.

Adeste Fideles	O come, all ye faithful
Ave Maria	Hail, Mary; a prayer addressed to Mary, the mother of Christ
Corpus Christi	the body of Christ
credo	in church, a statement of religious belief; also any system of personal or business beliefs (written with a lowercase *c*)
Dei gratia	by the grace of God
Deo gratias (D.G.)	Thanks be to God
Deo volente (D.V.)	God willing
Dominus	the Lord
ecclesia	church or congregation
Ego te absolve	I absolve you; used by a priest at the end of confession
ex cathedra	from the throne; a Catholic reference that says any pronouncement given *ex cathedra* by the pope is infallible
Fiat lux	Let there be light (Genesis 1:3)
Fidei defensor	Defender of the faith
imprimatur	let it be printed; church authorization for a book to be printed; now an official sanction of any kind
in nomine Domini	in the name of the Lord
in pace requiescat	may he rest in peace
mater	mother

Mater Dei	Mother of God
Noli me tangere	Do not touch me
Opus Dei	the work of God
ora pro nobis	pray for us
pater	father
Pater Noster	Our Father (the Lord's Prayer)
sanctus	holy
Te Deum	We praise Thee, God
Vox populi, vox dei	The voice of the people is the voice of God

A number of terms used in Christian services are often referred to by their Latin names. The *Gloria*, which begins *Gloria in excelsis Deo* (Glory to God in the highest), praises each part of the Trinity. During the *Credo* (I believe), which often comes after the sermon, churchgoers recite a number of religious tenets as they speak it in unison.

Checkpoint

Read the following selection and then substitute the appropriate Latin abbreviations, words, or phrases for the material in italics.

The lecturer had spoken *to a nauseating extent* _____ (*that is* _____, he'd been speaking for over two hours), and his topics were so disjointed that I wondered if he was *not of sane mind* _____. He blathered on about his *school from which he'd graduated* _____, and then said that he'd graduated *about* _____ 1995 and had weighed about 150 *pounds* _____. Discussion of an *academic conference* _____ he'd recently attended took another fifteen minutes.

Chapter 20

Foreign Languages in Everyday American English

"We don't just borrow words; on occasion, English has pursued other languages down alleyways to beat them unconscious and rifle their pockets for new vocabulary."—James Nicoll

20

English accepts—even welcomes—many terms from other languages. On occasion, theses words or phrases become so thoroughly assimilated into English that they no longer have their foreign flavor. Words like *negligee*, *camaraderie*, and *entourage* are now so commonly used in everyday English that we've forgotten their French etymology. However, due to the historical influence of immigrants and to today's increasing ease of communication, many books, documents, and other material that you may read are infused with foreign words and phrases.

Neighbors to the South: Spanish

Spanish is another one of the Romance languages; that is, it evolved from Latin (the language of ancient Rome). Beginning in northern Spain, it then spread to other parts of the country. More than 500 years ago, Spanish explorers and conquistadors brought the language to the New World.

Here's a news flash: In what is now the United States, Spanish was spoken many years before English was. If you remember your American history class, you'll think back to 1513, when Spaniard Ponce de León arrived in present-day Florida. Not until almost a hundred years later did the English establish their first permanent settlement, at Jamestown, Virginia.

FACT

Spanish questions are introduced with an inverted question mark (¿); Spanish exclamations are introduced with an inverted exclamation point (¡).

Even after English rule was established and its language adopted, Spanish influence permeated the colonies—and continues to do so. Today, Spanish is the second most common language in the United States, owing in large part to the influx of immigrants from the Spanish-speaking countries to the south and to increased commerce with these countries.

In many cases, Spanish words have been adopted into English with few changes. Some words, like patio, pimento, desperado, and mantilla, didn't change at all. Others, like guitar (from the Spanish *guitarra*) and ranch (from *rancho*) have so few changes that an English-speaking person can easily translate the word from its original form.

Commonly Used Spanish Terms

adiós	goodbye
¡Ay, caramba!	an expression of surprise, dread, displeasure, or disapproval
barrio	a Spanish-speaking neighborhood in a U.S. city
carne	meat
¿Cómo estás?	How are you?
¿Cómo se llama?	What's your name?
dinero	money
El Niño	a warming of the ocean surface that affects weather in many parts of the world
embarcadero	boat dock or pier
fandango	a type of music and dance
grande	large
gringo	any North American person, regardless of race
hacienda	a ranch-style country home
Hasta la vista	See you later
Hasta mañana	See you tomorrow
Hola	Hello
hombre	a man
mano a mano	(literally, "hand to hand") a face-to-face competition
Mi casa es su casa	literally, "My house is your house"; make yourself at home
nada	nothing
No comprende	I don't understand
no problema	although this is an incorrect usage of *no hay problema*, it's widely used in the United States to mean "no problem"
¿Qué pasa?	What's going on? What's up?

Que sera, sera	loosely translated "whatever will be, will be"
rodeo	a sport highlighting cowboy skills
¡Salud!	Cheers! (said when giving a toast)
siesta	a nap
Vamanos	Let's go
Vaya con Dios	Go with God

One of the most common contemporary influences of Spanish comes in Mexican, Tex-Mex, and Spanish cooking, which is popular in almost every area of the United States. Foods and drinks from these cuisines have become so commonplace that we hardly think that they're of Spanish origin. This includes tasty delights like tacos, tamales, tapas, paella, tortillas, chili con carne, enchiladas, guacamole, huevos rancheros, tequila, and sangria.

The French Connection

Picture this: You're sipping café au lait and nibbling on the specialty du jour. Since you want to stay au courant in haute couture, you open the newspaper and begin reading about a tête-à-tête between a famous femme fatale and a designer with great savoir-faire. You eagerly read on, and you understand what's being said because you're in the know about French terms that have made their way into everyday English.

Commonly Used French Terms

à la carte	ordering and paying for dishes separately in a restaurant
à la mode	fashionable; on a menu, "with ice cream"
à la	in the manner of
à propos	about, concerning
apéritif	a drink before a meal
attaché	a person assigned to a diplomatic staff; a carrying case
au contraire	on the contrary
au courant	up-to-date

au gratin	with cheese
au jus	in the meat's juice
au pair	a nanny
au poivre	with pepper
Bon appétit!	Enjoy your meal
bon vivant	person devoted to the sensuous things in life, especially good food and drink
bonne chance!	good luck
café au lait	coffee with milk
carte blanche	with complete and unlimited authority
coup de grâce	disastrous event or decisive act that brings about a far-reaching change
couture	high fashion
cul-de-sac	a street that has no outlet
de rigueur	required, obligatory
double entendre	a word or phrase with two meanings; usually one of the meanings is sexual
du jour	of the day
fiancé	someone engaged to be married; **fiancé** is male ; **fiancée** is female
faux	false
faux pas	social blunder
haute cuisine	food prepared in an elegant way
hors d'oeuvre	an appetizer
nom de plume	an author's pseudonym
raison d'être	purpose for existence
savoir-faire	the ability to speak or act appropriately in any situation
tête-à-tête	a private meeting
touché	an acknowledgement that another person has made a valuable point or criticism

French cuisine is famous the world over, and many of its terms are used in U.S. cookbooks. If you see cooking terms you're uncertain about, try the glossaries at

tinyurl.com/23doh9   tinyurl.com/yux6la
tinyurl.com/ypflt9

French, a Romance language spoken by millions of people worldwide, is the official language of thirty countries and of many international organizations. In the United States, French is the second most commonly studied foreign language (behind Spanish), and it's often heard in Louisiana, Maine, New Hampshire, and Vermont. You'll frequently see or hear French words and phrases, and some of the most commonly used phrases are listed in this section.

Achtung!—Paying Attention to German

In the United States, German immigrants often retained their mother tongue long after they settled here. That, however, changed with the anti-German sentiments connected with both World War I and World War II. Today, German linguistic influence can still be seen and heard in Pennsylvania (where Amish, Mennonites, and other sects speak Pennsylvania Dutch, a form of German), as well as in several states in mid-America and in metropolitan cities.

Interestingly, fifteen times as many German students study English compared to U.S. students who study German.

Commonly Used German Terms

Achtung!	Attention!
Angst	intense anxiety
Arbeit macht frei	Work will set you free
auf Wiedersehen	goodbye; until we meet again
Autobahn	motorway

Blitzkrieg	the German air bombing of London during World War II; now (with a lowercase *b*), any quick attack
danke	thank you
Deutschland	the German name for Germany
Doppelgänger	the ghostly counterpart of a living person; a double, an alter ego, or even another person who has the same name.
Ersatz	substitute, replacement, imitation
Führer	leader; usually refers to Adolph Hitler, who bestowed the title of Führer on himself in 1934
Geist	mind, spirit, or ghost; drive or motivation
Gestapo	literally, "secret state police"; the secret police force of Nazi Germany
Gesundheit	usually said after a person sneezes, this wishes the person good health
Hausfrau	housewife
Herr	sir, Mr.
jawohl	yes; of course
Kaffeeklatsch	a casual meeting for coffee and conversation
Kitsch	materials, often mass-produced, with overblown, sentimental, or tacky design
Kristallnacht	the night of November 9–10, 1938, a night of extreme violence against Jews
Lederhosen	leather trousers associated with Bavarian culture
Luftwaffe	the German Air Force during World War II
Meister	master of some sort of art or profession
Nazi	an abbreviation of the word **Na**tionalso**zi**alist; a follower or member of Hitler's National Socialist German Workers' Party (1933–45)
Poltergeist	a noisy ghost or spirit

Reich	realm, empire; usually used to refer to the Third Reich (Nazi Germany)
Schadenfreude	pleasure due to others' misfortune
über	super, over, about, superior
verboten	forbidden
Wehrmacht	German armed forces of the Third Reich
Wunderkind	child prodigy
Zeitgeist	spirit or climate of an era

German food and festivities have had a huge effect in the United States (have you ever visited an Octoberfest?). Americans heartily enjoy such German dishes as bratwurst, kohlrabi, kraut, liverwurst, muesli, pretzels, sauerkraut, strudel, wieners, wiener schnitzel, and even hamburgers and frankfurters, which are named after the German cities of Hamburg and Frankfurt.

FACT

Why do we say *"Gesundheit"* after a sneeze? Ancient Romans thought the soul left the body through the nose at death, and therefore powerful sneezing might be a harbinger of a life-threatening condition. Sneezing made a person open to evil spirits, and saying *"Gesundheit"* helped keep the spirits away. At the time of the bubonic plague, saying *"Gesundheit"* was employed as a method of driving off an infection.

Now, is your mouth watering? Maybe you'd like to whet your whistle with a pilsner, a spritzer, or lager in a stein—all of these are also German terms.

For the Italian in All of Us

In spite of Italian Christopher Columbus and his discoveries in the late 1400s, emigration from Italy to the Americas didn't reach full swing until almost four hundred years later. Many of the immigrants came during the

Great Migration (1880–1922), when they could find work easily and buy land cheaply. When Italians did begin to come—mama mia!—their influence took an immediate hold. Today, the U.S. Census Bureau says Italian-Americans comprise the fifth-largest ethnic group in the country.

Commonly Used Italian Terms

a capella	without musical accompaniment
al dente	slightly underdone; cooked firm but not soft
al fresco	dining outdoors
allegro	a quick and lively tempo
bambino	child
brio	vigor, vivacity, spirit
cantata	a musical composition (often sacred)
ciao	goodbye
cognoscente	someone having superior or refined taste
con	with
crescendo	gradually becoming louder
diva	a female opera singer; now also denoting a difficult-to-work-with star
finale	the final movement; in nonmusical terms, conclusion
forte	loud; in nonmusical terms, a person's strength or specialty
graffiti	(usually illegal) drawings made on walls or other surfaces
gusto	enthusiastic zeal
incognito	in disguise
largo	slow (musical term)
libretto	the text of an opera
lingua franca	a common or standard language between peoples
Machiavellian	having qualities like the Italian philosopher Niccolò Machiavelli, who wrote about expediency, craftiness, and dishonesty

Mafia	an organized crime syndicate in the United States and Italy
manifesto	a public declaration of principles or policy
molto	very
omertà	a code of silence in the Mafia
paparazzi	freelance photographers who sell pictures of celebrities to magazines and newspapers
pianissimo	very soft (musical term)
primo	the first; the best; the ultimate
quasi	resembling; in the style of
simpatico	compatible, physically pleasing

Food and drink are an integral part of Italian culture. Coffee drinks like espresso and cappuccino have become everyday necessities for many Americans, and Italian wines—whether created by big-name brewers or local villagers—have their devotees as well.

The food that complements the wine is even more famous. Pizza, of course, has become the food of choice for many Americans. Many pasta-based dishes (we'll skip the controversy about whether or not pasta originated in Italy) and other Italian favorites have become part and parcel of American households: spaghetti and marinara sauce, chicken marsala, beef carpaccio, penne with sauce, risotto, salami, bruschetta, panini, calzone, cannelloni, ravioli, prosciutto, tiramisu and gelato.

Come Together Right Now: Other Languages

Most documents written in English are, in fact, infused with terms from many other languages, languages of both Native Americans and immigrants. Settlers adopted Native American words for many discoveries—new places, new animals, new foods. Immigrants brought countless words from their homelands, then made those words part of their new community and therefore part of their new land. In fact, you'd be hard-pressed to find any language that has not sneaked at least one term into everyday English. The following are some of the more commonplace terms from a number of other languages.

Other Commonly Used Foreign Terms

agape	(Greek) spiritual, not sexual, love
aloha	(Hawaiian) a greeting used for both "hello" and "goodbye"; also a general term referring to affection, love, peace, and well-being
anime	(Japanese) a style of cartoon animation; interestingly, the Japanese word began as an abbreviation of the English word "animation"
apartheid	(Afrikaans) a former racial segregation policy in South Africa
bonsai	(Japanese) a short, ornamental tree grown in a small pot
donnybrook	(Irish) a public brawl; a free-for-all
Erin go Bragh!	(Irish) Ireland forever
ethos	(Greek) a set of values held by a person, group, or community
eureka	(Greek) an expression used in showing success or finding delight upon a discovery
fjord	(Norwegian) a narrow inlet of the sea, set between steep cliffs
glasnost	(Russian) an open and frank discussion
hoi polloi	(Greek) the common people
igloo	(Inuit) a dome-shaped structure or building, especially one built of packed snow
kosher	(Yiddish) keeping strict to dietary laws; slang, legitimate or authentic
kudos	(Greek) praise, approval
manga	(Japanese) a form of comic book or graphic novel
muumuu	(Hawaiian) a loose Hawaiian dress
ombudsman	(Swedish) a person appointed to investigate complaints
Oy, vey	(Yiddish) an expression of dismay or hurt

sauna	(Finnish) a small room or house to sit in and take advantage of wet or dry heat
schlep	(Yiddish) to haul or drag something
schmooze	(Yiddish) to make small talk
shtick	(Yiddish) the comic theme or gimmick
smörgåsbord	(Swedish) a buffet of dishes
spiel	(Yiddish) a speech usually intended to plead a case
taboo	(Polynesian) forbidden, banned
tsunami	(Japanese) a devastatingly large wave
ylang-ylang	(Tagalog) an aromatic tree; the oil or perfume from the tree

Checkpoint

Look at the words in bold print and then substitute the appropriate terms from this chapter. Check your answers in Appendix D.

Detective Darnetta Foster was **in disguise** _____ as she sat in the bar. This was a dangerous mission, and she reminded herself that she needed both **coolness under pressure** _____ and **the ability to speak or act appropriately in any situation** _____. Looking slyly at the people around her, Darnetta noted an Italian mother rocking her **child** _____ and saying **goodbye** _____ to a German **housewife** _____, an Irish man sporting an **"Ireland Forever"** _____ button, and a Hawaiian couple who were saying **a greeting used for both "hello" and "goodbye."** _____ None of these people figured into Darnetta's **number one** _____ problem: discovering clues about the recent robberies in town. (You finish the story.)

_____

_____

_____

_____

999 of the Most Commonly Misspelled Words

1. abdicate
2. absence
3. academically
4. accelerator
5. accessible
6. acclaim
7. acclimated
8. accommodate
9. accompanied
10. accomplish
11. accordion
12. accumulate
13. achievement
14. acknowledge
15. acoustics
16. acquaintance
17. acquitted
18. acute
19. adequately
20. adjacent
21. adjective
22. admission
23. admittance
24. adolescent
25. adultery
26. advantageous
27. adverb
28. advertisement
29. aerial
30. aerobic
31. aggravate
32. algebraic
33. alleged
34. allegiance
35. alliance
36. alliteration
37. allotting
38. almanac
39. already
40. altogether
41. amateur
42. ambassador
43. among
44. analogy
45. analysis
46. analyze
47. anecdote
48. angle
49. annihilate
50. annual
51. annul
52. antagonist
53. antithesis
54. apartheid
55. apartment
56. apologetically
57. apparatus
58. apparent
59. appearance
60. appositive
61. aptitude
62. arguing
63. argument
64. arrangement
65. ascend
66. aspirin
67. assessment
68. associative
69. assonance
70. asterisk
71. atheist
72. athletics
73. attendance
74. attitude
75. autumn
76. auxiliary
77. awfully
78. bachelor

79. balance
80. ballet
81. balloon
82. bankruptcy
83. barbarian
84. barbaric
85. barbecue
86. barbiturate
87. bargain
88. basically
89. battalion
90. bazaar
91. beautiful
92. beggar
93. beginning
94. behavior
95. beneficial
96. benefited
97. bilingual
98. biography
99. biscuit
100. bisect
101. bizarre
102. blasphemy
103. bologna
104. bookkeeper
105. bouillon
106. boulevard
107. boundary
108. boycott
109. bracelet
110. brackets
111. buffet
112. buoyant
113. bureaucrat
114. burial
115. calculation
116. camouflage
117. candidate
118. cantaloupe
119. caramel
120. caravan
121. carburetor
122. caricature
123. caring
124. cartographer
125. catalyst
126. catapult
127. catastrophe

128. category
129. cellar
130. centimeters
131. chagrined
132. challenge
133. changeable
134. changing
135. character
136. characteristic
137. chassis
138. chastise
139. chocolate
140. chord
141. chrome
142. chromosome
143. chunky
144. cigarette
145. cinquain
146. circumference
147. circumstantial
148. citizen
149. cliché
150. climbed
151. cliques
152. coefficient
153. coherence
154. coincide
155. collectible
156. colonel
157. colony
158. colossal
159. column
160. coming
161. commingle
162. commission
163. commitment
164. committed
165. committee
166. communication
167. commutative
168. comparative
169. compatible
170. compelled
171. competent
172. competition
173. complementary
174. completely
175. complexion
176. composite

177. concede
178. conceit
179. conceivable
180. conceive
181. condemn
182. condescend
183. conferred
184. congratulations
185. congruent
186. conjunction
187. connoisseur
188. conscience
189. conscientious
190. conscious
191. consensus
192. consequences
193. consistency
194. consolidator
195. consonance
196. constitution
197. consumer
198. continuous
199. contraction
200. controlled
201. controller
202. controversial
203. controversy
204. convection
205. convenient
206. coolly
207. coordinates
208. corollary
209. corporation
210. correlate
211. correspondence
212. counselor
213. courteous
214. courtesy
215. criticism
216. criticize
217. crowded
218. crucifixion
219. cruelty
220. curriculum
221. curtail
222. cyclical
223. cylinder
224. dachshund
225. daughter

226. debacle
227. decadent
228. decagon
229. deceit
230. deep-seated
231. deferential
232. deferred
233. definitely
234. dependent
235. depose
236. descend
237. describe
238. description
239. desirable
240. despair
241. desperate
242. detrimental
243. devastation
244. develop
245. development
246. diagonal
247. diameter
248. dictionary
249. difference
250. dilettante
251. diligence
252. dimension
253. dining
254. disappearance
255. disappoint
256. disastrous
257. discipline
258. discrimination
259. disdainfully
260. disguise
261. dispel
262. dispensable
263. dissatisfied
264. disservice
265. distinguish
266. diversified
267. dormitory
268. drugged
269. drunkenness
270. easily
271. economy
272. ecosystem
273. ecstasy
274. efficiency

275. eighth
276. either
277. electrolyte
278. electromagnet
279. elegy
280. elevation
281. eligible
282. eliminate
283. ellipsis
284. embarrass
285. emigrate
286. eminent
287. emperor
288. emphasize
289. empire
290. employee
291. empty
292. enamel
293. encouragement
294. encouraging
295. endeavor
296. enemy
297. enormous
298. enthusiastically
299. entirely
300. entrance
301. equality
302. equator
303. equipped
304. espionage
305. espresso
306. essential
307. exaggerate
308. excellence
309. excess
310. exercise
311. exhaustion
312. exhibition
313. exhilarate
314. expansion
315. experience
316. experiment
317. exponent
318. expression
319. extinct
320. extraneous
321. extremely
322. extrovert
323. exuberance

324. factor
325. fallacious
326. fallacy
327. familiarize
328. fantasy
329. fascinate
330. fascination
331. fascism
332. favorite
333. feasible
334. federation
335. feisty
336. felicity
337. feminine
338. fiction
339. fictitious
340. financially
341. financier
342. fiscal
343. fission
344. fluent
345. forcibly
346. foreign
347. foresee
348. foreshadowing
349. forfeit
350. formula
351. forty
352. fourth
353. frantically
354. frequency
355. fudge
356. fulfill
357. fundamentally
358. galaxy
359. gauge
360. genius
361. geography
362. government
363. governor
364. grammatically
365. grandeur
366. graphic
367. grievous
368. grizzly
369. grocery
370. guarantee
371. guerrilla
372. guidance

373. gyration
374. handicapped
375. happily
376. harass
377. heinous
378. heist
379. hemorrhage
380. heredity
381. heritage
382. heroes
383. hesitancy
384. hexagon
385. hierarchy
386. hieroglyphics
387. hoping
388. horizontal
389. hospital
390. humorous
391. hygiene
392. hyperbole
393. hypocrisy
394. hypocrite
395. hypotenuse
396. hypothesis
397. ideally
398. idiom
399. idiomatic
400. idiosyncrasy
401. ignorance
402. illogical
403. imaginary
404. imitate
405. immediately
406. immigration
407. immortal
408. implement
409. inaudible
410. incidentally
411. incredible
412. indicted
413. indispensable
414. individually
415. inequality
416. inevitable
417. influential
418. information
419. ingenious
420. initially
421. initiative

422. innocent
423. innocuous
424. inoculate
425. instantaneous
426. institution
427. insurance
428. insurgency
429. intellectual
430. intelligence
431. intercede
432. interesting
433. interfered
434. interference
435. interjection
436. interminable
437. intermittent
438. interrogate
439. interrupt
440. intricate
441. introduce
442. introvert
443. invertebrate
444. irony
445. irrelevant
446. irresistible
447. irritable
448. isosceles
449. isthmus
450. jealousy
451. jewelry
452. journalism
453. judicial
454. jugular
455. kaleidoscope
456. kerosene
457. kindergarten
458. kinetic
459. laboratory
460. laborious
461. lapse
462. larynx
463. latitude
464. legitimate
465. length
466. lenient
467. liaison
468. library
469. license
470. lieutenant

471. lightning
472. likelihood
473. likely
474. limerick
475. lineage
476. liquefy
477. literature
478. llama
479. longitude
480. lose
481. lounge
482. lovely
483. luxury
484. lyric
485. magistrate
486. magnificence
487. mainland
488. maintain
489. malicious
490. manageable
491. manufacture
492. mariner
493. martyrdom
494. mass
495. mauve
496. meadow
497. mean
498. meanness
499. median
500. medieval
501. mediocre
502. melancholy
503. melodious
504. metallic
505. metaphor
506. mien
507. migratory
508. mileage
509. millennium
510. millionaire
511. miniature
512. minute
513. mischievous
514. misnomer
515. missile
516. misspelled
517. monarchy
518. mosquitoes
519. mundane

520. municipal
521. murmur
522. muscle
523. myriad
524. mysterious
525. myth
526. mythology
527. naive
528. narcissism
529. narrative
530. nationalism
531. naturally
532. necessary
533. necessity
534. neighbor
535. neurotic
536. neutral
537. neutron
538. nineteen
539. ninety
540. ninth
541. nonpareil
542. noticeable
543. novelist
544. nowadays
545. nuclear
546. nucleus
547. nuisance
548. nutrition
549. nutritious
550. oasis
551. obedience
552. obsolete
553. obstacle
554. obtuse
555. occasionally
556. occurred
557. occurrence
558. octagon
559. official
560. omission
561. omitted
562. onomatopoeia
563. opaque
564. opinion
565. opossum
566. opponent
567. opportunity
568. oppose

569. opposition
570. oppression
571. optimism
572. optimistic
573. orchestra
574. orchid
575. ordinarily
576. origin
577. originate
578. outrageous
579. overrun
580. oxymoron
581. pageant
582. pamphlet
583. panicky
584. panorama
585. paradox
586. paralysis
587. paralyze
588. parenting
589. parliament
590. particular
591. pastime
592. patronage
593. pavilion
594. peaceable
595. peasant
596. pedestal
597. peers
598. penetrate
599. penicillin
600. peninsula
601. pentagon
602. perceive
603. performance
604. perimeter
605. permanent
606. permissible
607. permitted
608. permutation
609. perpendicular
610. perseverance
611. persistence
612. personal
613. personality
614. personification
615. personnel
616. perspiration
617. persuasion

618. pessimistic
619. pharaoh
620. pharmaceutical
621. phenomenon
622. Philippines
623. philosophy
624. physical
625. physician
626. picnicking
627. pilgrimage
628. pitiful
629. pixie
630. pizzazz
631. placebo
632. plagiarism
633. plagiarize
634. plague
635. planning
636. plausible
637. playwright
638. pleasant
639. pneumonia
640. politician
641. polygon
642. polyhedron
643. portray
644. Portuguese
645. possession
646. possessive
647. possibility
648. postscript
649. potato
650. potatoes
651. power
652. practically
653. prairie
654. precede
655. precedence
656. precipitation
657. precision
658. predation
659. predicate
660. preference
661. preferred
662. prefix
663. prehistoric
664. premier
665. premiere
666. preparation

667. preposition	716. quibble	765. reservoir
668. prescription	717. quiescent	766. resistance
669. presence	718. quinine	767. resources
670. prestige	719. quintessentially	768. responsibility
671. presumption	720. quipster	769. responsibly
672. prevalent	721. quizzes	770. restaurant
673. prime	722. quorum	771. restoration
674. primitive	723. quotation	772. resume
675. prism	724. quotient	773. retaliate
676. privilege	725. radioactive	774. retrospect
677. probability	726. rampage	775. reveal
678. probably	727. rampant	776. rheumatism
679. probation	728. rampart	777. rhombus
680. procedure	729. rarefy	778. rhyme
681. proceed	730. ratio	779. rhythm
682. professor	731. realistically	780. rhythmical
683. prognosis	732. realize	781. ridiculous
684. prominent	733. realtor	782. rotary
685. pronounce	734. rebellion	783. rotations
686. pronunciation	735. recede	784. sacrifice
687. propaganda	736. receipt	785. sacrilegious
688. propagate	737. receive	786. safari
689. protagonist	738. receiving	787. safety
690. protein	739. reception	788. salami
691. proximity	740. recession	789. salary
692. psalm	741. reciprocals	790. sanitize
693. psychoanalysis	742. recognize	791. sarcasm
694. psychology	743. recommend	792. satellite
695. publicly	744. rectify	793. satire
696. pumpkin	745. reference	794. saturate
697. pursue	746. referred	795. scalene
698. puzzling	747. referring	796. scenery
699. pyramid	748. reflections	797. schedule
700. pyrotechnics	749. refraction	798. scholastic
701. quadrant	750. regiment	799. scrimmage
702. quadrilateral	751. rehearsal	800. secede
703. quadruple	752. reign	801. sediment
704. qualify	753. reimburse	802. segregate
705. qualms	754. reincarnation	803. segue
706. quandary	755. relieve	804. seismic
707. quantity	756. relieving	805. seismograph
708. quarantine	757. religious	806. seize
709. quell	758. remembrance	807. sensitive
710. quench	759. reminiscence	808. sensory
711. querulous	760. remittance	809. sentry
712. query	761. repetition	810. sequence
713. quest	762. representative	811. sergeant
714. questionnaire	763. repugnant	812. serpent
715. queue	764. resemblance	813. severely

814. shady
815. shameful
816. shanghai
817. shepherd
818. sherbet
819. sheriff
820. shining
821. shish kebab
822. shrewd
823. siege
824. significance
825. simian
826. similar
827. simile
828. siphon
829. situation
830. skeptical
831. skimp
832. skinned
833. soliloquy
834. sophomore
835. souvenir
836. spasmodic
837. specifically
838. specimen
839. sphere
840. sponsor
841. spontaneous
842. stalemate
843. stamen
844. statistic
845. statistics
846. statue
847. stimulus
848. stopped
849. straitjacket
850. strategy
851. strength
852. strenuous
853. stretch
854. stubbornness
855. studying
856. stupefy
857. subcontinent
858. submersible
859. subordinate
860. succeed
861. success
862. succession

863. sufficient
864. summary
865. summed
866. superintendent
867. supersede
868. supervisor
869. supplementary
870. supposed
871. supposition
872. suppress
873. surround
874. surroundings
875. susceptible
876. suspicious
877. sustenance
878. Swedish
879. swelter
880. syllable
881. symbolic
882. symmetrical
883. sympathy
884. symphonic
885. synchronize
886. syncopation
887. synonymous
888. synopsis
889. synthesize
890. syringe
891. tachometer
892. taciturn
893. talkative
894. tangent
895. tangible
896. tapestry
897. tariff
898. technical
899. technique
900. technology
901. temperamental
902. temperature
903. tenant
904. tendency
905. terminator
906. terrain
907. tertiary
908. themselves
909. theology
910. theoretical
911. theories

912. therefore
913. thermal
914. thermodynamic
915. thesaurus
916. thorough
917. though
918. thought
919. through
920. tolerance
921. tomorrow
922. tortoise
923. tournament
924. tourniquet
925. traffic
926. tragedy
927. transcend
928. transferring
929. transitory
930. transparent
931. trapezoid
932. tried
933. trough
934. trousers
935. truly
936. twelfth
937. tyranny
938. ukulele
939. unanimous
940. undoubtedly
941. universal
942. unmistakable
943. unnatural
944. unnecessary
945. unscrupulous
946. usually
947. utopian
948. vaccine
949. vacuum
950. vagabond
951. valedictory
952. valuable
953. variation
954. vaudeville
955. vehicle
956. vendor
957. veneer
958. vengeance
959. ventriloquist
960. venue

961. veracity
962. versatile
963. vestige
964. village
965. vinegar
966. violence
967. visage
968. visible
969. warrant
970. warring
971. warrior
972. watt
973. weather

974. welcome
975. wherever
976. whether
977. whisper
978. whistle
979. whittling
980. wholesome
981. withhold
982. woman
983. women
984. writing
985. written
986. wrongful

987. wrung
988. xylophone
989. yacht
990. yawn
991. yea
992. yeah
993. yuppie
994. zenith
995. zephyr
996. zinnia
997. zodiac
998. zoological
999. zoology

Root Words, Prefixes, and Suffixes

Root Words

Word	Definition	Examples
arch	ancient	archaeology
aster/astra	star	astronomy, astronaut
audi	hear	inaudible, auditorium
bio	life	biology, biography
brev	short	abbreviation, brevity
chron	time	synchronize, chronological
cred, credit	belief, faith, confidence	creditable, credit card
cycle	wheel, circle	motorcycle, tricycle
fix	fasten	suffix, fixative
geo	earth	geology, geometry
graph	write/draw	photography, paragraph
hydro	water	hydropower, hydrate
illus	draw, show	illusory, illustrative
legis, leg	law, write	legislature, illegible
log, logue	word, thought	monologue, illogical
nega	deny	negative, negate
op, oper	work	cooperation, operator
path	feeling	pathetic, sympathy, empathy
phil	love	philosophy, philanthropic

phon	voice, sound	telephone, phonetic
phys	body, nature	physics, physiology
psych	soul, mind	psyche, psychiatric
quar	four	quart, quarto
quint	five	quintet, quintuplet
science	knowledge	conscience, conscientiousness
scrib, script	write	scribble, manuscript
sex	six	sextet, sextuplet
tact	touch	intact, tactile
tele	far off, distant	telephone, television
ten	to hold	tenure, tenant
ter, terr	earth	extraterrestrial, terrain
urb	city	urban, urbane
val	true	valid, invalidate
verb	word	verbal, reverberate

Prefixes

Word	Definition	Examples
a-, an-	without, not	asocial, anachronism
ab-	away, away from	abnormal, abductor
ad-	to, toward, near	adhere, adductor
agri-, agrio-	fields	agriculture, agribusiness
ambul-	walk, move around	ambulatory, ambulance
ami-, amic-	friend	amicable, amity
amor-	love, loving, fondness for	amorous, amoral
amphi-	round, both sides	amphitheater, amphibian
anima-, anim-	life, breath, soul, mind	animate, animal
anni-, annu-	year, yearly	annual, annuity
ante-	before, prior to	antecedent, antebellum
anti-	against	antipathy, anticlimax
aqua-	water	aquarium, aqueous
auto-	self, directed from within	automatic, automated
bi-	two, double	bipartisan, biennial
cardio-	pertaining to the heart	cardiologist, cardiogram
carni-	flesh, meat	carnivorous, carnivore
centi-, cent-	hundred	centigrade, centipede
cinema-	set in motion, movement	cinematography, cinematic
circum-	around, surrounding	circumference, circumspect
co-	with, together, jointly	cooperate, co-owner

contra-, counter-	opposed, against	contradict, contrary
corp-, corpus-	body	corpse, corporation
cour-	heart	courage, courageous
cur-	heal, cure	curative, curable
curr-, curs-	run, go	curriculum, cursive
de-	away from, downward	dethrone, depart
deca-	ten	decimal, decathlon
dei-, div-	God	deity, divine
demos-	people	democracy, demographic
dent-	teeth	denture, dentist
dia-	across, through	diagonal, diagnosis
dis-	not, apart, reversal	disrespect, disinherit
do-, don-	gift	donation, donor
dominus-	lord	dominant, dominion
dorm-, dormi-	sleeping	dormitory, dormant
duo-, du-	two, a number	duplicate, duologue
dyna-, dyn-	power, strength, force	dynamite, dynamic
dys-	bad, harsh, disordered	dysfunction, dyslexia
eco-	house, household affairs	ecology
ego-	I, self	ego, egomaniac, egocentric
en-, em-	in, into, to cover or contain	encipher, embody
epi-	upon, above, over	epidermis, epitaph
ergo-, erg-	work	ergometer, ergonomics
etym-	truth, true meaning, real	etymology, etymologist
ex-	out of, former	exterior, extract
extra-	beyond, outside, external	extracurricular, extramural
fidel-	believe, belief, trust, faith	fidelity
fin-	end, last, limit, boundary	finality, infinity
fluct-	flow, wave	fluctuation, fluctuant
fortu-, fortun-	chance, fate, luck	fortune, fortunate
frater-	brother	fraternity, fratricide
grad-	walk, step, move around	graduate, gradual
grav-, griev-	heavy, weighty	gravity, grievous
helio-, heli-	sun	heliocentric, heliostat
hemi-	half	hemisphere, hemistich
hetero-	mixed, different, unlike	heterogeneous, heteronym
homo-	same, alike	homonym, homogeneous
hyper-	above, over, excessive	hyperventilate, hypercritical
hypo-	under, below, less than	hypoglycemia, hypoallergenic

ideo-	idea	ideology, ideal
idios-	one's own	idiom, idiosyncrasy
il-	not, in, into, within	illogical, illiterate
im-	not	impossible, imperceptible
in-	in	incorporate, induction
inter-	between, among	interact, Internet
intra-	within, inside	intramural, intravenous
jet-	throw, send, fling, cast, spurt	jettison, jetsam
kilo-, kil-	one thousand	kilogram, kilometer
lav-, lava-	wash, bathe	lavage, lavatory
lexis-	word	lexicon, lexicography
liber-	free, book	liberty, liberal
loc-	talk, speak, speech	locution
lumin-, lum-	shine	luminescence, luminaries
luna-	moon, light, shine	lunar, lunatic
macro-	large, great, enlarged	macroeconomics, macrobiotics
magni-, magn-	large, big, great	magnificence, magnify
mal-	bad, ill, wrong, abnormal	maladjusted, malfeasance
mega-	large, great, big, powerful	megavitamin, megalomania
micro-	small, tiny	microscope, microfiche
milli-	thousand	millimeter, milligram
mini-, minut-, minu-	small, little	minuscule, miniature
mis-	bad, badly	mistrust, misspell
miso-, mis-	hate, hater, hatred	misogamy, misogyny
mono-	one, alone	monocle, monogamy
mor-, mori-	death, dead	mortician, morbid
multi-	many, much	multinational, multiply
neo-, ne-	new, recent, current	neoclassical, neophyte
non-	not	nonessential, nonfiction
oligo-, olig-	few, abnormally small	oligarchy, oligopoly
omni-, omn-	all, every	omnipresent, omnipotent
pac-	calm, peaceful	pacify, pacific
pachy-, pach-	thick, dense, large, massive	pachyderm, pachytene
pan-	all, every, completely	pantheistic, pan-American
pater-	father	paternity, patricide
photo-	light	photosynthesis, photoelectric
poly-	many, much, excessive	polygamy, polymorphous
post-	after	postscript, posterior
pre-	before	pregame, prenuptial

pro-	before, in favor of, forward	project, pro-American
pyro-, pyr-	fire, burn	pyromania, pyrotechnics
re-	restore, back, again	reassemble, redirect
retro-	backward, behind, back	retrospective, retrofit
sed-	sit	sedate, sedentary
semi-	twice, half	semiannual, semicolon
soli-, sol-	one, alone, only	solitary, solo
sono-, son-, sona-	sound	supersonic
spec-	see, look, appear, examine	spectator, spectacles
stereo-, stere	solid, firm, three-dimensional	stereograph, stereoscope
sub-	under, beneath	subterranean, subway
super-, supra-, sur-	above, over, excessive	supermodel, surcharge
syn-, sym-	together, with, along with	synchronize, symmetry
tacho-, tach-	fast, swift, rapid acceleration	tachometer, tachyarrthythmia
thermo-, therm-	heat	thermometer, thermostat
trans-	across, on the other side	transport, transatlantic
ultra-	extreme, beyond	ultraconservative, ultralight
un-	not	unsanctioned, unorthodox
uni-	one, single	union, unicycle
xeno-, xen-	foreign, strange	xenophobia, xenolith
zoo-	animal, living being, life	zoo, zoolatry

Suffixes

Suffix	Definition	Examples
-able, -ible	able, likely, can do	capable, visible
-ade	act, action	blockade, renegade
-al	characterized by, pertaining to	national, directional
-an, -ian	native of, pertaining to	Martian, Kentuckian
-ance	quality or state of being	protuberance, parlance
-ancy	action, process, condition	hesitancy, infancy
-ant	someone who or something that	observant, savant
-arch	ruler, chief	monarch, matriarch
-ary	related to, connected with	budgetary, planetary
-ation	action, result	syncopation, navigation
-cian	possessing a particular skill	musician, physician
-cide	kill	homicide, pesticide
-cracy	rule	democracy, theocracy
-dom	state of being, realm, office	freedom, wisdom
-ee	one who receives action	employee, refugee

-eer	worker, one who does	auctioneer, profiteer
-en	made of, resembling, become	maiden, harden
-er, -or	one who, that which	weaver, dictator
-ery	skill	bravery, embroidery
-escent	in the process of, becoming	adolescent, quiescent
-esque	in the manner of, resembling	picturesque, Romanesque
-fic	making, causing	terrific, scientific
-ful	full of, characterized by	cheerful, wonderful
-hood	order, quality, state of being	falsehood, brotherhood
-ial	characterized, pertaining to	presidential, industrial
-ify	make, cause	purify, vilify
-ism	condition, manner	feminism, nationalism
-ist	one who, believer, does	elitist, biologist
-itis	inflammation, burning sensation	bursitis, phlebitis
-ity, -ty	state of, quality	captivity, adaptability
-less	without	groundless, penniless
-ment	act of, result, means	disappointment, statement
-ness	quality, degree, state of	forgiveness, happiness
-ology	study of	psychology, ideology
-osis	action, process, condition	hypnosis, tuberculosis
-ous	marked by, having quality of	courteous, fibrous
-phobia	fear of	claustrophobia, agoraphobia
-ship	state, quality	relationship, dictatorship
-wise	in the direction of	clockwise, crosswise
-y	full of	blossomy, muddy

Suggested Substitutes for Wordy Phrases

Wordy Phrase	Suggested Substitute
a number of	some, several
absolutely essential	essential
according to our data	we find
adequate number of	enough
adverse impact on	hurt, set back
ahead of schedule	early
along the lines of	like
already exist	exist
am of the opinion	think
are in receipt of	have
are of the same opinion	agree
as a consequence	because
as a means of	to
as long as	if, since
as prescribed by	in, under
as regards	about
as to whether	whether
as well as	and, also
at all times	always
at the conclusion of	after

at the end of	after
at this point in time	now
be aware of the fact that	know
both of these	both
brief in duration	brief
by the use of	using
cancel out	cancel
come to an agreement	agree
comply with	follow, obey
costs a total of, costs the sum of	costs
desirous of	want, desire
despite the fact that	although, though
did not succeed	failed
during the time that	when
each and every one	each, all
except when	unless
exhibits the ability to	can
for a period of	for
give an account of	describe
give an indication of	show
in a position to	can, may, will
in accordance with	by, following
in advance of	before
in all cases	always
in an effort to	to
in case	if
in close proximity to	near, close, about
in excess of	more than
in large measure	largely
in lieu of	for, instead of
in no case	never
in order to	to
in possession of	have
in respect of	for
in some cases	sometimes
in the absence of	without
in the amount of	for

in the context of	in, about
in the field of	in
in the form of	as
in the midst of	during, amid
in today's society	today
inasmuch as	since, because
incumbent upon	must
interface with	meet
is able to	can
is capable of	can
is in a position to	can
it's often the case that	often
limited number	few
make a decision	decide
make a purchase	buy
make an assumption	assume
manner in which	how
not later than	by
off of	off
on behalf of	for
on no occasion	never
on the occasion of	on
on the part of	by, for
one of the	a, an, one
period of time	period, time
provided that	if
put an end to	end
realize a savings of	save
refer to as	call, name, term
relating to	about, on
some of the	some
take action	act
take the place of	substitute
that being the case	therefore
the fact that	that
the overall plan	the plan

the reason for	because, since, why
to the extent that	as much as
to whatever extent	however
under the provisions of	under
use up	use
utmost perfection	perfection

Appendix D

Checkpoint Answers

Chapter 1

1. wizards
2. pennies
3. wives
4. oxen
5. deer
6. abundance
7. believe
8. defendant
9. environment
10. February
11. grammar
12. knowledge
13. rhythm
14. separate
15. villain

Chapter 2

1. B
2. A
3. B
4. A
5. B
6. B
7. A

Chapter 3

Using Guideline #3:

1. Chris's computer
2. Lois's chair
3. Mrs. Williams's hairstyle
4. Mr. Harris's house
5. Katherine Mears's cards.

Using Guideline #4:

1. Chris' computer
2. Lois' chair
3. Mrs. Williams' hairstyle
4. Mr. Harris' house
5. Katherine Mears' cards

Chapter 4

One way to correctly punctuate the story starter is this:

It all started because I was so tired. I had my chapter notes in front of me, and what I had written said, "Test Monday on chapters 3–6 (pages 48–194)." I opened my history book to page 48, where I saw a picture of Robert Fulton (1765–1815).

I certainly learned quite a number of interesting facts. Among them (this was on page 57) was this:

"It [the *Clermont*, Fulton's first boat] sped along at the amazing rate of five miles an our. [*sic*]"

Chapter 5

One way to correctly punctuate the story starter is this:

Janet kept trying to get to the right Internet site. The URL that she had written down was <http://www.help-me-out.edu/hrcc/macleroy/>, but she was unsuccessful every time she tried that site. She just knew that if she went to that site, she'd find the words to "The Star-Spangled Banner," and she needed those words in order to get extra credit in her music class.

She began humming to herself, "Oh, say, can you see, by the dawn's early light,/ . . . O'er the land of the free and the home of the brave."

Chapter 6

Tom Swifties

1. darkly
2. wholeheartedly
3. icily
4. speedily
5. lackadaisically
6. finally
7. hotly
8. movingly
9. gamely
10. bravely

Chapter 7

1. Subject: Gail, Leo; Predicate: seemed = (linking) verb; Complement: nervous = predicate adjective
2. Subject: they; Predicate: were = (linking) verb; Complement: candidates = predicate nominative; Subject: they; Predicate: felt = (linking) verb
3. Subject: Gail; Predicate: called = verb; Complement: Leo = direct object
4. Subject: Gail; Predicate: is = (linking) verb
5. Subject: I; Predicate: will give = verb; Complement: you = indirect object; ride = direct object

6. Subject: need; Predicate: is = (linking) verb
7. Subject: I; Predicate: do have = verb; Complement: news = direct object

Chapter 8

1. A
2. H
3. J
4. D
5. I
6. G
7. B

Chapter 9

Problems with Pronouns

Here's one way that the story could be corrected:

Kerri received two letters today, one from Theresa and one from Vera. Kerri was happy to read that Vera would be coming for a visit soon. Vera's letter also mentioned that she [it's okay to use this pronoun since *she* has already been identified] would be bringing Andrea, somebody whom Kerri had never met. Kerri thought that the three of them could expect to have some fun-filled times because they [it's okay to use this pronoun since there's a clear reference whom *they* refers to] were all people who were always up for some kind of adventure.

More Problems with Pronouns

Here's one way the story could be corrected:

Looking out over the lake, Sarah was amazed to find that she and her sister seemed to be alone.

"It looks as if we two are the only ones still out. I saw Jody and Juan out in their boat just a few minutes ago. In fact, it was she who was rowing. Now I wonder what's happened to Jody and him." Sarah mused.

"Oh, I wouldn't worry about them. He and she both said they were getting hungry and would probably head for shore. But if you want to try to beat them, I know you can row faster than she."

Who? Whom?

1. Whom
2. whom
3. Who
4. whom
5. Who
6. Who
7. Who
8. Whom
9. whom
10. Who

Chapter 10

The reporter had just ~~bursted~~ **burst** on the scene, but already he could tell that the atmosphere was ~~more edgier~~ **edgier** than he had anticipated. He stopped some of the neighbors who were standing around and ~~sayed~~ **said**, "Is this the most ~~excitingest~~ **exciting** thing that's ever happened here on Elm Street?"

Mrs. Atcheson, one of the women in the group, turned to the reporter and said, "This ~~ain't~~ **is** nothing! You should have been here last week when two burglars ~~was~~ **were** holed up in my chimney. The ~~fattest~~ **fatter** one kept screaming for help, and the ~~skinniest~~ **skinnier** one kept whispering to him that he should be quiet."

Chapter 11

Here is one of several ways to make the sentences parallel:

Studying long hours, giving up fun-filled time with friends, and drinking lots of coffee were my habits when I was in school. My favorite classes were ancient Greek, quantum physics, advanced chemistry, and microbiology. At that time in my life, reading compelling subject matter was more important to me than playing cards with the rest of the gang. I wanted to get good grades, to retain my scholarship, and to work part-time at a job that would help my future career. I wanted not only to impress my instructors, but also to impress my boss. Because of this, I worked and studied industriously. I was constantly worried that my scholarship money would evaporate, that I'd lose my job, and that one of my coworkers would hamper my future career.

Chapter 12

I used to be better at saying no. I was supposed to be writing a report, but two friends called and asked if I wanted to go spelunking, which they had to explain meant exploring in caves.

Agreeing to go along with my friends, who were not experienced spelunkers, was my first mistake. When we got to the cave, there was a huge rock blocking the entrance. At first the rock seemed to be stationary, but using all the strength we had we were finally able to move it slowly and get inside. It was then that I should have left and gone home, but I didn't know whether my friends would be disappointed in me if I left them. My sole reason for staying was to keep face with them, and so the three of us formed a little spelunking troop and set off to explore.

Staying in the cave was my second mistake. When we were fairly deep inside, I became fascinated with a stalagmite that was shaped like a throne and decided to take a break and sit on it for a while. At that point, I realized I was hungry and decided to try to convince my friends that we should stop and eat the lunches we had brought.

Chapter 13

Sports Clichés

1. You'll be hearing *a lot from him*
2. They can really shoot *the three* or *from downtown*.
3. Nothing but *net*

Political Clichés

1. It's time for *a change* or *a new beginning*, or *real leadership*
2. This is turning into *a smear campaign* or *character assassination*
3. You have to question *the timing of this story*.

Chapter 14

Answers will vary.

Chapter 15

1. Her neighbors' cat bit the four-year-old child.
2. The doctor's assistant read the medical test results.
3. Julia approaches this problem in three different ways.
4. My new guitar is beside the chair.
5. Within five minutes of the accident, six police officers arrived on the scene.
6. Our ancestors certainly do not get the credit they deserve.
7. In the last fifteen years, many synthetic materials have come under scrutiny.

Chapter 16

Sentence that should be cut: "I was late because I hadn't felt well the night before and I'd forgotten to set the alarm clock."

Chapter 17

Possible answers:

1. The car sped/inched/crept up the hill.
2. Alfred is sneaking/running/charging around the corner.
3. Bobbie announced/whispered/screamed that she was leaving.

Chapter 18

1. understatement
2. allusion
3. onomatopoeia
4. cliché (also hyperbole)
5. simile
6. consonance
7. hyperbole
8. alliteration
9. metaphor
10. assonance

Chapter 19

to a nauseating extent = ad naseum

that is = i.e.

not of sane mind = non compos mentis

school from which he'd graduated = alma mater

about = circa

pounds = lb.

academic conference = symposium

Chapter 20

in disguise = incognito

coolness under pressure = sang-froid

the ability to speak or act appropriately in any situation = savoir-faire

child = bambino

goodbye = ciao

housewife= hausfrau

Ireland Forever = Erin Go Bragh

a greeting used for both "hello" and "goodbye" = aloha

number one = número uno

Index

subjects of. *See* Subjects

tenses of. *See* Tenses

Virgule/solidus/slash, 60–61

Voice, for writing, 155, 157, 211, 238, 246, 270, 330

W

Who and *whom*, 128–31, 132, 329

Wordiness, 207–8, 323–26

Words

choosing, 212, 238

commonly confused or misused, 184–200

homophone errors, 213–14

transitional phrases and, 180–84, 213, 237

Writing

anticipating audience, 229–30

asking questions to start, 221–22

bad, contest examples, 243–45

big-picture view, 234–35

brainstorming and, 219–21

Checkpoints, 231–32, 246, 260, 271, 330

choosing words, 211, 238

clustering or mapping, 222–23

common mistakes, 210–15, 309–16. *See also*

Sentence construction problems

defining purpose of, 227–28

first drafts, 226–31

freewriting sessions, 218–19

gender-based generalities and, 239–40

outlines, 223–26

paragraph construction. *See* Paragraphs

preliminary steps, 218–23

pronoun use, 237. *See also* Pronouns

proofreading, 213, 241–43

reviewing and revising, 234–41

sentences. *See Sentence construction references*

styles, 230–31

voice for, 155, 157, 211, 238, 246, 270, 330

Writing types and styles

abstracts, 252–53

argument essays, 262–63

autobiographical narratives, 266–67

business and technical writing, 253–54

cause-and-effect essays, 254–55

compare-and-contrast papers, 255–56

critical analysis papers, 263–64

description essays, 265–66

e-mail messages, 268–71

five-paragraph essay, 249–52

journals, 264–65

opinion pieces, 267–68

précis, 256–57

process papers, 257–58

research papers, 258–60

short papers, 248–53

single paragraphs, 248–49

THE EVERYTHING SERIES!

BUSINESS & PERSONAL FINANCE

Everything® Accounting Book
Everything® Budgeting Book
Everything® Business Planning Book
Everything® Coaching and Mentoring Book, 2nd Ed.
Everything® Fundraising Book
Everything® Get Out of Debt Book
Everything® Grant Writing Book
Everything® Guide to Foreclosures
Everything® Guide to Personal Finance for Single Mothers
Everything® Home-Based Business Book, 2nd Ed.
Everything® Homebuying Book, 2nd Ed.
Everything® Homeselling Book, 2nd Ed.
Everything® Improve Your Credit Book
Everything® Investing Book, 2nd Ed.
Everything® Landlording Book
Everything® Leadership Book
Everything® Managing People Book, 2nd Ed.
Everything® Negotiating Book
Everything® Online Auctions Book
Everything® Online Business Book
Everything® Personal Finance Book
Everything® Personal Finance in Your 20s and 30s Book
Everything® Project Management Book
Everything® Real Estate Investing Book
Everything® Retirement Planning Book
Everything® Robert's Rules Book, $7.95
Everything® Selling Book
Everything® Start Your Own Business Book, 2nd Ed.
Everything® Wills & Estate Planning Book

COOKING

Everything® Barbecue Cookbook
Everything® Bartender's Book, 2nd Ed., $9.95
Everything® Calorie Counting Cookbook
Everything® Cheese Book
Everything® Chinese Cookbook
Everything® Classic Recipes Book
Everything® Cocktail Parties & Drinks Book
Everything® College Cookbook
Everything® Cooking for Baby and Toddler Book
Everything® Cooking for Two Cookbook
Everything® Diabetes Cookbook
Everything® Easy Gourmet Cookbook
Everything® Fondue Cookbook
Everything® Fondue Party Book
Everything® Gluten-Free Cookbook
Everything® Glycemic Index Cookbook
Everything® Grilling Cookbook
Everything® Healthy Meals in Minutes Cookbook
Everything® Holiday Cookbook

Everything® Indian Cookbook
Everything® Italian Cookbook
Everything® Low-Carb Cookbook
Everything® Low-Cholesterol Cookbook
Everything® Low-Fat High-Flavor Cookbook
Everything® Low-Salt Cookbook
Everything® Meals for a Month Cookbook
Everything® Mediterranean Cookbook
Everything® Mexican Cookbook
Everything® No Trans Fat Cookbook
Everything® One-Pot Cookbook
Everything® Pizza Cookbook
Everything® Quick and Easy 30-Minute,
          5-Ingredient Cookbook
Everything® Quick Meals Cookbook
Everything® Slow Cooker Cookbook
Everything® Slow Cooking for a Crowd Cookbook
Everything® Soup Cookbook
Everything® Stir-Fry Cookbook
Everything® Sugar-Free Cookbook
Everything® Tapas and Small Plates Cookbook
Everything® Tex-Mex Cookbook
Everything® Thai Cookbook
Everything® Vegetarian Cookbook
Everything® Wild Game Cookbook
Everything® Wine Book, 2nd Ed.

GAMES

Everything® 15-Minute Sudoku Book, $9.95
Everything® 30-Minute Sudoku Book, $9.95
Everything® Bible Crosswords Book, $9.95
Everything® Blackjack Strategy Book
Everything® Brain Strain Book, $9.95
Everything® Bridge Book
Everything® Card Games Book
Everything® Card Tricks Book, $9.95
Everything® Casino Gambling Book, 2nd Ed.
Everything® Chess Basics Book
Everything® Craps Strategy Book
Everything® Crossword and Puzzle Book
Everything® Crossword Challenge Book
Everything® Crosswords for the Beach Book, $9.95
Everything® Cryptic Crosswords Book, $9.95
Everything® Cryptograms Book, $9.95
Everything® Easy Crosswords Book
Everything® Easy Kakuro Book, $9.95
Everything® Easy Large-Print Crosswords Book
Everything® Games Book, 2nd Ed.
Everything® Giant Sudoku Book, $9.95
Everything® Kakuro Challenge Book, $9.95
Everything® Large-Print Crossword Challenge Book
Everything® Large-Print Crosswords Book
Everything® Lateral Thinking Puzzles Book, $9.95

Everything® Literary Crosswords Book, $9.95
Everything® Mazes Book
Everything® Memory Booster Puzzles Book, $9.95
Everything® Movie Crosswords Book, $9.95
Everything® Music Crosswords Book, $9.95
Everything® Online Poker Book, $12.95
Everything® Pencil Puzzles Book, $9.95
Everything® Poker Strategy Book
Everything® Pool & Billiards Book
Everything® Puzzles for Commuters Book, $9.95
Everything® Sports Crosswords Book, $9.95
Everything® Test Your IQ Book, $9.95
Everything® Texas Hold 'Em Book, $9.95
Everything® Travel Crosswords Book, $9.95
Everything® TV Crosswords Book, $9.95
Everything® Word Games Challenge Book
Everything® Word Scramble Book
Everything® Word Search Book

HEALTH

Everything® Alzheimer's Book
Everything® Diabetes Book
Everything® Health Guide to Adult Bipolar Disorder
Everything® Health Guide to Arthritis
Everything® Health Guide to Controlling Anxiety
Everything® Health Guide to Fibromyalgia
Everything® Health Guide to Menopause
Everything® Health Guide to OCD
Everything® Health Guide to PMS
Everything® Health Guide to Postpartum Care
Everything® Health Guide to Thyroid Disease
Everything® Hypnosis Book
Everything® Low Cholesterol Book
Everything® Nutrition Book
Everything® Reflexology Book
Everything® Stress Management Book

HISTORY

Everything® American Government Book
Everything® American History Book, 2nd Ed.
Everything® Civil War Book
Everything® Freemasons Book
Everything® Irish History & Heritage Book
Everything® Middle East Book
Everything® World War II Book, 2nd Ed.

HOBBIES

Everything® Candlemaking Book
Everything® Cartooning Book
Everything® Coin Collecting Book
Everything® Drawing Book

Everything® Family Tree Book, 2nd Ed.
Everything® Knitting Book
Everything® Knots Book
Everything® Photography Book
Everything® Quilting Book
Everything® Sewing Book
Everything® Soapmaking Book, 2nd Ed.
Everything® Woodworking Book

HOME IMPROVEMENT

Everything® Feng Shui Book
Everything® Feng Shui Decluttering Book, $9.95
Everything® Fix-It Book
Everything® Green Living Book
Everything® Home Decorating Book
Everything® Home Storage Solutions Book
Everything® Homebuilding Book
Everything® Organize Your Home Book, 2nd Ed.

KIDS' BOOKS

All titles are $7.95

Everything® Kids' Animal Puzzle & Activity Book
Everything® Kids' Baseball Book, 4th Ed.
Everything® Kids' Bible Trivia Book
Everything® Kids' Bugs Book
Everything® Kids' Cars and Trucks Puzzle and Activity Book
Everything® Kids' Christmas Puzzle & Activity Book
Everything® Kids' Cookbook
Everything® Kids' Crazy Puzzles Book
Everything® Kids' Dinosaurs Book
Everything® Kids' Environment Book
Everything® Kids' Fairies Puzzle and Activity Book
Everything® Kids' First Spanish Puzzle and Activity Book
Everything® Kids' Gross Cookbook
Everything® Kids' Gross Hidden Pictures Book
Everything® Kids' Gross Jokes Book
Everything® Kids' Gross Mazes Book
Everything® Kids' Gross Puzzle & Activity Book
Everything® Kids' Halloween Puzzle & Activity Book
Everything® Kids' Hidden Pictures Book
Everything® Kids' Horses Book
Everything® Kids' Joke Book
Everything® Kids' Knock Knock Book
Everything® Kids' Learning Spanish Book
Everything® Kids' Magical Science Experiments Book
Everything® Kids' Math Puzzles Book
Everything® Kids' Mazes Book
Everything® Kids' Money Book
Everything® Kids' Nature Book
Everything® Kids' Pirates Puzzle and Activity Book
Everything® Kids' Presidents Book
Everything® Kids' Princess Puzzle and Activity Book
Everything® Kids' Puzzle Book
Everything® Kids' Racecars Puzzle and Activity Book
Everything® Kids' Riddles & Brain Teasers Book
Everything® Kids' Science Experiments Book
Everything® Kids' Sharks Book

Everything® Kids' Soccer Book
Everything® Kids' Spies Puzzle and Activity Book
Everything® Kids' States Book
Everything® Kids' Travel Activity Book

KIDS' STORY BOOKS

Everything® Fairy Tales Book

LANGUAGE

Everything® Conversational Japanese Book with CD, $19.95
Everything® French Grammar Book
Everything® French Phrase Book, $9.95
Everything® French Verb Book, $9.95
Everything® German Practice Book with CD, $19.95
Everything® Inglés Book
Everything® Intermediate Spanish Book with CD, $19.95
Everything® Italian Practice Book with CD, $19.95
Everything® Learning Brazilian Portuguese Book with CD, $19.95
Everything® Learning French Book with CD, 2nd Ed., $19.95
Everything® Learning German Book
Everything® Learning Italian Book
Everything® Learning Latin Book
Everything® Learning Russian Book with CD, $19.95
Everything® Learning Spanish Book with CD, 2nd Ed., $19.95
Everything® Russian Practice Book with CD, $19.95
Everything® Sign Language Book
Everything® Spanish Grammar Book
Everything® Spanish Phrase Book, $9.95
Everything® Spanish Practice Book with CD, $19.95
Everything® Spanish Verb Book, $9.95
Everything® Speaking Mandarin Chinese Book with CD, $19.95

MUSIC

Everything® Drums Book with CD, $19.95
Everything® Guitar Book with CD, 2nd Ed., $19.95
Everything® Guitar Chords Book with CD, $19.95
Everything® Home Recording Book
Everything® Music Theory Book with CD, $19.95
Everything® Reading Music Book with CD, $19.95
Everything® Rock & Blues Guitar Book with CD, $19.95
Everything® Rock and Blues Piano Book with CD, $19.95
Everything® Songwriting Book

NEW AGE

Everything® Astrology Book, 2nd Ed.
Everything® Birthday Personology Book
Everything® Dreams Book, 2nd Ed.
Everything® Love Signs Book, $9.95
Everything® Love Spells Book, $9.95
Everything® Numerology Book
Everything® Paganism Book
Everything® Palmistry Book
Everything® Psychic Book
Everything® Reiki Book
Everything® Sex Signs Book, $9.95

Everything® Spells & Charms Book, 2nd Ed.
Everything® Tarot Book, 2nd Ed.
Everything® Toltec Wisdom Book
Everything® Wicca and Witchcraft Book

PARENTING

Everything® Baby Names Book, 2nd Ed.
Everything® Baby Shower Book, 2nd Ed.
Everything® Baby's First Year Book
Everything® Birthing Book
Everything® Breastfeeding Book
Everything® Father-to-Be Book
Everything® Father's First Year Book
Everything® Get Ready for Baby Book, 2nd Ed.
Everything® Get Your Baby to Sleep Book, $9.95
Everything® Getting Pregnant Book
Everything® Guide to Pregnancy Over 35
Everything® Guide to Raising a One-Year-Old
Everything® Guide to Raising a Two-Year-Old
Everything® Guide to Raising Adolescent Boys
Everything® Guide to Raising Adolescent Girls
Everything® Homeschooling Book
Everything® Mother's First Year Book
Everything® Parent's Guide to Childhood Illnesses
Everything® Parent's Guide to Children and Divorce
Everything® Parent's Guide to Children with ADD/ADHD
Everything® Parent's Guide to Children with Asperger's Syndrome
Everything® Parent's Guide to Children with Autism
Everything® Parent's Guide to Children with Bipolar Disorder
Everything® Parent's Guide to Children with Depression
Everything® Parent's Guide to Children with Dyslexia
Everything® Parent's Guide to Children with Juvenile Diabetes
Everything® Parent's Guide to Positive Discipline
Everything® Parent's Guide to Raising a Successful Child
Everything® Parent's Guide to Raising Boys
Everything® Parent's Guide to Raising Girls
Everything® Parent's Guide to Raising Siblings
Everything® Parent's Guide to Sensory Integration Disorder
Everything® Parent's Guide to Tantrums
Everything® Parent's Guide to the Strong-Willed Child
Everything® Parenting a Teenager Book
Everything® Potty Training Book, $9.95
Everything® Pregnancy Book, 3rd Ed.
Everything® Pregnancy Fitness Book
Everything® Pregnancy Nutrition Book
Everything® Pregnancy Organizer, 2nd Ed., $16.95
Everything® Toddler Activities Book
Everything® Toddler Book
Everything® Tween Book
Everything® Twins, Triplets, and More Book

PETS

Everything® Aquarium Book
Everything® Boxer Book
Everything® Cat Book, 2nd Ed.
Everything® Chihuahua Book

Everything® **Cooking for Dogs Book**
Everything® Dachshund Book
Everything® Dog Book
Everything® Dog Health Book
Everything® Dog Obedience Book
Everything® Dog Owner's Organizer, $16.95
Everything® Dog Training and Tricks Book
Everything® German Shepherd Book
Everything® Golden Retriever Book
Everything® Horse Book
Everything® Horse Care Book
Everything® Horseback Riding Book
Everything® Labrador Retriever Book
Everything® Poodle Book
Everything® Pug Book
Everything® Puppy Book
Everything® Rottweiler Book
Everything® Small Dogs Book
Everything® Tropical Fish Book
Everything® Yorkshire Terrier Book

REFERENCE

Everything® American Presidents Book
Everything® Blogging Book
Everything® Build Your Vocabulary Book
Everything® Car Care Book
Everything® Classical Mythology Book
Everything® Da Vinci Book
Everything® Divorce Book
Everything® Einstein Book
Everything® Enneagram Book
Everything® Etiquette Book, 2nd Ed.
Everything® **Guide to Edgar Allan Poe**
Everything® Inventions and Patents Book
Everything® Mafia Book
Everything® **Martin Luther King Jr. Book**
Everything® Philosophy Book
Everything® Pirates Book
Everything® Psychology Book

RELIGION

Everything® Angels Book
Everything® Bible Book
Everything® **Bible Study Book with CD, $19.95**
Everything® Buddhism Book
Everything® Catholicism Book
Everything® Christianity Book
Everything® Gnostic Gospels Book
Everything® History of the Bible Book
Everything® Jesus Book
Everything® Jewish History & Heritage Book
Everything® Judaism Book
Everything® Kabbalah Book
Everything® Koran Book

Everything® Mary Book
Everything® Mary Magdalene Book
Everything® Prayer Book
Everything® Saints Book, 2nd Ed.
Everything® Torah Book
Everything® Understanding Islam Book
Everything® **Women of the Bible Book**
Everything® World's Religions Book
Everything® Zen Book

SCHOOL & CAREERS

Everything® Alternative Careers Book
Everything® Career Tests Book
Everything® College Major Test Book
Everything® College Survival Book, 2nd Ed.
Everything® Cover Letter Book, 2nd Ed.
Everything® Filmmaking Book
Everything® Get-a-Job Book, 2nd Ed.
Everything® Guide to Being a Paralegal
Everything® Guide to Being a Personal Trainer
Everything® Guide to Being a Real Estate Agent
Everything® Guide to Being a Sales Rep
Everything® **Guide to Being an Event Planner**
Everything® Guide to Careers in Health Care
Everything® Guide to Careers in Law Enforcement
Everything® Guide to Government Jobs
Everything® **Guide to Starting and Running a Catering Business**
Everything® Guide to Starting and Running a Restaurant
Everything® Job Interview Book
Everything® New Nurse Book
Everything® New Teacher Book
Everything® Paying for College Book
Everything® Practice Interview Book
Everything® Resume Book, 2nd Ed.
Everything® Study Book

SELF-HELP

Everything® **Body Language Book**
Everything® Dating Book, 2nd Ed.
Everything® Great Sex Book
Everything® Self-Esteem Book
Everything® Tantric Sex Book

SPORTS & FITNESS

Everything® Easy Fitness Book
Everything® **Krav Maga for Fitness Book**
Everything® Running Book

TRAVEL

Everything® **Family Guide to Coastal Florida**
Everything® Family Guide to Cruise Vacations
Everything® Family Guide to Hawaii
Everything® Family Guide to Las Vegas, 2nd Ed.
Everything® Family Guide to Mexico
Everything® Family Guide to New York City, 2nd Ed.
Everything® Family Guide to RV Travel & Campgrounds
Everything® Family Guide to the Caribbean
Everything® **Family Guide to the Disneyland® Resort, California Adventure®, Universal Studios®, and the Anaheim Area, 2nd Ed.**
Everything® **Family Guide to the Walt Disney World Resort®, Universal Studios®, and Greater Orlando, 5th Ed.**
Everything® Family Guide to Timeshares
Everything® Family Guide to Washington D.C., 2nd Ed.

WEDDINGS

Everything® Bachelorette Party Book, $9.95
Everything® Bridesmaid Book, $9.95
Everything® Destination Wedding Book
Everything® Elopement Book, $9.95
Everything® Father of the Bride Book, $9.95
Everything® Groom Book, $9.95
Everything® Mother of the Bride Book, $9.95
Everything® Outdoor Wedding Book
Everything® Wedding Book, 3rd Ed.
Everything® Wedding Checklist, $9.95
Everything® Wedding Etiquette Book, $9.95
Everything® Wedding Organizer, 2nd Ed., $16.95
Everything® Wedding Shower Book, $9.95
Everything® Wedding Vows Book, $9.95
Everything® Wedding Workout Book
Everything® **Weddings on a Budget Book, 2nd Ed., $9.95**

WRITING

Everything® Creative Writing Book
Everything® Get Published Book, 2nd Ed.
Everything® Grammar and Style Book
Everything® Guide to Magazine Writing
Everything® Guide to Writing a Book Proposal
Everything® Guide to Writing a Novel
Everything® Guide to Writing Children's Books
Everything® Guide to Writing Copy
Everything® **Guide to Writing Graphic Novels**
Everything® Guide to Writing Research Papers
Everything® Screenwriting Book
Everything® Writing Poetry Book
Everything® Writing Well Book